Daoism

A SHORT INTRODUCTION

'In less than two hundred pages Miller provides detailed
coverage of Daoist tradition, from its prehistoric roots
up to contemporary Daoist movements (Falun Gong,
the burgeoning Taiji Quan "recreation" industry) and
practitioners (Mantak Chia, Moy Lin-Shin) ... This book
has a host of strengths, not the least being its combination
of brevity and thoroughness. Writing such a book is not
easy and Miller has done us all a great favor.'
Teaching Theology and Religion

D1332577

RELATED TITLES PUBLISHED BY ONEWORLD

Confucianism: A Short Introduction, John H. and Evelyn Nagai Berthrong,
ISBN 1–85168–236–8

The Wisdom of the Tao, ISBN 1–85168–232–5

The Wisdom of the Confucians, ISBN 1–85168–259–7

Daoism

A SHORT INTRODUCTION

James Miller

ONEWORLD

OXFORD

DAOISM: A SHORT INTRODUCTION

Oneworld Publications
(Sales and Editorial)
185 Banbury Road
Oxford OX2 7AR
England
www.oneworld-publications.com

ISBN 1–85168–315–1

Cover design by Design Deluxe, Bath
Typeset by LaserScript Limited, Mitcham, UK
Printed and bound by WS Bookwell, Finland

For the faculty, staff and students of
Queen's Theological College

Contents

Preface   ix
Acknowledgements   xiv
Timeline of Daoist History   xvi

HISTORICAL INTRODUCTION   1
    Proto-Daoism   4
    Classical Daoism   7
    Modern Daoism   11
    Contemporary Daoism   13
    Suggestions for further reading   15

1 IDENTITY   16
    Daoism as Chinese Religion   17
    Daoism as Lineages of Transmission 26
    Daoism as Universal Path   29
    Conclusions   34
    Suggestions for further reading   35

2 WAY   36
    Way   37
    Power   45
    Communication   46
    Suggestions for further reading   52

3 BODY   53
    Qi: The Breath of Life   54

Correlation, synchronicity and resonance 60
Longevity practices 65
Transcendent bodies 71
Suggestions for further reading 73

4 POWER 75
Daoist Millenarianism 78
Daoist Messianism 82
Daoism in contemporary China 87
Negotiating with destiny 89
Suggestions for further reading 92

5 LIGHT 93
The development of Shangqing Daoism 93
Light practices 96
Contemporary visualization practices 104
Suggestions for further reading 106

6 ALCHEMY 107
Alchemy and the quest for immortality 108
Laboratory alchemy 109
Internal alchemy 112
The Way of Complete Perfection 114
Transformation 118
Suggestions for further reading 121

7 TEXT 122
The religious origins and functions of Daoist texts 123
Transformations of meaning in Daoist texts 132
Suggestions for further reading 138

8 NATURE 139
Natural space as sacred space 140
Marvellous nature 147
Caverns and texts 148
A Daoist aesthetic of spontaneity 150
Suggestions for further reading 151

Glossary of Chinese Terms 152
Bibliography 157
Index 164

Preface

Daoism is an organized religious tradition that has been continuously developing and transforming itself through China, Korea and Japan for over two thousand years. It has now spread around the globe from Sydney to Toronto and includes among its followers people from a whole range of ethnicities and cultural backgrounds. Day by day, Daoism is truly becoming a world religion, but as it does so, it seems to resist being pinned down in neat categories. Not many people know what Daoism is, and when people do have an understanding of it, often it is quite different from someone else's. One reason for this is that the history of Daoism is a marvellous history of continuous change rather than a linear progress or development. Daoism has no single founder, such as Jesus or the Buddha, nor does it have a single key message, such as the gospel or the four noble truths. Rather Daoism bears witness to a history of continuous self-invention within a vast diversity of environmental contexts.

In fact the human experience of change or transformation in our bodies and in the world around us lies at the heart of the Daoist experience in much the same way that faith in an eternal, unchanging deity lies at the heart of the Jewish–Christian–Islamic religious system. Whereas Western religionists seek to place their trust in an unchanging and invisible stability that somehow transcends the fleeting experience of time, Daoists recognize and celebrate the profound and mysterious creativity within the very fabric of time and space itself.

The most influential Daoist text, *Daode jing* (Scripture of the Way and its Power, *c.* fourth century BCE) names this mysterious creativity 'Dao', which can be translated quite straightforwardly as 'way' or 'path'.

The first line of the standard version of the text enigmatically warns, however, that 'Dao can be spoken of, [but it is] not the constant Dao.' No wonder, then, that Daoism has taken a vast array of forms within the East Asian cultural context. This book is a short introduction to Daoism that takes seriously the task of naming the Dao, all the while acknowledging the constant change that continues to take place within Daoism. The way I have chosen to do this is to settle on eight keywords or fundamental themes that I believe lie at the heart of Daoism in its various cultural and historical forms. In each chapter I focus on one of these themes using it as a lens or a spotlight to illuminate a key aspect of the Daoist tradition.

Perhaps a more conventional way of explaining Daoism would be simply to offer a history of the development of Daoism, placing it in its changing socio-cultural context. The value of this approach would be that it would give the reader all the necessary facts about Daoism, however it would not do so well at the task of understanding what Daoism means as a historical and living religious tradition. I have chosen to concentrate on this latter task: to try to introduce what Daoism means, and more specifically to introduce what it means to someone, like myself, who lives in the twenty-first century Western cultural context. This is not to say that the standard historical approach is not as useful, but there is already a good introduction to Daoism that takes a historical approach: *Daoism and Chinese Culture* (Kohn, 2001). My aim is to offer a different sort of perspective, and I would like to explain why.

When teaching Daoism in universities, my experience has been that in order for students to understand Daoism it is necessary for them to change their expectations as to what religion is all about. To be sure there are gods and priests and beliefs and rituals in Daoism – and these categories are the bread and butter of religious studies – but I have discovered that approaching the study of Daoism with these traditional categories at the forefront of one's mind is an unprofitable strategy. The fact is that Daoists construct their way of being religious in quite different ways than we might expect. For instance Daoists have gods, but these gods are not usually the superhuman creators of the world, nor are they the religious symbols for natural forces. In fact most Daoist deities are simply human beings who have learned to transcend the horizons of space and time, or worthy ancestors whose spirits deserve veneration. To understand what Daoism means, then, it is instructive to pay attention to our own cultural milieu, the values and concepts that we take for granted in our day-to-day lives. But on the other hand we must also look for the ways in which the various Daoist traditions operate quite differently than the cultures we are familiar with. By shuttling backwards and forwards between these two perspectives I hope to weave a picture of Daoism that is historically accurate and also culturally enlightening.

In order to grasp the many radical differences between our own worldview and that of Daoism it is necessary to look closely at some of the core values that inform classical Chinese culture. Such root metaphors and core motifs are embedded deep within the collective consciousnesses of the world's divergent cultures, setting the terms of reference for the subsequent flourishing of its various traditions. This does not mean that cultures are forever bound to work out the destinies set thousands of years ago, for clearly cultures interact and are transformed by each other. Nevertheless the core motifs do play a significant role in how cultures develop, and it is important for the student of religions to pay attention to them so as to understand the fundamental differences between one religious worldview and another. If we fail to pay sufficient respect to these core motifs, then we will be more likely to misunderstand the culture or civilization in question, more likely to represent it in our own terms, and our own categories.

As the history of colonialism has demonstrated, it is a tendency of any civilization to construct representations of other cultures in ways that it deems convenient. Convenience has its many uses, which is, no doubt, why you are reading a short introduction to Daoism and not a long one. But convenience must also be balanced by attention to context. It may well be convenient to explore the wonderful exhibits in the British Museum on a wet Tuesday afternoon, but the intellectual value of that convenience depends on how well the curators contextualize their exhibits.

Although the academic study of religion generally holds that it is desirable that everyone in the world should become more acquainted with the world's religious traditions, it also holds that academics, as stewards of public learning, have a special responsibility to ensure that the picture they paint of other cultures is properly contexualized and also intelligible to representatives of that culture. Of course the substance of scholarship is the debate over the various contexts in which scholars place their interpretations, and scholars often disagree with adherents of religious traditions who have their own agenda in representing their traditions in certain ways. But progress in understanding is only made through dialogue, and dialogue begins in listening to what the other has to say.

So rather than try to understand Daoism in the conventional terms of the Western academic study of religion, I decided to focus on the key themes that have surfaced with insistent regularity in my own study of Daoism: identity, way, body, text, power, light, alchemy, text and nature. Some of these themes are common to many religions, others are particular to Daoism. All of them recur in different forms and different contexts throughout Daoist history. By focusing on these key themes and showing the wide range of meanings they have, I aim to give you the tools to develop your own understanding of Daoism. I hope this strategy proves to be a provocative and illuminating way of grasping some of the most important features of the Daoist tradition.

Readers will also note that since the overall plan of the book does not follow a linear historical scheme, the actual text of the book also does not follow a strict linear scheme. You are thus invited to leap backwards and forwards through the chapters to pursue whichever themes or lines of thought are interesting, and from time to time in the text suggestions for how to do this are given. Of course it is also possible to start at the beginning and work your way forward, in which case readers will find themselves coming back to the same Daoist movements, but each time looking at them from a different perspective. In this way the text aims to mirror something of the recursive quality that the great scholar of Daoism Isabelle Robinet noted in her history of Daoism (1997, pp. 2–3). Before beginning the book, however, it is worthwhile acquainting yourself with some of the basic facts of Daoist history so that you will have a better understanding of what is going on in each chapter. To help you do this I have provided a very brief summary of some of the key Daoist movements that you will encounter throughout this book.

DAOISM OR TAOISM?

The English language uses the Roman alphabet to make a phonetic transcription of the way words sound. Chinese, in contrast, uses characters that mostly convey the meaning of a word, not its pronunciation. About 5000 characters are in common usage, and it usually takes only one or two characters to convey the equivalent of an English word. In spoken Mandarin Chinese, each written character is pronounced using one of only 416 syllables, but the pronunciation of that syllable varies according to the dialect throughout China. A further complication lies in the fact that each syllable can be pronounced using a variety of tones, which also vary from dialect to dialect. The result is that the 1.2 billion Chinese people share a common written language, but there are many different spoken languages.

There are two common systems for representing Chinese using Roman letters. Both systems attempt to convey the pronunciation that is used in Modern Standard Chinese, commonly called Mandarin, the official language of the People's Republic of China. The older system, called Wade–Giles after its inventors, is common in Taiwan and the United States. The newer system, called Hanyu pinyin, or just Pinyin for short, was developed by Chinese people for use in China, and is now increasingly common throughout the world. This book uses the Hanyu pinyin system throughout the text, but includes the Wade–Giles version in the Glossary of Chinese Terms, which precedes the Bibliography.

The Chinese character for 'Way' is Romanized as 'Tao' in the Wade–Giles system, and from this older Romanization system came the English word 'Taoism'. In the more modern Hanyu pinyin system, however, 'Tao' becomes 'Dao'. The sound they both intend to convey is like the Dow of the Dow-Jones Index, though slightly more aspirated. When Western scholars started to use the newer Romanization system, they also had to decide whether to keep using the older English term 'Taoism' or to coin a new word 'Daoism'. Many scholars prefer the more familiar term 'Taoism' arguing that it is now an English word in its own right and should not be affected by changes in linguistic fashions. The term 'Daoism' is, however, becoming increasingly popular. One recent book that I coedited, *Daoism and Ecology*, contains an important explanation for the adoption of the new term, namely that 'earlier discussions of the Daoist tradition were often distorted and misleading – especially in terms of the special Western fascination with the "classical" or "philosophical" *Daode jing* [Tao-te-ching] and the denigration and neglect of the later sectarian traditions' (Girardot, Miller and Liu, 2001, p. xxxi). This book follows that lead and similarly uses the word 'Daoism' in order to distinguish itself from what 'Taoism' represented in the twentieth-century Western imagination.

Acknowledgements

In the West, the study of Daoism is very young. It only became feasible to write a book such as this three years ago, when scholars around the world joined forces to produce the monumental *Daoism Handbook* (Kohn, 2000) under the leadership of my teacher, Livia Kohn. I owe a debt of gratitude to her and to all the scholars who collaborated with her in producing the first major English-language resource that examines the Daoist tradition in its entirety. The picture of Daoism that is painted in this book is largely my own attempt to synthesize and interpret the wealth of data that they originally presented. I have also drawn on work that I have published elsewhere in more specialist books, reworking ideas to fit into the general presentation offered here. Chapter 5 draws on my essay, 'Living Light: Shangqing Daoist Cultivation in Theory and Practice', forthcoming in *Daoist Cultivation*, edited by Louis Komjathy. Chapter 8 makes use of ideas articulated in my 'Daoism and Nature' in *Nature Across Cultures: Non-Western Views of Nature and Environment*, edited by Helaine Selin (2003).

I also acknowledge with gratitude the many people who have helped me in other ways with this book. In particular I would like to thank the faculty and staff of Queen's University Department of Religious Studies and Queen's Theological College who have given me a much-appreciated academic home. Thanks are also due to John Berthrong who first suggested this book to me, and to Victoria Roddam at Oneworld, who has been unfailingly efficient and admirably helpful. Various people have shaped the way that I express my ideas in this book, either as students in my courses at Queen's University or as readers of earlier drafts. Kate

Cohen provided helpful comments, and Eric Tang edited an early draft, but most of what is good about this book I owe to my teachers in Durham, Cambridge and Boston, and in particular to Livia Kohn and Robert Cummings Neville.

James Miller
Toronto, April 2003

Timeline of Daoist History

1046–221 BCE	**Zhou dynasty**
552–479 BCE	Traditional dates of Confucius
Fourth century BCE	Probable dates of earliest versions of *Daode jing* and the *Zhuangzi*
350–270 BCE	Zou Yan formalizes system of five phases
Third century BCE	Qu Yuan composes shamanic-inspired *Chuci*
Third century BCE	Probable date of bamboo-strip version of the *Daode jing* discovered in the Guodian excavations
221 BCE	Qin ruler proclaims himself 'First Qin Emperor' (Qin shi huangdi)
206 BCE–9 CE	**Former Han dynasty**
168 BCE	Date of the silk cloth version of the *Daode jing* discovered in the Mawangdui excavations
141–187 BCE	Reign of the Wu emperor of the Han dynasty, said to have been fascinated by immortality
60 BCE	First record of the ingestion of an alchemical elixir of immortality
25–220 CE	**Later Han dynasty**
142	Way of Orthodox Unity (*Zhengyi dao*) founded in 142 CE by Zhang Ling

200	*Xiang'er* commentary on the *Daode jing*
215	Zhang Daoling's grandson, Zhang Lu, cedes power to Cao Cao, effectively ending the original Way of Orthodox Unity
Third–fifth centuries	Taiqing (Great Clarity) alchemical movement flourishes
226–249	Wang Bi, philosopher and commentator on the *Daode jing*
283–343	Ge Hong, literatus and alchemist
330–386	Yang Xi, religious visionary and medium
364	Shangqing revelations begin through Yang Xi
390s	Ge Chaofu, descendant of Ge Hong, compiles Lingbao scriptures
365–448	Kou Qianzhi (365–448), Daoist instrumental in establishing the theocracy known as the Northern Celestial Masters
406–477	Lu Xiujing, Lingbao reformer and compiler of early Daoist canon
440	Kou Qianzhi invests Northern Wei dynasty Emperor with Daoist registers and proclaims him the Perfected Lord of Great Peace
450	Daoist theocracy dismantled
520	Daoists engage Buddhists in the first of a series of formal debates
456–536	Tao Hongjing, Shangqing patriarch
581–618	**Sui Dynasty**
618–906	**Tang dynasty**
647–735	Sima Chengzhen, Shangqing patriarch
721	Sima Chengzhen ordains the Tang dynasty Xuanzong Emperor (713–756)
960–1279	**Song dynasty**
1113–1170	Wang Zhe (aka Wang Chongyang) founder of the Way of Complete Perfection

1115–1234	Tartar Jin dynasty rules in the north
1119–1182	Sun Bu'er, famous female Daoist and disciple of Wang Zhe
1130–1200	Zhu Xi, Neo-Confucian philosopher and polymath
1148–1227	Qiu Changchun, disciple of Wang Zhe, who travels to meet Chinggis Khan
Mid-thirteenth century	The thirty-fifth Celestial Master was given authority over the ordination of Highest Clarity priests
Mid-thirteenth century	Daoists lose a series of debates held at the Khan's court
1280	**Yuan dynasty** established when Chinggis Khan's grandson, Kublai assumes the throne of China
1317–1328	Liu Dabin (last major Shangqing patriarch) active
1368–1644	**Ming dynasty**
1445	Compilation of the Daoist Canon
1644–1911	**Qing dynasty**
1656	Establishment of the Dragon Gate (Longmen) branch of the Way of Complete Perfection
1911–1948	**Republic of China** (continues in Taiwan after 1948)
1949–	**People's Republic of China** (PRC) proclaimed in mainland China
1966–1976	Great Proletarian Cultural Revolution; many Daoist temples destroyed
1980–	Liberalization of religion in the PRC begins under Deng Xiaoping
1997	Hong Kong reverts to PRC
1999	Macao reverts to PRC

Historical introduction

There is no established consensus on how to divide up the history of Daoism, and any scheme of periodization inevitably reflects the particular judgements of the individual historian. The present chapter contains a fairly standard historical survey of Daoism in China. It largely ignores the history of Daoism in Korea and other East Asian countries where Daoism flourishes in dialogue with, but independently from, Chinese Daoism (for the history of Korean Daoism see Jung, 2000). The reason for this largely reflects the fact that Daoism has been studied in the West almost exclusively in reference to China, because the bulk of historical documents dealing with Daoism are written in classical Chinese.

The history of Daoism can conveniently be divided into four periods: proto-Daoism, classical Daoism, modern Daoism and contemporary Daoism. Although these labels tend to suggest a gradual historical development, it does not follow from this that Daoism has been steadily developing in a linear fashion towards some ideal state, nor is this meant to imply that the 'classical' period is somehow 'better' than the 'modern' period.

The first period, proto-Daoism, covers the time from antiquity up to the second century CE. The reason why this period is called 'proto-Daoism' is that we have no knowledge of any formal Daoist religious organizations at this time. Despite this fact, it is necessary to include this period in any understanding of Daoism because many of the core values and motifs of Daoist philosophy and religion were shaped during this period, and one of the most important Daoist texts, the *Daode jing*, was written during this period. Evidence for our understanding of proto-Daoism derives largely from textual materials and archaeological evidence about the functioning of ancient Chinese religion.

The second period, that of classical Daoist religion, starts in 142 CE when Zhang Daoling established the Way of the Celestial Masters, also known as the Way of Orthodox Unity, the first successful organized Daoist religious system. Daoist priests today claim to be ordained in a lineage that stretches back to this original founder. Two other important movements developed later during this period of classical Daoist religion: the Way of Highest Clarity (Shangqing Daoism) and the Way of Numinous Treasure (Lingbao Daoism). This period, between the second and the seventh centuries can be called the classical period because scholars of Daoism look back to this time (known also as the medieval period of Chinese history) as the era in which many Daoist practices, texts and rituals initially took shape. Also during this period, Buddhism was brought to China by missionaries from India and Tibet. Buddhist ideas and practices were absorbed into Daoism (and vice versa) but there were also periods of intense rivalry between Daoists and Buddhists. The classical period of Daoism ends with the Tang dynasty (618–906), one of the high-points of Chinese civilization from the point of view of the development of art and culture. During the Tang dynasty Daoism became fully integrated with the imperial court system, particularly under the reign of the Xuanzong Emperor (713–56). During this time Daoism functioned as the official religion of the imperial court and exerted supremacy over Buddhism.

The Tang period is also important in Daoist history because Daoist missionaries were also sent to Korea by the Tang court in the seventh century, in part to help the Korean court restrict the spread of Buddhism in Korea. According to the Korean Daoist history, the *Haedong chŏndo rok* written by Han Muwae (1517–1610), two Korean monks also went to China to study Daoism, and brought back their teaching to Korea. These types of officially sanctioned exchange were no doubt facilitated by the fact that Daoism had an identifiable role at the imperial court.

The third phase of Daoism may be said to begin with the break-up of the Tang empire, and the increasing syncretism between Buddhism, elite Daoism and localized religious cults that have been documented from the Song period (960–1279) onwards. This modern period also witnessed the founding of the Daoist movement known as the Way of Complete Perfection (Quanzhen dao) by Wang Zhe (1113–70). The Way of

Complete Perfection is the major monastic form of Daoism that exists to this day alongside the more community-based priesthood of the Celestial Masters. The Way of Complete Perfection is devoted to the practice of internal alchemy, in which the energies of the body are refined through breathing and other forms of meditation into ever subtler forms, thus promoting longevity and even, in a few rare cases, the possibility of totally transcending the ordinary finitudes of human existence. The Way of Complete Perfection is also marked by its aim to 'harmonize the three teachings' of Confucianism, Daoism and Buddhism, and became highly influential under the Mongol Yuan dynasty after Wang Zhe's disciple Qiu Changchun (1148–1227) undertook a three-year journey to the court of the Mongol warlord, Chinggis Khan. Despite the rhetoric of harmonization, further acrimonious debates with Buddhists developed at this time, and when the Daoists lost a series of these debates in 1281 many Daoist texts were burned. Despite this setback, Daoism flourished during the subsequent Ming dynasty (1368–1644) and the year 1445 saw the compilation of the Daoist Canon (*Daozang*), a compendium of some 1500 Daoist texts, under the patronage of the Yongle Emperor. In the Qing dynasty (1644–1911) Daoist ideas and practices became more entrenched in popular religious culture. Perhaps it would be more accurate to say that we have better historical evidence of the way popular religion functioned since many popular Daoist morality texts were published and the practice of Daoist-inspired arts such as taiji quan (Tai Chi) and Qigong (Ch'i-kung) became increasingly widespread.

The fourth period, since the advent of Western colonial powers in the nineteenth century, has been a near-total catastrophe for Daoism, particularly during the period of the Great Proletarian Cultural Revolution (1966–76) when many Daoist temples were destroyed and the overt functioning of the religion to all intents and purposes ceased to exist in mainland China. Since 1980 Daoism has begun to be practised openly again in China and a new generation of Daoists are struggling to rebuild their temples and recover their tradition. On the other hand, through the emigration of many Chinese people across the world, Daoist temples have been established in Europe, the Americas and elsewhere and many popular Daoist practices such as *Qigong* and *taiji quan* (Tai Chi) have taken root in the West. Until recently it was not certain that Daoism had survived this cataclysmic upheaval, but the study and practice of Daoism is flourishing once again in China and throughout the world.

PROTO-DAOISM

Laozi and the Daode jing

The person most revered in the whole of Daoism is known to us simply by the epithet Laozi, which can be translated as 'the Old Master'. The earliest biography of the Old Master is contained in the *Shiji* (Records of the Historian *c*. 90 BCE) by the great Han dynasty intellectual Sima Qian (145–86 BCE). Sima Qian identifies Laozi as an archivist named Li Er or Li Dan at the Zhou dynasty court (1046–221 BCE). During his life he is said to have instructed the Chinese philosopher Confucius (traditional dates 552–479 BCE) on matters of ritual. When Laozi retired from the court, he set off on a journey west, but was stopped at the Hangu Pass by the gatekeeper, Yin Xi, who asked him to compose a text outlining his philosophy of dao (way) and de (power, or virtue). The result was the text known to us as the *Daode jing* (The Scripture of the Way and its Power) or simply as the *Laozi*. The *Daode jing*, along with the Bible, is one of the most widely translated books in the world and continues to exert a profound influence on Chinese culture.

Sima Qian's biography formed the kernel out of which grew the most important myth surrounding Laozi as a manifestation or incarnation of the Dao itself. According to this myth Laozi continued his journey west and appeared in India, as the Buddha, and in the far west, as Mani, the prophet who founded the influential dualistic Christian sect known as Manichaeism. This myth moreover was used to lend authority to those Chinese rulers and revolutionaries who shared Laozi's surname, Li, and thereby claimed the mandate of heaven to govern the Chinese empire.

Apart from Sima Qian's biography and the myth of Laozi's transformations, we have very little historical evidence about Laozi in his original guise, but we do know more about the book that is attributed to him. The *Daode jing* is a compilation of terse aphorisms about the Way (*dao*) and its Power (*de*), that totals some 5000 Chinese characters. Some of its sayings, such as 'The journey of a thousand miles starts with a single step' are well known. Others are obscure and difficult to comprehend. The text exists in a standard edition made by the commentator Wang Bi (226–49 CE), but recent archaeological finds at Mawangdui and Guodian have unearthed earlier versions on silk and bamboo strips, respectively. The standard edition is divided into eighty-one chapters and two parts. Part I (chapters 1–37) is known as the

Daojing (Scripture of *Dao*); Part 2 (chapters 38–81) is known as the *Dejing* (Scripture of *De*).

The text speaks of Dao as the formless and ineffable Way that is the wellspring of creative power for a universe of constant transformation. The Dao is the mother of heaven and earth and is the spontaneously self-generating life of the universe. Everything in the universe has its own virtue or power (*de*) which, if permitted to flourish, brings a natural order and harmony to the world. Human beings, however, have the capacity to deviate from or simply ignore this natural order by imposing their will upon the world and by giving free rein to powerful emotions such as desire, hatred and greed. When human beings abandon the natural way they develop large-scale societies governed by draconian rulers at war with each other. The enlightened ruler or sage, however, can cultivate order and harmony within a small community by cultivating spontaneity within himself and by following a path of non-aggressive action. By virtue of his own charismatic power, order will naturally arise within human societies, because in the feudal hierarchy of ancient China, the ruler was seen as the foundation and embodiment of the whole people. The text of the *Daode jing* and the myth of Laozi as the supreme sage and recurring manifestation of the Dao together lay the foundation for an important theme in Daoist history, though one which is not so evident today, namely the close and often antagonistic relationship between Daoist religion and Chinese imperial authority (see chapter 4).

The Zhuangzi

The *Zhuangzi* is one of the most popular classics of Chinese literature, and revels in a philosophical dexterity and rhetorical sophistication that ranks with the highest achievements of many cultures. It is supremely witty and imaginative. Although this work has always been classified as a Daoist text, it is interesting to note that it has never been particularly important as a Daoist religious scripture. Rather, within Chinese and Western culture the text represents a form of Daoism centred upon the Daoist sage as the supremely self-realized individual who wanders free from the conventions of culture and society. This work has a universal appeal that can readily be appreciated by those with little or no background in Daoist thought and religion. The work does, however, contribute to our understanding of Daoism because its view of the perfected person (*zhenren*) was instrumental in the development of Daoism as a personal spiritual quest.

In this form of Daoism the sage is not viewed in socio-political terms as the ruler of a nation, but rather as someone who is utterly unperturbed by whatever might happen to him and apparently unconcerned with all the affairs of politics and business. In the *Zhuangzi*, the sage is thus a supremely self-realized person who roams freely throughout the world impervious to the vagaries of his or her fate.

The edition of the *Zhuangzi* that we rely upon today was put together by a commentator, Guo Xiang, around 300 CE. The Han dynasty historian Sima Qian attributes the text to a man known as Master Zhuang (Zhuangzi) who lived in the third century BCE. It is evident, however, that the thirty-three chapter text as we have it today has gone through several processes of editing, and thus the whole text is usually referred to as 'the *Zhuangzi*' in order to distinguish it from 'Zhuangzi', the sage who is probably the author of most of the first seven chapters, known as the 'inner chapters'.

The emphasis in the *Zhuangzi* is on the spontaneous transformation of things in the natural world and the impossibility of fixing words or human principles onto this world. The text thus ridicules the attempts of philosophers and statesmen to impose some sort of human order onto the world and instead speaks of meditative practices such as 'sitting in oblivion', 'breathing through the heels' and 'fasting the heart-mind'. These practices aim to break down the conventional distinctions between self and world. The result is that the realized or perfected individual will be instinctively attuned to the spontaneity of the Dao and able to accept all that befalls him or her with absolute equanimity. Moreover such a perfected person has plumbed the depths of the Dao and possesses a holistic wisdom that is beyond conventional knowing. Such a person 'wanders freely' on the Dao, roaming in a kind of liberated, ecstatic state. Commentators have also drawn parallels between this type of 'wandering' and the voyages of the soul conducted by shamans, in which the practitioner engages in a vision quest or journey to the spirit world.

In the Daoist tradition, the text was profoundly influential upon the Shangqing (Highest Clarity) Daoist movement that began in the fourth century CE. Shangqing Daoists adapted some of its key practices such as 'sitting in oblivion' into spiritual practices that aimed to unite the adept with the full range of spiritual powers in the cosmos. Uniting with these spirits, imaged as the constellations of stars in the night sky, freed the individual from the conventional bounds of life and death and transformed him into a celestial immortal.

Most Western commentators have focused on the philosophical aspects of the *Zhuangzi*, particularly its brilliant arguments for epistemological scepticism and moral relativism. Zhuangzi argues that words cannot adequately grasp the reality of things, which are in constant flux, and consequently there is no way for people to decide on what is true. Debates are merely exercises of rhetoric in which the winner is simply the one who is more skilled in speaking. Ultimately there is no way to know whether our language really matches reality at all. This line of argument may be viewed as developing out of the first stanza of the *Daode jing* which states that 'the way that can be told is not the constant Way'.

The Neiye (inward training)

The third 'proto-Daoist' text that is important for understanding the foundations of Daoism is the *Neiye* (inward training). This text is contained within a broad-ranging compendium known as the *Guanzi*, and, for a long time was not considered an important proto-Daoist work. Recently, however, scholars have come to reconsider the text and to see it as a forerunner of the longevity practices and breath meditation that became an important constituent of the later Daoist tradition (see Roth, 1999). Like the *Zhuangzi*, the text is more concerned with the individual than society. The 'inward training' to which the title of this work alludes is a training of the internal energy systems of the human body so as to produce a refined and potent form of the vital energy (*qi*) that makes up the cosmos. This refined form of vital energy is known as vital essence (jing). Cultivating vital essence within the body enhances the circulation of qi. This text is considered an important Daoist text because by guiding and directing the energy of the human body it is possible for the body to become more aligned with the vital energy of the cosmos and in so doing the practitioner of inward training will have 'attained the Dao'.

CLASSICAL DAOISM

The three proto-Daoist texts mentioned above (the *Daode jing*, the *Zhuangzi* and the *Neiye*) give us a strong clue as to how the Daoist tradition came to develop. Their themes of social harmony, mystical realization, and biospiritual cultivation are all present to some extent in the formal Daoist religious movements that emerged in the second century (CE) towards the end of the Han dynasty. These movements, beginning with the Way of Great Peace and the Way of Orthodox Unity, were the first Daoist religious movements that we know of with a reasonable degree of historical accuracy.

The Way of Great Peace and the Way of Orthodox Unity

The Way of Great Peace was the name of the ideology espoused by a revolutionary religious–political community known, because of their distinctive headdress, as the Yellow Turbans. The Yellow Turbans, led by Zhang Jue in the east of China, organized an unsuccessful rebellion against the ruling Han dynasty in 184 CE. At the same time as the Yellow Turbans were being organized in the east of China, the most important Daoist religious organization was being organized in the West. Known as the Way of Orthodox Unity (Zhengyi dao) or the Way of the Celestial Masters (Tianshi dao), it was founded in 142 CE by Zhang Ling, later known as Zhang Daoling, revered as the first Celestial Master and founding patriarch of Daoist religion. The Way of Great Peace and the Way of Orthodox Unity are often discussed together because they shared many features in common, despite the fact that they emerged at opposite ends of the Chinese empire. Both organizations were established as theocracies in which the civil administration and the religious adminis- tration were one and the same. Both organizations held the expiation of sins as an important public ritual. Both organizations revered the divinized Laozi as a key personage in their pantheon.

Although the Way of Great Peace was bloodily suppressed by the Han dynasty, the Celestial Masters' movement was able to flourish in Sichuan province in the more remote western part of China. Zhang Ling organized his territory into twenty-four parishes each headed by a religious functionary known as a libationer. Offices were hereditary, and overall control of the movement passed on to Zhang Ling's son and grandson over a period of seventy-three years from 142 to 215 when the grandson, Zhang Lu, in a widely criticized move, ceded power to the powerful local warlord Cao Cao. At this point the followers spread or were forcibly moved throughout China, organizing themselves and integrating themselves into local communities.

The Way of Orthodox Unity is said to have originated in a vision of the divinized Laozi that was granted to Zhang Ling while he lived as a hermit on Mount Heming. According to tradition, Laozi presented

Zhang with an 'awesome covenant'. Within the framework of this covenant, Zhang and his followers claimed privileged access to a network of celestial powers or spirit–bureaucrats who regulated the fates of people in this world and the next. Members of the community contributed a tax of five pecks of rice or millet and were invested with a register that contained the names of the various spirits upon whom they could call for assistance. Those who were highest up in the community had the longest registers with the most names and the most powerful spirits at their command. In its original form every member of the community was thus an ordained Daoist with an important liturgical function. Nowadays only Celestial Masters' priests possess these registers, and they make a living by performing rituals for people in which they make use of the registers to call upon the spirits for assistance with whatever problem a person or community faces.

The Way of Highest Clarity

In the late fourth century an important new Daoist movement emerged among an aristocratic milieu in southern China. A religious visionary called Yang Xi received a revelation of texts from a Daoist immortal known as Lady Wei. Yang Xi was an official in the household of the Xu family who lived on Mount Mao (Maoshan) near present-day Nanjing. The scriptures were passed on through the Xu family and were eventually gathered together by Tao Hongjing (456–536). From Tao's efforts at reconstructing this revelation emerged the Shangqing school, or the Way of Highest Clarity. This form of Daoism was less communal in orientation than the original way of the Celestial Masters, though its exponents were themselves ordained priests in that tradition. What distinguished the Shangqing revelation was an emphasis on personal self-cultivation and on deities associated with the stars of the Big Dipper. Through a complex multi-coloured process of internal meditation, these deities were envisioned as descending into the organs of the body to aid in the process of transforming the adept into a celestial immortal.

The Way of Numinous Treasure

Another new direction in Daoism emerged from the encounter between Buddhism and Daoism that developed in the Lingbao (Numinous Treasure) sect. It is thought that the term Lingbao referred originally to spirit guardians, that is, shamanic figures who were able to interact easily with the realm of the ancestors. Subsequently the term came to refer to talismanic objects, usually texts or diagrams, that were imbued with spiritual powers and guaranteed the protection of the spirits to their owner. The Lingbao school evolved into tradition based on five of these sacred diagrams, each associated with the five directions (north, south, east, west and centre), which were incorporated in a collection of texts allegedly composed in the 390s by Ge Chaofu, heir to an important family of Daoists. When these texts were made public in 401 they were immediately popular and exerted a wide influence on the development of Daoism. The influence of Buddhism came to be seen in the application of these texts and talismans for the salvation of all living beings. What originally began as a movement to assist in the liberation and transformation of the individual practitioner evolved into complex liturgies designed to save everyone from a Buddhist-inspired complex of purgatories and hells in which the individual suffered retribution for the karmic guilt accumulated during his or her lifetime.

One of the most important figures in this stage of Daoist evolution was the seventh celestial master, Lu Xiujing (406–77) who classified the corpus of Lingbao scriptures, and standardized Daoist ritual into three major forms: ordinations (*jie*), fasts (*zhai*) and offerings (*jiao*). These rituals formed the basis for the official religion that came to be practised at the imperial court, but Lu also developed rituals for lay people, thus ensuring the widespread popularization of Daoism. Thanks to Lu's efforts, Daoism began to exert a deep influence on Chinese religious life rather than remain the preserve of isolated communities or aristocratic families. To this day the *jiao* ritual is the main public ritual performed by Daoist priests, and elements of it still date back to Lu's liturgy.

The influence of Buddhism is also evident in the development of Daoist monasteries. Although Daoism had already a long tradition of eremitism in which individuals would leave their families (*chujia*) and devote themselves to a monastic life often in the mountains, Daoism had no formal monastic organization until Lu developed a set of precepts specifically for Daoist monks. These precepts included vows to abstain from meat and sexual intercourse.

Daoism under the Tang

All of the above Daoist movements were finally integrated into a coherent whole under the Tang dynasty. In the seventh century Daoism was established as the official religion, and imperially sponsored monasteries were established throughout China. This was partly a nationalistic reaction against the foreign religion of Buddhism and partly an attempt to give religious legitimation to the authority of the Tang emperors. On the one hand this period in Chinese history represents the high-point of Daoist history in which Daoism fully penetrated Chinese culture, inspiring poets, painters and philosophers; on the other hand it could be argued that this marked a watershed in which Daoism lost its political independence and became chiefly an ideological tool of the political elite.

MODERN DAOISM

The period of modern Daoism begins with the Song Dynasty (960–1279), during which time the boundaries between elite Daoist religion, Buddhism, and local cults begin to be increasingly blurred (Davis, 2002). Based on the syncretism that began in this period, it becomes increasingly difficult to separate out Daoism as a religious category from the popular Chinese religious culture as it functions on the ground. In terms of elite Daoism, however, the most significant event is the formation of the Way of Complete Perfection by Wang Zhe and his seven disciples in the twelfth century. Modern Daoism can be traced back to this period as the modern Daoist emphasis on the importance of both internal energy practices and the cultivation of personal morality was definitively put into place by Wang's disciples' insistence on the dual cultivation of mind and nature. This religious philosophy thus mirrored the trend towards syncretism that was taking place in popular religion, and incorporated the Daoist cultivation of the body with Buddhist-style meditation practices and a Confucian insistence on spiritual and ethical integrity. Furthermore it consolidated the pursuit of personal transcendence as the central goal of Daoist cultivation. All these are the hallmarks of Daoism as it evolved in the modern period and became popularized throughout China.

The Way of Complete Perfection

The origins of the Way of Complete Perfection can be traced back to the summer of 1159, when, according to tradition, the founder Wang Zhe encountered Zhongli Quan and Lü Dongbin. Zhongli Quan and Lü

Dongbin were Daoist immortals – human beings who had engaged in a lifetime of cultivation and, through a process known as internal alchemy, transmuted into the form of transcendent spiritual beings not subject to the ordinary limitations of space and time. Zhongli and Lü chose Wang as their disciple and instructed him in the cultivation of the internal energies of his body. Wang then left his family, and engaged in a life of extreme asceticism that at one point involved digging himself a 'living grave' in the ground in which he lived and meditated. When he emerged from his grave he gathered seven disciples and established the Way of Complete Perfection that exists to this day.

The most important of Wang's seven disciples was Qiu Chuji (1148–1227) who met with Chinggis Khan – the Mongol warlord who had successfully invaded northern China – and whose grandson Kublai established the Yuan dynasty in 1280. Chinggis Khan put Qiu in charge of all religions in China and gave Complete Perfection monasteries tax-exempt status. The movement flourished immediately. Also important among the seven disciples was Sun Bu'er (1119–82), the only woman. She is widely revered by women as the most important female Daoist role-model.

Through the network of monasteries that were established by Wang's followers, the methods of internal alchemy became more widespread throughout China. The quest for immortality had previously been the goal of the elite few, but this goal now became accessible to many in the form of breathing and other energy practices that aimed to stimulate and guide the flow of qi in the body. Of course few people attained the goal of immortality, and those who did are now honoured as divine beings – but many people were able to use the practices developed in the monasteries to improve their ordinary lives.

During the Ming dynasty (1368–1644) Daoism received regular patronage at the imperial court. As a result Daoism became more and more integrated into the civil life of Chinese society. Daoist priests officiated at civil religious temples, and popular deities were adopted into the Daoist pantheon. An important example of this is the Daoist adoption of the city gods (Chenghuang). Each city usually had its own city god who was responsible for the well-being of the city. The fact that these deities were adopted into Daoism indicates the blending of official civic religion and Daoist religion that was taking place. Another example of this is the way in which the Yongle Emperor promoted Mount Wudang (Wudang shan) as a Daoist centre. Mount Wudang was the centre of a religious cult devoted to the martial deity Xuanwu or Zhenwu (Dark Warrior or Perfected Warrior). Again this deity was thoroughly adopted into the ever-expanding pantheon of Daoist deities and was welcomed by both Complete Perfection monks and Celestial Masters' priests. It is one of the most important Daoist centres today.

The subsequent Qing dynasty (1644–1911) was marked by the increasingly unsuccessful attempts of the government to exert a rigid control over the functioning of religion. The result of their policies was an explosion of popular lay religious cults and a relative decline in importance of official Daoist religion. The last two hundred years, in particular, have witnessed an explosion in popularity of energy practices such as *taiji quan* and qigong. The rise in popularity of these Daoist-inspired arts can in part be attributed to the strict control over religion exercised by the state in the Qing dynasty. During this period religion seemed to flourish more in the form of lay movements rather than monastic organizations. The important exception to this rule was the establishment of the Dragon Gate (Longmen) branch of the Way of Complete Perfection in 1656. This branch of Daoism, based at the White Cloud Monastery (Baiyun guan) in Beijing is the dominant form of monastic Daoism today.

CONTEMPORARY DAOISM

The contemporary period in Daoism is marked by the influence of the West. In the nineteenth century, the Qing government struggled unsuccessfully to stave off the encroachment of foreign powers onto Chinese territory. Through war and threats of war, European colonial powers exacted concessions of territory and trading rights from the Qing government. The Chinese elite saw itself as weak and in need of modernization. Intellectuals led the struggle to reform China's traditional attitudes and to embrace Western science and technology. Modernization of China's feudal society came violently in the form of the overthrow of the Qing government in 1911 and the subsequent establishment of the Republic of China. Following a bitter civil war between the nationalists led by Chiang Kai-Shek and the communists led by Chairman Mao Zedong – interrupted by the Japanese invasion of 1937 and the Second World War – the communists gained the upper hand and the nationalists fled to the island of Taiwan. In 1949 Mao proclaimed the establishment of the People's Republic of China.

This event fundamentally changed the nature and functioning of Daoism in two ways. On the one hand, Daoism was effectively banned in China as a feudal superstition, its monks sent out to work, the monasteries closed or destroyed, and its priests forbidden from conducting rituals. On the other hand through the emigration of millions of Chinese throughout the world, Daoism began to be established more and more in the West. As it has done so it has increasingly adapted itself to, or been appropriated by, Western cultural forms, and is less to be found as a traditional organized religion than as a collection of philosophical ideas accompanied by health practices.

Daoism is once again in flux. On the one hand it seems quite clear that the popularized forms of Daoist cultivation practices are ever more widespread, and now these practices are being repackaged to make them more accessible to Westerners and are being sold over the Internet. At the same time Westerners have developed a dissatisfaction with many traditional Western forms of philosophy and religion and are eagerly turning to ancient proto-Daoist philosophies such as those found in the *Daode jing* and the *Zhuangzi*. On the other hand institutional Daoism in the form of Complete Perfection monasteries and Celestial Masters' priests has suffered a terrible blow in China. Since the relative liberalization begun under Deng Xiaoping's regime in 1980, Daoism has begun to function again in China and many temples and monasteries have been reopened, but the bitter loss of a whole generation of the transmission of Daoism cannot be underestimated.

Now younger Daoist monks are struggling to rebuild their religion and some are enrolling in university courses to try to recapture their history and doctrines. On a recent visit to China, I interviewed one bright, young monk who was doing research into Lingbao Daoism. He chose to research Lingbao Daoism because it was the Lingbao reformer Lu Xiujing who established the foundations and basic principles for Daoist ritual. Today many rituals are carried out in Daoist temples in China without the meaning of those rituals being fully understood by the participants. By returning to the historical roots of Daoist ritual, he hopes to restore the understanding that was lost when the transmission of Daoism was interrupted by the Cultural Revolution in the 1960s and 70s.

At the end of this swift survey of Daoist history one thing is quite clear: Daoism is hard to define. It has few essential characteristics that remain constant from one generation to another. It has disparate origins, has borrowed extensively from other religions and our understanding of it has been further complicated by the effects of Western colonialism and Western-inspired communism. All this flux is reflected in the current debate in Western scholarship about Daoist identity. What exactly is Daoism and how can we define it? Before we proceed any further in our investigation of Daoism we must first of all explore the question of Daoist identity.

SUGGESTIONS FOR FURTHER READING

Kohn, Livia. 2001. *Daoism and Chinese Culture*. Cambridge, MA, Three Pines Press
Robinet, Isabelle. 1997. *Taoism: Growth of a Religion*, trans. Phyllis Brooks. Stanford, Stanford University Press.

1

Identity

家

What is Daoism? Who is a Daoist? The ways in which Daoist creativity is acknowledged and embodied in ritual and culture vary so widely that these questions are frustratingly difficult to settle. Nonetheless, Daoists and scholars of Daoism have historically sought to understand Daoism and Daoist identity in three main ways: 1) as the indigenous religion of China; 2) as a lineage of transmission; and 3) as a universal path. In all these cases, however, it is important to bear in mind that Daoist identity is always something that is constructed and asserted by human beings and human communities. Moreover, the question of identity always involves aspects of power and authority because identity is a form of demarcation in which some people are included and others are excluded. In all the cases that we will be considering it is important to know who is defining Daoism and what interests they have in constructing their own particular definitions. Even though it is difficult, it is still necessary to attempt a definition of Daoism, otherwise there is no way for us to come to a clear understanding in our own minds.

Before beginning a somewhat complex investigation into the ways in which scholars have historically understood what Daoism means, it is worth investigating first of all the range of terms that are used in English and Chinese to represent the various phenomena under investigation. The Western understanding of Daoism is undergoing a sea-change at the moment, and a century of neglect of the Daoist religion and its dismissal as magic and superstition is being replaced by a renewed respect and less prejudiced understanding.

Whether one uses the 'Taoist' or 'Daoist' spelling, both of these terms refer to three Chinese terms that need to be explained: daojia, daojiao and daoshu, which may be translated respectively as the 'school of the Way', the 'traditions of the Way', and the 'arts of the Way'. The earliest of these terms is the first one and was used initially as a bibliographical classification for books such as the *Daode jing* that concerned themselves with the Way. This term is often translated into English as 'Philosophical Daoism', but it would be misleading to suggest that the content of these books is what you would expect from the English term 'philosophy' for they deal with wisdom, meditation and statecraft rather than logic and metaphysics. The second of these terms is often translated as 'Religious Daoism'. It is used in Chinese to refer to the transmission of Daoist teachings chiefly within an institutionalized, religious setting that takes place when priests in the tradition of the Celestial Masters are trained and ordained. The third term refers mostly to Daoist practices such as breathing meditation or energy movements that may be undertaken either in a formal religious context, or on one's own or under the auspices of a lay Daoist organization.

The interesting point about all this is that different people have different ideas as to which of these three sorts of 'Daoism' legitimately deserve the label 'Daoism' in English. Broadly speaking, the move in the West has been to acknowledge that 'Daoism' is a legitimate religion (daojiao) and not just a classical philosophy. There is, however, no consensus as to whether the term 'Daoism' may also be applied to the Daoist arts such as *Qigong* that are increasingly prevalent in the West. In this book I use the term 'Daoism' in the widest sense possible, to include all three Chinese terms, but it is important to understand the distinctions between them, and to understand why there is something of an acrimonious debate about Daoist identity. In order to understand this debate it is necessary to understand something about the history of the Western scholarly understanding of the term 'Daoism', and how Daoism has historically been defined by scholars.

DAOISM AS CHINESE RELIGION

The most important definition of Daoism that has been drawn up by scholars is that Daoism is the organized, indigenous religion of China. This definition links the religion of Daoism with the geographic space that is China and, by extension, the cultural and racial identity of

Chinese people. This definition is sometimes used as an ethnic-cultural definition, but it is also used as a racial-genetic definition. But what exactly is China, and who exactly are the Chinese people? These are both complex questions that deserve further investigation.

The Chinese term for China translates into English as 'The Middle Kingdom'. This suggests that China is not something that has an essential identity in and of itself, but is a term that is defined by its relationship with other geographic and cultural spaces. The assertion of Chinese identity is thus an assertion over and against other geographic and cultural spaces that are by definition peripheral, or, in traditional Chinese terms, 'barbarian'. These 'barbarian' spaces, whether the icy plains to the north, the fiery deserts to the west, or the dense jungles to the south, are not simply geographical locations, but important cultural markers. They define whatever 'the Middle Kingdom' is not: inhospitable to human flourishing and civilization. Conversely, the ideology of 'the Middle Kingdom' asserts a unified, centralized identity, a refuge from, and bulwark against, those other, 'dangerous', peripheral spaces.

All of this perhaps suggests that China and Chineseness is something that has historically had to be asserted or manufactured to resist a far different reality – that of an extraordinary internal diversity within China, and a long history of cultural exchange with non-Chinese peoples. But why has the idea of a unified Chinese identity been manufactured in this way? One answer to this question takes us back to the period in Chinese history when China, as we now know it, came into being. Known as the Warring States period (seventh to third centuries BCE), it was a time of disunity and warfare between several smaller states that occupied the central area of what we now call China. Each of these states had its own traditions, culture and language, and the literary documents that we now possess suggest that people looked back to a golden age of the former Zhou empire. Eventually the period of disunity ended when the state of Qin successfully conquered the other states in 221 BCE, imposed a single legal administration, standardized weights and measures and the writing system, and began construction of the Great Wall of China. The English word 'China' derives from the Chinese 'Qin', and so also the cultural idea of 'China' may be seen as deriving from the success of the Qin in unifying central China, the Middle Kingdom, and separating itself from the outer 'barbarian' states.

More recently, however, there has been a different attempt to assert the unity of Chinese identity. This attempt arose as a result of Western colonial interest in China during the nineteenth century, which led to a rise in Chinese nationalism. As nationalist Chinese scholars struggled to understand their own national identity they turned to a racial definition that based Chinese identity upon the notion of a 'yellow race'. The importance of race as a biological category was brought to China by the Western colonialists and was rooted in scientific ideas that came to China through the translation of the works of Charles Darwin and Thomas Huxley towards the end of the nineteenth century. These works gave rise to the idea of the human species being divided into several races, each competing with the other in a struggle for genetic superiority. Of course now we know that genetic diversity is spread throughout different races and that, from an evolutionary point of view, race contains nothing of biological importance. At the time, however, racial purity and eugenics were seen as vital scientific enterprises. We should not be surprised to learn, therefore, that the notion of the 'yellow race' had no connotations of racial inferiority in China. In fact the reverse was the case, for the colour yellow corresponds to the idea of the centre in the Chinese symbolic universe. Yellow is the imperial colour, the most august and splendid colour. Thus the notion of a yellow race reinforced the idea of cultural superiority over and against peripheral races, whether white, brown or black.

Moreover this nineteenth century period in Chinese history saw the rise in importance of extended clans based on shared patriarchal lineages within Chinese society. The way to unite the Chinese people against foreign domination was sought in the myth of the Yellow Emperor, the legendary founder of China and patriarch of the Chinese race. This myth was employed by nationalists in order to foster the notion of a single Chinese race, known as the Han. This powerful notion was used not only to assert Chinese racial identity in the face of Western aggression, but as an ideological weapon against the corrupt Qing dynasty government which was of Manchu origin. The overthrow of the Manchu Qing dynasty in 1911 only contributed to an upsurge in Han Chinese nationalism that came to be expressed in many literary and cultural forms of the era. A typical example is the nationalistic poem by the famous poet, Wen Yiduo:

> I am Chinese, I am Chinese
> I am the divine blood of the Yellow Emperor
> I come from the highest place in the world,
> Pamir is my ancestral place,

My race is like the Yellow River,
We flow down the Kunlun mountain slope,
We flow across the Asian continent,
From us have flowed exquisite customs.
Mighty nation! Mighty nation!

(trans. Dikötter, 1997, p. 23)

In this way European colonialism came to foster an extremely powerful Chinese nationalism based on the quasi-biological assertion of Chinese identity that derived from an ultimately mythical patriarch. It is no surprise to learn, therefore, that the earliest Western investigators of religion in China defined it racially, as though there were some intrinsic connection between race and religion. There was no distinction made at the time between the biological category of race and the cultural category of ethnicity, and thus it was that eminent scholars of religion and anthropology conducted their research along essentially racialist lines. It would be surprising for Westerners to come across a book on 'European Religion' that sought to present a synoptic overview of some supposed intrinsically European tradition, because Westerners are readily attuned to ethnic and religious diversity within Europe. But Westerners do not seem to be surprised by books or university courses on 'Chinese Religion'. Perhaps this is simply because Westerners – and also Chinese people facing Western colonialism – have been trained to think of China as a single cultural unit.

Early works in the study of religion in China include Marcel Granet's *The Religion of the Chinese People* (1922) and J.J.M. De Groot's *The Religion of the Chinese* (1910). We must not infer from the titles of these works that these scholars were in any way racially prejudiced – indeed their works are pioneering and still valuable today – but it is legitimate to infer that for them, race was an essential category for understanding religion. De Groot writes in the introduction to his book: 'China's religion proper, that is to say, apart from Buddhism, which is of foreign introduction, is a spontaneous product, spontaneously developed in the course of time. Its origin is lost in the night of ages. But there is no reason to doubt, that it is the first religion the Chinese race ever had' (1910, p. 1).

Work such as this has given rise to the impression that there is – without any question – a single Chinese people who share a common cultural and religious heritage. Of course as Chinese nationalism continued into the twentieth century this view becomes increasingly correct, as Chinese people themselves asserted a unity that was never before present in China. Increasingly Mandarin or Modern Standard Chinese is spoken throughout China, and with the introduction of simplified Chinese characters as an aid to improving literacy, the People's Republic of China sees itself as more and more a single, cohesive, powerful nation state. For this reason it vehemently opposes the recognition of Taiwan as a separate nation state, and views itself as the true motherland of all Han Chinese people, whether or not they are citizens of other countries. The People's Republic of China also recognizes that approximately seven per cent of its population is non-Han people, of various ethnic nationalities, ranging from the Muslim Uighurs and Buddhist Tibetans in the west to a multitude of small ethnic groups in the south and south-west.

Given all of the above, does it make any sense to speak of Daoism as a Chinese religion? The answer to this question is yes, but with important qualifications. One of the most important reasons for answering yes is that traditional Daoist scriptures are written in Chinese script. This is true for Korean and Japanese Daoists as much as it is for Chinese Daoists. This also means that academics who wish to study Daoism must spend a lot of time learning classical Chinese, and historically Daoism has been most studied in departments of East Asian studies by people who are trained first and foremost in understanding Chinese texts rather than religious ideas and practices. But increasingly it must be recognized that Daoism is also a non-Chinese religion with followers who do not speak a word of Chinese, and, although many people will be surprised to learn this, there are now Daoist priests who are of African and European descent. Moreover as our knowledge of early China grows through archaeological discoveries, there is increasing evidence of wide diversity within the early Chinese cultures that gave rise to Daoism as an organized religious system.

Popular Chinese religion and culture

Any understanding of Daoism as Chinese religion also has to take into account the complex relationship between Daoism and the religious/ cultural practices of the Chinese people. All religions in China have traditionally functioned in relation to a common substrate of popular religion. The characteristics of this popular Chinese religion are relatively simple to identify. Its main components are a calendar that takes into account both lunar and solar elements; a set of festivals based on that calendar; and a way of respecting one's deceased ancestors. Together these three elements constitute the foundation for the everyday cultural-religious practices that are common to most people who consider themselves ethnically Chinese, and also to many people throughout South-East Asia in the zone of Chinese cultural influence. Daoism has had a varying relationship with this popular religious culture, at times being fully integrated into it, and at times wishing to distance itself from it. In order to understand these differences it is first necessary to go into some detail about the Chinese calendar and the traditional festivals.

The most important difference between Chinese timekeeping and Western timekeeping is the system of marking years. Western time is marked in reference to the year of Jesus' birth, whereas Chinese time is traditionally marked by reference to a sixty-year cycle based originally on the twelve years that it takes the planet Jupiter to make a complete circuit of the night sky. The sixty-year cycle was created combining a decimal system known as the ten 'stems' with the duodecimal cycle of the twelve 'branches', originally houses of Jupiter, each of which is further associated with an animal of the Chinese zodiac.

Stem	Branch	English Equivalent	Numerical Value
jia	zi	A – rat	1
yi	chou	B – ox	2
bing	yin	C – tiger	3
ding	mao	D – hare	4
mou	chen	E – dragon	5
yi	si	F – snake	6
geng	wu	G – horse	7
xin	wei	H – sheep	8
ren	shen	I – monkey	9
gui	you	J – rooster	10
(cycle repeats)	xu	A – dog	11
	hai	B – pig	12
	(cycle repeats)	C – rat	13
		D – ox	14
		E – tiger	15
		⋮	⋮
		H – rooster	58
		I – dog	59
		J – pig	60
		(cycle repeats)	(cycle repeats)

Traditionally it is claimed that the entire system was invented by the legendary Yellow Emperor in 2637 BCE. We are thus in the middle of the seventy-eighth cycle of sixty years, which began in 1984. The seventy-ninth cycle will begin with the next jiazi year, in 2044.

The confusing part comes in with the fact that to divide up each year the Chinese calendar combines both lunar and solar elements. In this respect it is similar to the Jewish calendar, but unlike the Western calendar (solar) and the Muslim calendar (lunar). The lunar element of the Chinese calendar comes from dividing the year into twelve lunar months of three ten-day weeks. The solar element comes from the parallel division of the year into twenty-four solar houses. Two Chinese festivals are based on the solar calendar: the Qingming (grave-sweeping) festival, which usually falls on 5 April; and the midwinter festival, on 21 December. Other Chinese festivals, including the new year and the mid-autumn festival are based on the lunar year. Overall the lunar and the solar calendars are combined to create the important festivals of the Chinese calendar. For instance the new year festival begins with the new moon (from the lunar calendar) that falls closest to the spring equinox (from the solar calendar). Moreover, in order to reconcile the lunar year of 360 days with the solar year of 365¼ days it is necessary to insert an intercalary, thirteenth leap month seven times every nineteen years. Not surprisingly the calendar improved with advances in mathematics and astronomy and was reformed in 1280 under the influence of Muslim astronomy and again in 1645 by the Jesuit astronomer Adam Schall (Aslaksen, 2002).

The reason this is important is that the Daoist calendar is identical to the traditional Chinese calendar, and influences the functioning of Daoist ritual. For instance Daoist priests celebrate an enormous jiao festival once every sixty years on the *jiazi* year that marks the beginning of the cycle. For Daoists this festival and the year it marks represent the rebirth of the cosmos and the renewal of life. One reason why Daoism seems so tied into Chinese culture is that it is impossible to appreciate the significance of this and many other Daoist rituals without understanding how they are tied to the various solar and lunar cycles of the traditional Chinese calendar. The *jiazi* year is also significant within Daoist political history. The central ideology of the Yellow Turbans movement, for instance, was underpinned by the goal of instituting a utopian era of peace and prosperity in 184 CE. That year was chosen because it too was a jiazi year.

The second important area of convergence – and difference – between Daoism and popular Chinese religion lies in the treatment of deceased ancestors. In traditional Chinese culture, an ancestor is venerated in two ways based on the Chinese cultural belief in two souls – an earthly, material soul called the *po* soul and a heavenly, more ethereal soul called the *hun* soul. The *po* is interred with the body in the grave and stays with the body for several days after death. Funeral rites must be conducted correctly so that the *po* safely leaves the body and has a successful journey into the underworld. If the *po* is in any way disturbed or troubled it may return as a 'hungry ghost', a disturbing psychic force that may bring misfortune on the family. The *hun*, on the other hand, separates from the body at death and is thought to ascend to heaven. The *hun* of the ancestor is traditionally venerated in the form of a tablet that records the ancestor's name and his or her image in the form of a photograph or other likeness. The most spectacular case of care given to the soul can be seen in the famous terracotta warriors, some six thousand of them who were buried to protect the grave of the first Qin Emperor (Qin shi huangdi, r. 221–210 BCE). A more conventional way of ensuring the successful afterlife of the *po* in the underworld was by offering the blood of sacrificed animals and other desirable goods. Nowadays the most common form of offering is fruit and other comestibles, but offerings can also take the form of burning paper money and credit cards at the graveside. It is the responsibility of each family or extended clan to look after the souls of its own ancestors. Additionally, the souls of particularly eminent figures such as the teacher Confucius, the legendary Yellow Emperor, or particularly important local figures may be venerated in civic temples.

Daoism, by contrast, proposes a different attitude to death. First of all it raised the possibility for some people to escape the ordinary death that most people go through, in which the body and the souls are separated. Some people are able to keep their souls intact and to enter a transcendent plane of existence frequently symbolized as a heavenly or an island paradise. These people, known as immortals, are thus an entirely different class of spiritual being than the ordinary ancestor whose soul must be laid to rest in the underworld. In this way the personalities in the Daoist pantheon are of a different order than the deities in the ordinary popular Chinese pantheon of emperors, ancestors and worthies. According to Anna Seidel (1987) the Daoist approach to death must be considered an innovation over the traditional Chinese attitude because it proposed that the ancestors' souls might not only be comforted (and therefore kept at bay) in the underworld, but that they might in fact be liberated from it.

The possibility for this sort of liberation was established in the religion of the Celestial Masters. Daoist priests ordained in the lineage of the Celestial Masters possess a privileged access to the functionaries of the transcendent realm in the form of registers (lu) that contain the names of these spirit-officials that govern the fates of mortal men and women. The priest, acting as a sort of funerary bureaucrat, addresses a written memorandum to the appropriate spirits requesting that the deceased be permitted entry to the celestial realms. The deceased is then buried along with this 'grave contract' so as to ensure the liberation of his or her soul, or the memorial is burned to speed its message heavenward in the form of smoke. Although the extent to which this 'post-mortem liberation' was an innovation has recently been challenged (Nickerson, 2002), and is clearly a question of interpretation, the fact remains that Daoist priests, at least at some points in their history, aimed to distinguish themselves from other religious popular functionaries by the type of rituals they performed and the class of spiritual officials to which they claim access. In this regard a Daoist funeral conducted by Daoist priests offers a different type of salvation than that offered by, say, a Catholic funeral mass or by Buddhist monks.

The problem with this definition is that it does not hold true throughout Daoist history, and is particularly problematical in the modern period from the Song dynasty onwards (960–1279) when Daoist priests came to occupy overlapping ritual spaces with Buddhists and also popular religious functionaries such as spirit-mediums (Davis, 2002). This practical ambiguity that developed in Chinese history has persuaded the Daoist academic Kristofer Schipper to argue that Daoism in actuality is nothing more (or less) than a specifically institutionalized form of popular Chinese religion (Schipper, 1993, p. 2). The confusion arises partly out of the multiplicity of perspectives from which Daoism is studied, and the truth of the matter is more likely that Daoism's relationship with popular Chinese religion is both 'antagonistic and symbiotic' (Davis, 2002, p. 11). Attempting to define Daoism based on categories of ethnicity and race, or on function and ritual are clearly important perspectives, but each one has its own limitations.

DAOISM AS LINEAGES OF TRANSMISSION

An alternative to the ethnic and functional perspectives outlined above is to regard Daoism in terms of its genealogy, that is, the lineages of transmission and ordination that are claimed by Daoist priests. The advantage of this is that it is less dependent on the racial or ethnic categories surrounding the notion of 'Chinese religion'. Daoist priests trace their lineage back to the first Celestial Master, Zhang Daoling. According to Daoist tradition, in 142 CE Zhang was living as a hermit on Mount Heming in present-day Sichuan province in China's fertile west. He was said to have been searching for an elixir of immortality when he was granted an audience with the deity Laozi. 'Suddenly there was a heavenly being descending with a thousand chariots, ten thousand riders and golden carriages with feathery canopies drawn by countless dragons on the outside and tigers on the inside. Sometimes he called himself the Archivist; at other times he called himself the child of the Eastern sea. He then gave Ling the newly emerged Way of Orthodox Unity and the Awesome Covenant' (Ge Hong, 'Biography of Zhang Daoling' in *Shenxian Zhuan* [Biographies of Divine Immortals]).

This covenant was a method for modelling human communities on a vast celestial bureaucracy with which it was in intimate, sympathetic relation. This theocracy divided the community into parishes each led by priests known as 'libationers'. Originally, each member of the community was invested with a register that recorded his or her name and rank within the hierarchy. Each register also listed the names of the celestial spirits upon which the individual was able to call. One's status depended upon the number of spirits under one's control, and status was conferred by being ordained or invested with registers that listed the names of these spirits.

This system of ordaining all members of the Daoist community no longer exists in China, but its legacy endures in the form of a system of priestly ordinations. At their ordination ritual, Daoist priests are invested with scriptures, talismans and registers that grant them privileged access to members of a celestial bureaucracy that, to a large extent, functions just like any other government administration. The celestial powers are stirred to action by submitting petitions or memoranda correctly inscribed in conformity with the complexities of celestial protocol, by a duly ordained priest. Such priests continue today to offer petitions on behalf of human beings who are in any situation that needs the help of spiritual powers. The most common times when Daoist priests are employed are at birth and death or at moments of crisis in personal lives or in the life of a community. These priests see themselves in a direct line of transmission from Zhang Daoling whom they revere as the first Celestial Master.

In the light of this system of ordination, it is quite easy to answer the question, 'Who is a Daoist?' A Daoist is someone who has been ordained into a lineage of transmission and has been invested with registers that record the names of the celestial powers that can be invoked when needed. Daoists are trained by their teachers in the arts of submitting petitions and may be viewed as functionaries or civil servants within a splendid celestial network that is ordinarily inaccessible to most human beings. This view has been most forcefully articulated by Michel Strickmann:

> Zhang Daoling and his followers clearly effected a religious revolution. They inaugurated a new dispensation that defined itself, then as now, not in relation to Buddhism or 'Confucianism', but rather in antithesis to the false gods whom the benighted populace worshipped with blood offerings. Though the early Daoists spoke of high antiquity, of the Yellow Emperor, Yu the Great and the famous immortals of the Zhou dynasty ... the social history of the Daoism begins with the founding of the Way of the Celestial Master in the second century AD.
>
> Thus I am proposing to use the word *Daoist* only in referring to those who recognize the historical position of Zhang Daoling, who worship the pure emanations of the Dao rather than the vulgar gods of the people at large, and – I may add – who safeguard and perpetuate their own lore and practices through esoteric rites of transmission. (Strickmann, 1979, pp. 165–6; quoted in Nickerson, 2002, p. 58)

A major advantage of this way of defining Daoist identity is that it releases Daoism from the problem of its relation to the problematic category of 'Chinese religion'. This is particularly important given the fact that the Celestial Masters' movement originated in what we know to be an ethnically diverse part of China (present-day Sichuan province) and developed in partnership with the local Ba minority culture. In fact the noted sinologist Terry Kleeman has recently argued that 'the earliest Celestial Masters community was truly multiethnic, accepting people from a variety of ethnic backgrounds as equal members of the new faith. This was an unprecedented event in Chinese history and deserves far more recognition than it has received' (Kleeman, 2002, p. 28). Moreover, as Kleeman goes on to explain, one of the major forms of Daoism today is practised by the Yao minority people who originally lived in southern China but now are more prominent in Thailand, Laos and Vietnam. Every member of the Yao is ordained into a form of Daoist priesthood and invested with registers, in a strikingly similar fashion to what we know took place in the original Celestial Masters' community (2002, pp. 32–3). Within Chinese ethnic culture today, only priests are ordained as Daoists, not the whole of the religious community.

Strickmann's definition of Daoist identity equates Daoism with ordination. Although this way of defining Daoist identity has the advantage of clarity and precision, and avoids the problems of ethnic-based definitions, the problem is that it does not adequately reflect the sociological situation of Daoism in the modern period, with its development of monastic Daoism and lay Daoist associations. The narrow Strickmann definition thus represents only one major strand of the teachings and practices that have traditionally fallen under the rubric of 'Daoism'. The other major line of teachings that continues today is based on the Way of Complete Perfection, the monastic religion that encourages people to leave their homes and spend time in a monastery learning cultivation practices from senior practioners. These practices centre on learning to cultivate the qi-energy of the body in a form of internal alchemy that gradually transforms the body into an ever more subtle and refined form, which eventually operates as though all distinctions between the body and the world have dissolved away. Those who approach this level of perfection in their personal cultivation become utterly tranquil in their attitude, and neither attached nor unattached to the goings on around them. This is quite a different sort of Daoism than the Daoism of the Celestial Masters' religion, but there is no getting around the fact that both types of Daoist communities, while sociologically distinct, have always considered themselves to be Daoist and have always been accepted as Daoist. Moreover there is a clear historical connection between these two distinct religious forms.

In this second monastic form of modern Daoism it is still important to remember that Daoists are trained and initiated under the guidance of experienced masters who themselves were trained and initiated by experienced masters before them in a lineage of transmission that too stretches back over centuries. Although the emphasis is not on the control of celestial powers through a religious bureaucratic system, this does not mean that we can in any way discount the importance of lineage in Complete Perfection Daoism. The difference lies in the content of the transmission: in Complete Perfection the content of the transmission is primarily methods of cultivating the body; in Celestial Masters' Daoism, the content is primarily registers and talismanic scriptures, and the training in how to use them.

Although these two styles of Daoism seem to be very different in their content, in fact the difference is perhaps less than it seems. The fact is that both styles of Daoism are concerned with the renewing and refining of the body. For the Orthodox Unity priests, the body is often construed as the body of the community, which may be disturbed by individual actions or by natural events such as deaths or floods. In either case the goal is restoring harmony and balance to the life of the body. In the case of Complete Perfection Daoists, their quest is clearly more individualistic in nature, but at a deep level Daoists argue that the many different dimensions of reality that tend to get separated in our everyday experience of the world – the heavens, the earth, the village, the body – are in fact reflections of each other. A modern way of interpreting the Daoist world is by analogy with a hologram or a fractal function in mathematics such as the Mandelbrot Set. In both cases, what is important is that a part contains an image of the whole within itself. No matter how many times you break each part down, the image of the whole is still preserved. Whereas we are often used to thinking about relationships in terms of parts which combine together to make a whole, Daoist thought and practice tends to hold on to this alternative way of understanding relationships in which each part retains something of the whole within itself – just like the DNA in each individual cell contains the complete DNA for the whole organism. So, if one branch of Daoism attends primarily to imbalances in large-scale environments such as human communities, and another branch of Daoism attends primarily to the refining of the individual body, we should not see these as being in any way opposed to each other. For this reason these two major branches of transmission deserve to be, and have always been, classified as Daoism even though from the perspectives of Western sociology of religion they may seem to be vastly different in function.

DAOISM AS UNIVERSAL PATH

The third way of understanding Daoism is as a universal mystical path that exists and functions independently of any particular lineage of transmission or cultural context. Although this way of understanding Daoism is particularly prevalent in the contemporary West, it has definite roots in Daoist tradition too.

This view of Daoism concentrates particularly on two of the earliest and most influential texts that were classified as belonging to 'Dao-school' writings. These texts, the *Daode jing* and the *Zhuangzi* were probably put together towards the end of the Warring States period (fourth century BCE), though the standard versions that we use today date from as late as the third century CE. Recent archeological finds at Mawangdui and Guodian have provided us with earlier versions of parts of the *Daode jing* written on silk cloth and strips of bamboo respectively. Although we will be looking in more detail at these texts later, what is important to ask here is how it came to be that for the best part of a century these earlier texts stood for the whole of Daoism in the Western imagination.

One answer to this is that these works are of extraordinarily high philosophical and literary value, so much so that the *Daode jing* is said to be the most translated work in the history of human culture, after the Bible. These texts are works of rare genius that are readily appreciated beyond Chinese culture. The *Daode jing* speaks of a way of acting that is in concert with the natural flow of things in the world, and advocates harmony and balance between *yang* and *yin*, the two poles of reality that depend each upon the other like sun and shade, day and night. The *Zhuangzi* contains a brilliant and sophisticated collection of stories that advocate equanimity in the face of fate, the advisability of refusing to engage in the business of government, and scepticism that philosophy can ever attain an adequate description of a world that is characterized by spontaneous, creative transformation.

Aside from the mass appeal of these works, they also have a profound and enduring influence on Chinese culture. During imperial times when Confucian principles of right relationship and proper social order were the official basis of government administration, these texts provided a welcome antidote to the necessarily formulaic nature of official public life. In contrast to the religious bureaucracy of the Celestial Masters, this classical 'Daoist' philosophy thus came to represent a sort of official counter-culture that was sanctioned by its inclusion in official libraries and its ready availability to all who could read. As a result, these texts were widely copied and commented upon within Chinese culture and were simply more accessible to China's wider cultural milieu than were the texts and rituals of Daoist priests that were handed down from generation to generation in secret ordinations. Thus even within China the type of Daoism that has most deeply pervaded Chinese intellectual culture is the proto-Daoist wisdom literature.

There exists, however, a further set of reasons as to why these texts took first place in the popular understanding of Daoism in the West. To understand this we have to look at the colonial attitudes that shaped the encounter of China and the West in the nineteenth century and the desires of popular Western culture in the twentieth century.

First, many of the earliest Western students of Chinese religion were Christian missionaries. First came the Catholics, both Jesuits and Dominicans, in the seventeenth and eighteenth centuries, and then the Protestants in the nineteenth and twentieth. The Catholic missionaries were mostly concerned with understanding the official, Confucian culture, since they recognized that this was the substance and the form of the imperial system. They sought a way to Catholicize the state apparatus without destroying it, but their efforts were frustrated by the Vatican, which insisted that converts to Catholicism must do away with all of the traditional Confucian ritual apparatus, especially reverence for one's ancestors. The Protestant missionaries by and large were directed more towards the common people and, in common with the spirit of the age, saw Protestant Christianity as a far more modern and 'scientific' form of religion that had done away with what they saw as the ritualistic excesses of Catholicism. Thus they focused on the local, popular religious cults and saw in them a terrible superstition that had to be eradicated. The view of these missionaries also became the view of Chinese modernizers, including especially the Chinese Communist Party, for whom religion is by and large a superstitious product of feudal culture that has no place in a modern, enlightened socialist state.

The Christian religion is also a religion that focuses on a book – the Bible – and the Western academic system is similarly biased towards engaging reality through words and ideas. Thus in their sincere attempt to understand Chinese culture, missionaries and academics both turned towards its classic texts, and in so doing came across a 'Daoism' that was found in the *Zhuangzi* and the *Daode jing*. When later scholars came to realize that there was a religious system also called 'Daoism', scholars wondered how it was that these two things were connected. To answer this question, they adopted the mindset of Protestant Christians who had argued that the Bible represented a form of pure, idealized Christianity that, through centuries of Roman Catholicism, had degenerated into a collection of rituals and social controls that served only to advance the interests of the Vatican establishment over the kings and rulers of European countries. So also, these academics believed, Daoism had existed in an originally pure philosophical form that had somehow degenerated into a ritualistic religion that was nothing more than pure superstition. This religion might be of interest to anthropologists and ethnographers, but not to scholars of the world's great religions, not to those who occupied themselves with the lofty sentiments of the Buddha, Jesus or the Prophet Muhammad.

A further development in the Western study of Daoism came about during the crisis in Western civilization that followed the Second World War and that threatened to engulf the world in nuclear holocaust. During this period the 'East' came to stand in many people's minds as the antidote to the 'West'. This dichotomy had always been present in the colonial period, where the West symbolized the place of enlightenment, science and democracy, and the East (or the South) symbolized the place of superstition, ignorance and primitive barbarism. In the 1960s and 70s, however, this polarity was reversed in popular counter-cultural movements in the West. The 'East' suddenly found itself to be the place of deep wisdom, tranquil philosophy and a timeless mystical insight into the true nature of reality. Driven by the understandable desires to reject their colonialist past, Westerners turned to the East not as it truly was, but as the inverse image or the negative of Western civilization. In a sense they continued the colonialist legacy of mirroring the 'other' as the antithesis of 'oneself'. Whereas in the past the 'other' was dark, dirty and in need of civilization, suddenly the 'other' was wise, benevolent and a beacon of enlightenment to the world.

It didn't take long before this enlightened, mystical wisdom was defined in its essential, ideal aspects. In fact this enterprise had been undertaken a few decades earlier by advocates, notably Aldous Huxley, of what is known as the 'perennial philosophy'. Advocates of this philosophy hold that there is an eternal, unchanging Reality that underlies the fleeting phenomena of temporal existence. Human beings have access to this Reality in the innermost part of their soul, and, through mystical practice (sometimes aided with psychoactive drugs) can achieve a union between the Soul and Reality. In the mystical bliss of spiritual union the seeker discovers that in fact the Soul and Reality are the very same eternal Oneness. When the seeker comes down from a spiritual high, he or she sees the world in a new light in which all of its parts are viewed as fragments of the same Oneness. No longer is the world a world of Self and Other, Us and Them; instead All is One. This extremely powerful and understandably attractive philosophy is sometimes referred to as the Perennial Philosophy because its adherents claim that it surfaces across (or lurks within) all world cultures in all periods of history under a variety of guises: in Islam, it is called Sufism; in Christianity it is present in the mystical philosophy of Meister Eckhart; in Hinduism it is in the Advaita Vedanta philosophy of Sankara; in Buddhism we call it Zen. In 'Chinese religion' it was called 'Taoism', meaning by this a sort of philosophical interpretation of selected aspects of the *Daode jing* and the *Zhuangzi* that sought a transcendental wisdom beyond the shallow teachings of conventional philosophy.

As people began to study this 'Taoism' more and more, it gradually took hold within the Western imagination as an antidote to the business of life and commerce that came to be held responsible for the environmental degradation perceived in the late twentieth century. The Western 'instrumental rationality' perceived all things as means to some desirable end, towards which it was one's duty to work hard, whereas 'Taoism' counselled a respect for the buzzing creativity of nature and cautious restraint or 'inaction' in which things should be permitted to take their natural course rather than being forced into cramped alignment with an unnatural human view of what was good or bad.

As the individual body and health culture of the 1990s soared in response to the failure of public health systems and global efforts to curb environmental degradation, so also did Westerners come to look carefully at Eastern physical cultivation practices. Westernized forms of Indian Yoga became immensely popular, and so also did Chinese health practices and martial arts. Today the world headquarters of the Taoist Tai-Chi Society is in Toronto, and Daoist practitioners such as Mantak Chia have adapted their own brands of physical cultivation practices and inner alchemy to suit Western markets. Whereas in the past it was Daoist philosophy that inspired a generation, now it is Daoist practices. In both these cases the ideas and the practices are being de-Chinesed and repackaged to suit Western consumers. Some scholars have reacted negatively towards this, claiming that what is being presented to Westerners as Daoism is nothing more than an American or Western Daoism that emphasizes traditional Western values such as individualism, commerce and freedom over traditional Chinese values such as respect for the lineage of transmission from which these teachings come. Perhaps the most apparent difference in the way these practices are being transmitted to the West is the readiness with which Western practitioners feel free to combine different Chinese practices they have learned or invent new ones to suit their needs or the needs of their commercial enterprises. In all of these cases, Daoism is seen as belonging to a universal human culture that has no intrinsic and essential connection with Chinese culture. In some cases practitioners feel that they are rescuing these Daoist practices from the hands of Chinese communists who generally permit them to take place only under official sanction, and have no compunction in putting a stop to them if, like Falun gong, they seem threatening to the status quo.

CONCLUSIONS

So what is Daoism? Is it a Chinese religion, a lineage of transmission, or a universal path that has nothing essentially Chinese to it? It is not really the business of scholars to tell people who claim to be Daoist whether or not they in fact count as Daoists. The interesting scholarly question is: who claims to be a Daoist, and why do they make those claims? The fact is that people assert identity as an attempt to understand their location within the social fabric and as an attempt to distinguish themselves from other people. The reasons why people call themselves (or others) Daoists thus vary throughout history in accordance with the social situation of the people who are making the assertion of identity. It is important for students of Daoism to realize that what they call Daoism has something to do with who they are, and where they are located within the world as well as the content of Daoism if, indeed, we are able to isolate what that content might be. The fact is, too, that 'Daoism' is an English word and has a life of its own within the English-speaking world, and perhaps covers a wider range of meaning than does the Chinese term 'Daojiao' which refers to traditions or lineages of Daoist practice that usually go under the English term 'Daoist religion'.

What is clear is that earlier attempts to distinguish Daoist philosophy from Daoist religion depend on Western views about the content of 'philosophy' and 'religion', and, usually, the value of the former over the latter. This internal Western conflict has no place in Daoism because Daoism views the body as a single organism in which mental, emotional and physical activities take place in constant interaction with each other.

Wisdom means knowing how to act, (or not to act), and acting well makes us wise. Given this fact, Daoists are usually quick to criticize Western studies of Daoism particularly because the Western study of religions holds that you do not have to be a believer or a practitioner in order to study a religion. Daoists strongly deny this and claim that understanding is a function of the whole body, not just the mind, Thus much Western writing about Daoism has failed not because of 'colonial this' or 'Western that' but because the Western writers simply had not experienced the Dao as a bodily practice, concentrating only on the part of their understanding that took place in their brain. Thus Daoists insist on what I call the 'hermeneutics of the body' – the notion that our bodies can be a repository of meaning and a medium of knowledge. This emphasis on embodiment constitutes a profound challenge to Western academic intellectualism.

SUGGESTIONS FOR FURTHER READING

Clarke, John James. 2000. *The Tao of the West*. New York, Routledge

Kleeman, Terry F. 1998. *Great Perfection: Religion and Ethnicity in a Chinese Millennial Kingdom*. Honolulu, University of Hawai'i Press

Kohn, Livia and Harold Roth, eds. 2002. *Daoist Identity: History, Lineage and Ritual*. Honolulu, University of Hawai'i Press

Paper, Jordan. 1995. *The Spirits are Drunk: Comparative Approaches to Chinese Religion*. Albany, State University of New York Press

2
Way

道

The distinguished philosopher of science, Karl Jaspers, observed that many of the world's great literary civilizations underwent a radical transformation at roughly the same time in human history, about the sixth–fifth centuries BCE. He termed this period the Axial Age, for it was during this time that the fundamental 'axial' questions of morality and value were raised right across the world. The Axial Age marks the transition from religions based primarily on sacrifice and ritual to religious traditions where human values and ethical principles are equally important. This was the time of the great Greek philosophers, the Hebrew prophets, the Buddha, Confucius and Laozi. All these figures were decisive in shaping the world's cultural traditions and in setting the terms of the debates that their philosophers and religionists would subsequently engage in. Since one of the hallmarks of modernity is cultural and religious pluralism, it is not surprising that many contemporary intellectuals have come to re-examine the teachings of these extraordinary figures and classic works that have framed the vastly different approaches to the human enterprise across the world.

During the Axial Age period in China, the basic categories of thinking were shaped by the various philosophical schools of the time and written down in classic texts that were classified and edited by subsequent intellectuals. In fact our main means of access to these ancient thinkers is through the lens of these later scholars. This unfortunately makes it even more problematical to arrive at a historically accurate understanding of these thinkers and their cultural background, and this is why archaeological investigations are such an important part of research into ancient Chinese culture. Despite all these problems of interpretation, we do have a basic understanding of the core values and motifs that characterized the ancient Chinese worldview, which framed the context out of which the Daoist religion emerged.

All these core values were shaped by the socio-historical context of the Axial Age era in China. At this time, the society had a patriarchal feudal social structure in which land and authority were controlled by aristocratic clans organized through a pattern of shifting alliances into various feudal states, each vying with each other for territory and power. The old imperial system of the Shang and the Zhou dynasties had broken down and China was then comprised of several warring states each governed by a king and the various noble families that supported him. This period lasted for roughly five hundred years until the leader of the state of Qin conquered the empire in 221 BCE and declared himself the 'first emperor'.

WAY

From the uncertain context of the warring states period flourished an intellectual culture devoted to the pressing practical question of the day: how might harmony and order be restored to the empire? The way this question was phrased by the leading thinkers of the time was like this: 'Where is the Way?' The question of the Way (in Chinese 'Dao') is the single most important question that shaped Chinese religious civilization. It is important to appreciate how different this question is from the questions that have shaped Western civilization, namely the questions generated in classical Greek philosophy and Semitic religion. The questions that arose in Greek philosophy, such as 'What is truth?' or 'What is goodness?' suggest that wisdom consists in understanding fundamental abstract categories or first principles, which can then be applied to specific situations. From these abstract categories emerged the great Western disciplines of logic, metaphysics, law and science. The questions that arose in Semitic religions, such as 'How may I obey the will of the creator?' led to a religious life centred on the relationship between one god and a community of believers founded upon commandments and ethical precepts. When approaching Daoism, it is important to understand that Daoism is shaped neither by the categories of logical philosophy nor by the categories of belief in a monotheistic god who created the world out of nothing. In this regard it is possible that Western philosophers or students of religion would not recognize Daoism as philosophy or religion, at least in the conventional sense of these terms.

Turning to the questions of the Warring States period, we discover that the question of the 'Way' is basically a searching for guidance within a landscape that has become distressingly unfamiliar, as though suddenly all the signposts have disappeared and the people no longer know where they are in relation to each other. This, roughly, is what you would expect if a nation experienced the gradual dissolution of its traditional bonds of unity and kinship, as did China during this period. Figuratively speaking, the territory was no longer familiar and new maps had to be made.

Various practical schools of thought emerged in response to this situation. The response of Confucius was that the nation required a systematic programme of reorientation and harmonization. This programme, known as the 'rectification of names' sought to re-establish the social and cultural signposts so that everyone would know where they stood. This, thought Confucius, would bring stability and order to a divided nation. The genius of Confucianism was that the re-establishment of cultural markers was not something simply to be imposed from on high by a despot, but something to be worked out in the relationships that comprised the social fabric. For Confucius, therefore, finding the way lay in normalizing the five cardinal relationships upon which his patriarchal society rested: ruler–minister, father–son, older brother– younger brother, husband–wife and friend–friend. These bonds, though understood hierarchically, were to be based on the principle of reciprocity. Thus it was the duty of ministers to be loyal servants of their rulers; but it was also the duty of rulers to act so as to command a natural loyalty from their ministers.

Accompanying this moral revolution was an effort to recover and renovate the foundational rituals or stylized ceremonies (*li*) that underpinned the place of the emperor and the state within the cosmos. Of particular importance in this regard was the music and dance that played an important part in the official ceremonies of the state. Although it is perhaps surprising that music and morality were seen as being two sides of the same coin, it must be remembered that the overall goal was harmony, a term that can be readily applied to the arts as much as to social morality. This emphasis has led certain thinkers in the West, notably Roger Ames and David Hall, to a radical reinterpretation of the whole of the Confucian project as first and foremost an aesthetic endeavour. There is much to be commended in their interpretation. Too often Western students of ancient Chinese philosophy have only investigated the ways in which it most closely resembles Western philosophy and, consequently, have neglected entire areas of Confucian thinking that did not seem to fit in with their preconceptions as to what a moral or philosophical system ought to look like. In this aesthetic light the 'Way' is not in the first instance a set of moral prescriptions, but a way of acting so as to optimize the social tapestry. At the basic level, Confucianism is about etiquette, that is, the basic conventions that are necessary for the smooth functioning of society. Confucius understood that it is not laws that make society, but rather rituals and social conventions.

An important Western interpretation of this was developed by the philosopher Herbert Fingarette. Fingarette came to understand the power of the Confucian idea of ritual by teaming it with the theory of performative utterances developed by the British linguistic philosopher J.L. Austin. An example of a performative utterance is the way in which a couple becomes actually married by saying 'I will' in a public ceremony performed in a socially sanctioned context. The saying of the words in the right context creates a new social fact – the marriage of the couple. In this way ritual codes of conduct are not narrow restrictions upon the ways that human beings can act in society but, as Confucius realized, nothing less than the fabric that makes up a society. In fact every society is already highly ritualized, it is just that we do not realize that we are performing time-honoured social rituals when we shake someone's hand, or reply to a dinner invitation, or buy someone a beer at the pub. Each of these acts is a particular 'way' that together make up the complete web of social interactions that constitutes a culture or civilization.

Given the hierarchical nature of the society, the importance of rituals varied in proportion to the social status of the person. That is, the question of ceremony was most important for the king and his court. If the king could set the right tone and harmonize the court, then this harmony would trickle down through the social ranks until eventually the whole empire would be at peace. Confucius travelled through the country trying to find a feudal lord who would implement his plan, but he was unsuccessful. Instead he gathered about himself a group of students who transmitted his teachings in the form of conversations, which are recorded in Confucius's *Analects*.

It turned out for Confucius that these conversations were not only the medium but the message: the way is to be sought in the shared pleasures of learning and friendship. The *Analects* begins with the phrase 'Learning and its timely practice: is this not delightful? To have a friend come from a distant place: is this not a pleasure?' These phrases set the tone for the rest of the text, which is no doubt why they were placed at the beginning by its editor. On the basis of Confucius's dedication to teaching and learning in the company of friends and disciples, an entire cultural edifice was constructed and, equally importantly, for Confucian philosophers and political theorists, the shared norms of family and society were in fact the best way in which a culture and a civilization could be reconstructed.

Following the reforms of the great neo-Confucian philosopher Zhu Xi (1130–1200), the Confucian classics became the basis of the imperial civil service examinations. Confucian thinking was thus established for much of China's history as the foundation of its social, economic and political life. China's decline relative to the West in the nineteenth century led to the near-collapse of Confucian thought as Chinese intellectuals began to embrace Western philosophy, science and technology. Part of the blame that was attached to Confucianism lay in its inherently conservative nature, and for this reason the radical Chinese communist party conducted several anti-Confucianism campaigns during the twentieth century. The reason why Confucianism is inherently conservative lies in the fact that if we are to speak of the way and somehow to realize it in our society, then we must already be inside some established social, semiotic, and political system. We simply cannot invent the way out of nowhere, but only discover, renew and transmit it in discourse and conversation. But for Confucians, our language and our culture – that which was transmitted to us by our parents – is far from being a stumbling block to progress and reform. In fact these inherited values are to be celebrated as our only means of intercourse with, our only Way towards that which is real, true and valuable. Human beings are always and irrevocably social and institutional creatures. The Way is thus always a social and an institutional process.

An alternative response to the question of 'Where is the Way?' is recorded in texts that were subsequently grouped together under the bibliographical classification of 'Dao-school' (*daojia*). These 'Dao-school' texts, including the *Daode jing* (Classic of the Way and its Power) and the *Zhuangzi*, emphatically denied that the Way was something encoded within human culture – ceremonies that shape the social order. Rather these Daoists argued that the Way lies naturally and spontaneously within the natural world. To follow the Way means to harmonize oneself with the natural flow of water which, though soft, overcomes all obstacles in its path. National unity, moreover, is not something that can be imposed from without, nor is it something that can be artificially generated within ritualized codes of human conduct. Rather it lies present within the natural tendency of things; the task, then, is to permit it to manifest itself in human beings.

According to the *Daode jing*, the chief means of doing so was by practising a kind of non-assertive action (*wuwei*) that promoted, and did not disrupt, the natural tendency of things to be in harmony and unity with each other. This Daoist view of harmony was just as much an aesthetic and hierarchical view of harmony as its Confucian counterpart. The difference is that for the Daoists this 'way' was already embedded – as it were 'genetically' – within the natural tendency of things to spontaneously organize themselves into an organic whole. It is as if the *way*, the right direction, is encoded within the *ways* of life itself. It is not surprising that Chinese intellectuals came to see these ways as something more than just the natural paths that are evident in the environment, but as evidence of a unifying and transcendent force – the Way – that is the fundamental principle of the cosmos. The Dao as a cosmic principle, moreover, forms the connection between the natural philosophy of proto-Daoist texts and the complex religious system of the classical Daoist movements, depending on whether you view the Dao in its multiplicity of natural, immanent aspects, or in its 'one', transcendent aspect.

In order to understand this more cosmic view of the transcendent Dao, it is worthwhile examining chapter 25 of the *Daode jing*, which contains perhaps the most poetic hymn to Dao as the mother of the universe:

> There is a being – in chaos yet complete.
> It preceded heaven and earth.
> Silent, it was, and solitary;
> Standing alone, never changing.
> Moving around, yet never ending.
> Consider it the mother of heaven and earth.
>
> I do not know its name.
> To call it something, I say *dao*.
> Forced to give it a name, I say great.

Great – says it departs.
Depart – says it is far.
Far away – says it returns.

Therefore *dao* is great, heaven is great,
Earth is great, humans too, are great.
In the universe there are four 'greats'
And humans make their residence in the whole of them.

Humans are modelled on earth.
Earth is modelled on Heaven.
Heaven is modelled on *dao*.

Dao is modelled on its own spontaneity.
(translation adapted from Kohn, 1993, p. 17)

Of course such a beautiful and complex passage is open to many interpretations, but it is worthwhile trying to work out some of the basic themes that it expresses, for they are fundamental to the flourishing of the classical Daoist religion that emerged later.

First the Dao is to be understood as the mother – the matrix of life; and second life is understood to take three major forms: heaven, earth and humankind. This sets the basic framework for Daoist religion, the boundaries within which the religion was established and continues to function, and can be summed up in the form of a question: how are we to understand and to live out the basic patterns and relationships between human beings, our natural environment (earth), and the world of spiritual powers that rules over life and death (heaven)? All Daoist religion is based on the notion that there is a way, a logic or a rationale that governs the relationships between humans, the earth and the heavens. This is the Way, the evolving cosmic process in which these three dimensions of life are interrelated, and mutually constituted. Daoism, like science, generally rejects the notion that things are the result of some capricious trickster-like spirit or chaotic force, but rather asserts that there is a basic principle of organic communication within the evolving universe. This principle of communication is perhaps an article of faith for Daoists in the same way that science is based on the faith that the world is fundamentally explainable. For Daoists the world is explainable and there exists a principle of communication between the various types of life in the universe because all forms of life and power depend upon the Dao as their mother or matrix. Importantly, this is true for gods and spiritual beings, just as much as it is for human beings and fish. This is why the Daoist pantheon, unlike the West Asian religions of Judaism, Christianity and Islam, contains no supreme creator god: in Daoism all deities, like every other life form, are manifestations of the primordial Way.

One way of understanding the relationship of classical Daoist religion to the proto-Daoism of the *Daode jing* is to see the various forms of the Daoist religion as pathways of communication between humans, the earth and the heavenly spirits, all of whom are clothed in the same fabric of the Dao. It is quite uncertain – and frankly doubtful – that the person who composed these lines in the *Daode jing* could ever have supposed that they should be influential in the evolution of some later religious system. Perhaps a better way of seeing these lines is as expressing a fundamental conviction or 'absolute presupposition' about the nature of the universe that was inherited by those who went on to elaborate the various forms of Daoist religion. Thus the later religious systems maintained the conviction – first articulated in the *Daode jing* – that even the heavens themselves form part of the continuing evolution of the Dao.

If humans are subject to the authority of the heavenly powers, and the heavenly powers are themselves modelled on the Dao, what then is the foundation of the Dao itself? The answer to this question can be found in the last line of chapter 25: the Dao is modelled on its own spontaneity. The original Chinese term that 'spontaneity' translates is '*ziran*' the basic meaning of which is 'self-so'. If the Dao is 'self-so' it means that it has no foundation for itself except itself. The image that this evokes is that of a fountain that is constantly overflowing with water yet never dries up, or of a sun that constantly radiates energy but never seems to burn out. Again the implication is that the Dao is filled with life, a life that is constantly developing and evolving. It is not difficult to see how this constantly life-giving power could evoke a deep respect on the part of humankind, and even a religious awe.

One further point about this passage deserves comment and that is the theme of progress and return. The second and third stanzas speak of the nameless 'Dao' that 'departs', 'is far', and then 'returns'. This suggests a journey that arrives back where it started, and this cyclical motion reflects the universal theme of the basic rhythm of life that arises from the ground, flourishes, decays and eventually returns to its point of origin. Daoism takes this pattern to be a foundational pattern for the way all life operates. The universe is dynamic and alive, but it dances to a clearly discernable pulse, a binary pulse or a cosmic heartbeat according to which everything around us is undergoing a process of expansion and contraction. Nothing in the world stays the same. Transformation is constant, but this transformation is regular and in principle understandable.

The name for this pattern in Daoism – and in all of Chinese culture – is yin and yang. The words themselves refer originally to the shady side of a hill and the sunny side of a hill respectively. Of course the important feature of this idea is that the shady and the sunny sides of the hill are constantly changing: the side that is in the sun in the morning will be in the shade in the afternoon and vice versa, and this goes to show how nothing in the world ever stays the same. The basic yin-yang dynamic is thus summed up in the famous yin-yang symbol that is on the front cover of this book. Moving anti-clockwise from the top the white segment, representing yang, increases in strength until it reaches its maximum point. When yang is at its maximum, at the bottom of the circle, the power of yin begins to increase until it too attains its maximum at the top of the circle. The cycle begins again in a continuous process of arising and decaying.

From this basic pattern two important points emerge about the nature of the Dao. The first, as will already be clear, is that everything is constantly transforming itself. The second is that opposites in the world are complementary. Thus there can be no black without white and vice versa, no good without evil, no strength without weakness, no male without female, no boom without bust, and no joy without sadness. When one fully internalizes this realization, it becomes clear that the goal towards which human beings should strive is balance and harmony rather than the ultimate victory of one perspective over another – since there are no ultimates.

It is easy to see why this sort of philosophy might have a wide New Age appeal in the post-modern West where traditional values and authorities have been called into question. The philosophy of the Dao seems to resonate with a counter-cultural distrust of absolutes. However, although this desire for balance and harmony has been a constant factor within the history of Daoism, it has been manifest in thoroughly structured and often rigid ways that might surprise the contemporary Westerner. One must never forget that Daoism evolved as a religious institution with its own hierarchies, precepts, rituals and structures. While it may be tempting to think of proto-Daoist texts as espousing ideals that the reality of Daoism failed to live up to, this would be a mistake. The proto-Daoist view of the Way is not an 'ideal' but rather one of several ingredients that together constituted the classical religion that evolved later. From the point of view of many Daoist religious movements, what is more important than the intellectual values of the *Daode jing* is the fact that the Way is believed to manifest itself in the person of Laozi, the supposed author of the text. From this religious perspective the figure of the Old Master is just as important as the values that the *Daode jing* transmits, similar to the way in which Christians worship the figure of Jesus as well as revere his message. According to this later religious tradition the figure of Laozi stands as one of the most important manifestations or transformations of the Dao.

POWER

The term that is used when the 'way' is manifested in a human being is *de* (pronounced like 'durh') which can be translated as 'virtue' both in a moral sense, and in the sense of the power inherent within a thing. The term 'de' is related semantically to another Chinese character, also pronounced 'de', which means 'to attain'. This Daoist concept of virtue may thus be defined as the power obtained when the Way is attained. The basic implication of this is that finding the way has a real effect upon the individual. In fact one may look at the whole of the Daoist religion as an ongoing study of this power attained by men and women in their search for the Dao, and the way it transforms their lives and their environment.

Although chapter 4 goes into more detail about this idea of power, particularly as it relates to political authority, it is helpful to understand how this term relates to the functioning of the Way in the proto-Daoist period. One of the central concerns of Warring States' thought was the question as to what virtues or powers an individual must have in order to be a successful ruler. The theory was that if the ruler had the right sort of virtue or power, then Heaven would, in an act of divine reciprocity, confer upon him the authority or mandate to rule. In the *Daode jing*, power is obtained by adopting a policy of 'non-action' or 'actionless-action' (*wuwei*). This political philosophy arose from the view that power is something that is naturally present within things in the universe. Each thing has the power to grow and develop so long as it is properly nourished and looked after.

From this idea develops one of the key metaphors of the Daoist symbolic universe that applies to the concept of power in ordinary people's lives, namely, cultivation. Daoists may be viewed as the gardeners of the cosmos, those who slowly shape their life and environment through a process of planting, nourishing, weeding and then letting nature take its course. Given the right conditions, something marvellous will flourish. This flourishing is inherent in the nature of things, if only they are given the chance. Thus the idea of virtue or power that arose in the context of the political philosophy of the mandate of heaven came to be much more widely applied in people's religious lives.

Daoism thus embraces an important paradox, and this paradox runs throughout its history: on the one hand the way is actively to be sought and to be attained; on the other hand the flourishing of things is achieved by letting them be. All of this suggests that the Daoist world has an irreducibly reciprocal character of continuous action and re-action. The harmony that is sought in the Daoist worldview is thus not a static harmony, but a dynamic creative harmony that is far more than the sum of its parts. Often this harmony is symbolized in ways that might seem magical or superstitious to the Western mind, but this appearance stems from our failure to appreciate the radically dynamic and self-transformative nature of the Daoist universe – a universe in which caterpillars 'magically' turn into butterflies, and fish 'magically' evolve into birds. All these things are possible not because of some divine power that exists beyond the limits of human understanding, but because this radical creativity or 'supernatural' power is built into the natural constitution of the universe.

Realizing that the world is actually like this leads naturally to a sense of awe and wonder. Where does all this extraordinary power come from? The answer is that it lies in the Dao, the Way itself. That is, the power of transformation that is inherent within things does not – so far as we can tell – come from any external source or creator, but rather 'wells up' within things causing them to have life and to grow. Thus the Way is nothing more than the Power that lies within things, and the Power is itself the manifestation of the Way. Without the universe there would be no Way, and without the Way there would be no universe. This is just another example of the inherently reciprocal character of the Daoist world.

COMMUNICATION

The idea of a 'way' can also be explained by reference to the secondary meaning of the word 'dao' in classical Chinese, which is 'to speak'. If we understand 'dao' not only as the cosmic way, but at a fundamental level as an act of 'speech' then we can construct an interpretation of 'dao' not only as the matrix of the universe, but also a means of communication between the three fundamental realities of the universe: humans, the earth and Heaven. It was this root meaning of the Way as a pathway or a means of communication that the Daoist religious traditions fully exploited. The Way is thus not only a cosmological principle but also an active form of communication that takes place between humans, the earth and Heaven.

An important way of viewing religion is as a way for human beings to communicate with gods, spirits and ancestors. Daoism is quite compatible with this idea of religion, but it has some interesting ideas and profound theories about how this communication takes place. The word for communicate is pronounced *tong* in Mandarin Chinese, and Daoists have explained how religious communication takes place by means of a close homonym, *dong*, which is usually translated as 'cavern' or 'grotto'. The (perhaps surprising) idea is that caves are important ways of communicating with Heaven.

There are two ways in which communication takes place through caves in Daoism: the first is that many Daoist immortals seem to have spent parts of their lives living in caves in the mountains and found them to be sources of spiritual power; the second is that the caves had a symbolic function as representing vaults that contained secret Daoist texts. Caves thus represent physically and symbolically the secret paths that lead the religious traveller from the ordinary plane of existence to a more transcendent plane. They are passageways or 'daos' to Heaven. For this reason many Daoist temples and monasteries are situated on mountains and even on the site of caves.

It is interesting to consider why caves should be seen as a symbol of the Dao in the physical world. One of the most important temples on Mount Qingcheng in Sichuan province is called the 'Grotto of the Celestial Master' (Tianshi dong). The temple is built on top of a cave where, according to tradition, the first celestial master, Zhang Daoling, is supposed to have lived. Although one cannot go into the cave any more, the entrance to it has been converted into a sacred space and pilgrims are able to offer worship at an historically and religiously important pathway or cavern. But why is it that the celestial master should have wanted to live in a cave? One answer might be seen in the way that caves seem to be living and breathing features of the natural landscape that closely mirror our internal human physiology.

> Despite a singular solidity, their physical permeability in terms of air- and water-flow reflects the inner workings of the human body. Blood equals water; air equals breath. Spermatic liquids form pools; walls constitute shapes like inner organs or viscera. Their resident, left windowless and in an enclosed void, experiences the dignity of complete independence and autarky. (Hahn, 2000, p. 695)

This physical aspect of caves is thus an important feature of the way in which the Dao came to be experienced by Daoists in the natural world in a physical, even visceral sense. More information on caves, placed in the context of the complex relationship between Daoism and nature, is given in chapter 8.

The second reason why caverns or grottos are important symbols of the Dao is that caves are considered to be repositories for Daoist texts. This idea falls neatly in line with the secondary meaning of 'dao' as the verb 'to speak'. When the great Lingbao reformer Lu Xiujing made the first compilation of Daoist scriptures in the fifth century he arranged them into three 'caverns': the Cavern of Mystery, the Cavern of Perfection and the Cavern of Spirit. These caverns were thought to be vaults or libraries of the original texts, presided over by deities, who transmitted them to earth at various times and places. The caverns, as 'libraries', thus represent the chief means of communication between the celestial and earthy realms in Daoism, namely, scripture.

Perhaps it is stating the obvious, but one of the most important things to consider when trying to understand a text such as the *Daode jing* is that it is regarded by Daoists as a canonical scripture (jing), that is as a manifestation of the Dao itself. Thus when trying to understand what the Dao means in Daoist religion, a key element is that the Dao is revealed in the form of scripture as well as in the form of important personages such as Laozi. Although the role of texts is discussed in more detail in chapter 7, one thing is worth mentioning at this point: the ultimate purpose of this communication according to some Daoist traditions is not to 'save' or 'liberate' human beings from their finitude (though this may be one result) but rather more grandly, to assist in the continuing evolution of the cosmos. According to Daoist theology, the capacity for language has endowed human beings with a privileged role in shaping the world. This fact was well recognized in Daoist movements going back as far as the Way of Great Peace in the second century. This early Daoist movement envisioned the role of human beings as facilitators of a 'central harmony' in the cosmos. The central text of that movement, known as the Scripture of Great Peace, asserts that 'it is our human mission to preserve, protect, and circulate harmonious communication between the realms of cosmos and humanity' (Lai, 2001, p. 104).

There are two chief aspects to the way in which Daoists continue to promote such a 'harmonious communication': communal ritual and self-cultivation. These two activities though different sociologically and phenomenologically can be understood as sharing a common theological purpose, namely to promote the dynamic exchange of power and vitality within the three levels of the cosmos, heaven, earth and humanity, so as to achieve a level of optimal harmony among them.

Given the fact that we are dealing with a three-way communication, there are thus three basic areas to which Daoist ritual and cultivation attends. The most mundane level is that of ensuring that the physical environment has room to breathe. The early Celestial Masters' movement, for instance, included in its list of 180 precepts injunctions against sealing off pools and wells and drying up marshes (Schipper, 2001, p. 81). Ge Hong's (283–343) biography of Zhang Daoling, the first Celestial Master, also relates how the community was instructed to keep the roads and bridges clear and puddles drained of water. More information about the complex relationship between Daoism and nature is found in chapter 8.

The second area of this dao of communication is perhaps a more familiar one to students of religion, that of maintaining a harmony between human life and the heavens. This too is a large topic which obviously recurs throughout the book but there are two aspects to this line of communication that deserve mentioning at this point. The first aspect of human–heavenly communication is evident in Daoism's appropriation of the phenomena of mediumism and shamanism. Shamanism (the word is of Mongolian origin) is a religious phenomenon found all over the world and is particularly visible in indigenous (i.e. non-Axial age) religious cultures. A shaman is someone who through a variety of techniques (often involving drugs or dancing) enters into a state of ecstasy and makes a journey to the spirit world to encounter one or several deities. Shamans are generally different from mediums in that mediums channel, or are possessed by, the spirits of the dead whereas shamans make the journey themselves to see the spirits. Very often the spirit and the shaman develop a relationship known as a hierogamy or sacred marriage, and often the spirit and the shaman are of the opposite sex. The popular practice of shamanism was generally denounced by

Daoists, a fact that leads us to suspect that it functioned as a problematic boundary-line between Daoism and popular religion (Davis, 2002, p. 9).

From a beautiful anthology of poetry known as the *Chu ci* (Songs of Chu – a region in the south of China) we have evidence of a shamanic tradition that had a strong influence on the development of Daoist religion. The songs were composed by Qu Yuan around the third century BCE (see Hawkes, 1959; Waley, 1955). One of the poems, entitled 'The Far-Off Journey' describes the astral journey of one who is worn down by the cares of the world. As he journeys towards the stars his body is transformed into an ever more illustrious and resplendent being.

The corollary to the phenomenon of shamanism is the cult of mediumism, in which a person, often a young boy, is possessed by a spirit and, for a temporary period, becomes the medium through which that spirit communicates. The practice of spirit-possession takes place to this day at the local level in China. Ordinarily it would be correct to think of Daoist priests as functioning in a completely different social and ritual space to those specialists in spirit-possession: Daoist priests are highly educated, literate and deal with powerful spirits who hold important jobs in the celestial bureaucracy. The fact is, however, that from the Song period (960–1279) onwards, the boundaries between Daoism and local, popular religion began to blur, and there emerged a class of Daoist ritual specialists who operated at a local level and employed the techniques of spirit-possession to conduct funeral rites or exorcisms (Davis, 2002).

Both mediumism and shamanism are evident in the development of the Way of Highest Clarity (Shangqing dao). The texts of Highest Clarity were revealed by an immortal, Lady Wei, through a medium, Yang Xi, to the Xu family in southern China. Conversely, the texts prescribe a form of meditation in which adepts visualize themselves on journeys to the stars of the Big Dipper and in which the gods of the Dipper descended into the organs of their body. This visualization practice is explained in further detail in chapter 5.

The third aspect of human–heavenly communication lies in the formalized communications or public liturgies performed by Daoist priests. Although the exact form of these liturgies has varied throughout history, it is possible to give a general explanation of the underlying structures of communication that have historically been important in Daoism.

As we saw in chapter 1, one of the ways in which scholars assert a distinction between the earliest Daoist movements and the religious system that preceded it lies in Daoism's rejection of blood sacrifices. Under the system of blood sacrifices, the powerful chaotic forces of gods, spirits and ancestors were to be venerated and assuaged by sacrificing animals and offering meat to them. The king or emperor as patriarch of the nation was responsible for conducting these sacrifices and thereby ensuring peace and stability. The gods of the Daoist pantheon, by contrast, were largely vegetarian and in Daoist temples today fruit and incense are the staples that are offered to the statues of the gods.

The earliest Daoist movements, the Way of Great Peace and the Way of the Celestial Masters, however, instituted the expiation of sins as a new rite that was designed to promote harmony within the universe and also as a method of healing the sick. Human sins, it was thought, blocked effective communications between heaven, earth and humans. These sins, according to the Scripture of Great Peace, accumulated over generations, resulting in a catastrophic interruption in the normal 'dao' of communication between heaven, earth and humans. The result of this blockage was natural disasters such as earthquakes and thunderstorms, political instability, and human illness. Confessing one's sins, by contrast, functioned so as to unblock this 'inherited guilt' and to restore harmony to the world. In the religious system operated by the early Celestial Masters, the individuals were required to enter a 'quiet chamber' and list their own sins as well as the sins of their ancestors. Following the confession, a written record of the confessions was made in triplicate by a priest who ritually submitted it along with a formal plea for pardon to the spirits of earth, water and heaven. One copy was buried in the ground, one copy put in water, and one copy was burned. The priest thus functioned as an intermediary between the people and the spirits, in charge of ensuring harmony between the two realms. If a confession was duly received and pardon granted by the spirits, harmony would be promoted on the earth and the penitent would be healed of all illness.

Most contemporary Daoist ritual, however, is based on the reforms that were undertaken in the Way of the Numinous Treasure (Lingbao Daoism). Under the influence of Buddhism, the notion of ritual communication was greatly expanded to include all living beings. The ritual of confession or expiation was standardized by Lu Xiujing as a ritual of purification (*zhai*) and involved the purification of the body through bathing and fasting, the purification of the heart through the confession of sins, and a communal feast celebrating the re-established harmony between the people and the gods. Usually the *zhai* was a large-scale public affair carried out in the open air around a temporary Daoist altar (*daotan*) erected for the occasion by the priests.

The other main form of ritual communication was the *jiao* offering, an act of communal renewal that is the main Daoist ritual carried out today. In the *jiao* offering today an altar is erected, written invitations are sent to the gods, the gods descend into the sacred space around the altar, incense is offered and an audience takes place between the sponsors of the ritual and the gods. When the audience is concluded, the gods are thanked, they return to their homes, and the altar is disassembled (Dean, 2000, p. 675). The ritual can last from a day to several weeks, depending on the importance of the occasion, and is accompanied by a symphony of music and movement performed by as many acolytes as the sponsors wish to pay for, all under the expert direction of the master of ceremonies, the Daoist priest.

The purpose of all this ritual communication is to restore the world to the state of the primordial Dao in which heaven, earth and humanity flourish together in creative harmony. This movement of restoration or reversion is a key theme in Daoist cultivation and is a component of the theory that underlies Daoist alchemy (chapter 6). The transformative effects of renewal are not only experienced in an abstract way as a feeling of harmony between oneself and the universe. Daoists also experience transformation viscerally in their bodies in the form of the healing of diseases and also in the experience of the subtle body, that is, the network of energies that are believed to constitute our vitality at a sub-physical level. In the next chapter, we will go on to examine how this religious experience takes place within the human body. To do so we will have to examine Daoist notions of what the human body is, how it functions, and how it is related to the flow of the Dao.

SUGGESTIONS FOR FURTHER READING

Allan, Sarah. 1998. *The Way of Water and Sprouts of Virtue*. Albany, State University of New York Press

Graham, Angus Charles. 1986. *Disputers of the Tao*. La Salle, Open Court

Schwartz, Benjamin. 1985. *The World of Thought in Ancient China*. Cambridge, Belknap Press

3

Body

體

Two common synonyms for religion are 'faith' and 'belief'. Both these words suggest that religion is about the intangible and unknowable aspects of life: whether there is a god; what happens after we die; whether there is any ultimate justice. Many of the world's religions propose their own theological ideas about these great imponderable questions and fit nicely into this view of religion as faith and belief. But it is a safe generalization to say that these great questions of faith and belief have not been strongly thematized or voiced within the Daoist tradition. Part of the reason for this is that Daoism is fundamentally a religion that has to do with the whole of one's body. To be sure beliefs and attitudes are important, but they are only one aspect of our embodied being. The operations of the mind and the spirit are understood in Daoism as organic functions of the energy systems of our bodies. Daoists are thus concerned with what they do with their bodies just as much as what they believe in minds or feel in their hearts.

All religions have to deal with the fact that we are embodied creatures. As Michel Foucault has demonstrated, an ideology (whether religious or not) is not just a system of beliefs, but a social and institutional mechanism for regulating those beliefs; judicial processes are put in place to restrain and discipline the bodies of heretics and dissenters – those who openly reject the tenets of the system (Foucault, 1995). Religions explicitly regulate what goes in and out of our bodies – what we can eat and drink; when we can have sex and with whom – and provide purification mechanisms to deal with the fact that we break the rules. Daoism is unusual, however, in that it makes our entire human physiology, from brains to livers, a central theme of its spirituality. The body in fact is the pre-eminent space in which Daoism operates. The body is the object of many Daoist practices and also the means by which Daoists engage in their spiritual life and cultivate their nature.

The classical Daoist approach to cultivating one's nature thus stands in contrast to the Confucian philosophers who took the principal location of our nature to be in the heart-mind (*xin*), which was viewed as the affective and intellectual organ of the body. Thus the most important task for Confucians is to cultivate one's heart-mind so as to promote harmonious relationships between oneself and one's environment, whether construed narrowly as one's kith and kin, or more abstractly as the natural world or the cosmos. An important question that developed in Confucian thought then was how best to develop the goodness that is inherent in our nature and to restrain or discipline the negative aspects of our nature.

Daoists, however, never accepted that the heart was the most important seat of our nature. Instead they took the view that human nature is to be understood as the vitality that flows throughout the body and that could be cultivated in a variety of ways from simple physical exercise, to subtle forms of meditation, to elaborate communal rituals. Thus it is not surprising that Daoism developed in close concert with Chinese medicine: both are based on a similar understanding of the body. In order to understand Daoist practices it is essential, therefore, to have a good understanding of the way in which Daoists understand the functioning of the human body. Consequently this chapter does not contain much information about Daoism itself, but rather the range of ideas about the body that Daoist cultivation draws on.

QI: THE BREATH OF LIFE

The starting point for the Daoist view of the body is qi (pronounced 'chee'). Qi is often translated as 'vital energy', 'breath', or 'pneuma' and it is quite literally the stuff of life. If a Daoist were to come across the story of how the god of the Bible breathed life into Adam, he or she would say that the divine creator was transferring qi energy to him. In Daoism, however, qi is not bestowed by some almighty creator, but is simply the natural operation of the universe, the basic pattern of expansion and contraction, the rhythm of the Dao. When the qi or breath is flowing in and out then we have life; when the qi or breath stops moving then we have death. Flexibility and movement are thus key to maintaining life. As the *Daode jing* puts it:

> The stiff and strong
> Are Death's companions
> The soft and weak
> Are life's companions.
> Therefore,
> The strongest armies do not conquer,
> The greatest trees are cut down.
> The strong and great sink down
> The soft and weak rise up.
>
> (*Daode jing*, ch. 76; trans. Addiss and Lombardo, 1993, p. 76)

Early on in Chinese civilization came the discovery that qi can be flexed and cultivated so as to promote vitality and longevity. The proto-Daoist text *Inward Training* is a training manual that details a rudimentary form of qi cultivation through a controlled breath meditation and a controlled diet (not too much or too little food). Regulating one's breathing and eating are the primary means of regulating the energy that enters our bodies. As the text explains, when vital essence is stored within the chest, it spontaneously generates vital energy which circulates freely through the body, entering and exiting through the nine apertures of the body (eyes, ears, nostrils, mouth, anus and penis or vagina). A person whose energy circulates freely can 'exhaust the heavens and the earth and spread over the four seas' (*Neiye*, 15, trans. Roth, 1999, p. 74). This poetic concept introduces an important theme in Daoist cultivation, namely making one's body 'translucent' or 'transparent' to the cosmos (a feature described by Lisa Raphals (2001, p. 312) as the 'porosity of the self'). This means that people who are far advanced in the cultivation of their qi seem hardly to be affected by external events: the experience they have of their own body is that it extends to incorporate the things that lie around them. It is as though they have a much expanded sense of self, a cosmic body. In fact one way of looking at Daoism from ancient philosophy to contemporary religious movements is simply as the cultivation of oneself and one's reality. Thus when Daoists engage in self-cultivation, they are at the same time engaged in the cultivation of the reality of the Dao that enfolds them.

It is hardly surprising, therefore, that commentators have made a connection between these energy practices and the phenomenon of mysticism that has been discerned throughout the world's religions. In fact, as theoretical research into mystics and mysticism developed in the West, increasingly that category has come to be applied to the whole of Daoism. A landmark book in this regard was Livia Kohn's *Early Chinese Mysticism* (1992), which linked together proto-Daoism from the fourth century BCE and classical Daoism up to the ninth century CE by demonstrating that mysticism and mystical experience played a foundational role throughout the development of Daoism.

But what in fact is mysticism or mystical experience? One of the foundational studies of mystical experience is William James's *The Varieties of Religious Experience* ([1902] 1999). James recognized that to understand religion it is more important to look at the actual religious experiences of people than all their doctrines and rituals and sacred texts. He aimed to uncover commonalities that could be generalized across all religious traditions, and thereby discover the essential qualities of human religious experience. For him, the defining characteristics of mystical experience are: 1) ineffability – it defies our ability to speak of it; 2) a noetic quality – it gives fundamental insights into the world; 3) transience – it lasts a short time; and 4) passivity – the mystic experiences a sense of powerlessness as he or she is utterly caught up in the experience. From this starting point other scholars attempted to investigate the phenomenon of mysticism across many different religious cultures. Their investigation has proceeded along philosophical or metaphysical lines (what does the insight of mystics tell us about the nature of the world and our place in it?) and psychological lines (how can mysticism be defined as a type of psychological experience?). Broadly speaking, the experience of many mystics points towards the notion of an ontological unity between the self and ultimate reality (God, or the Universe). This basic concept can be found in a whole range of cultures, from Indian Vedanta philosophers such as Sankara, Islamic mystics such as Al-Ghazzali, and Christian mystics such as Meister Eckhart. The reason why we do not ordinarily experience this unity is because our mind has become clouded over by mental concepts, linguistic categories and cultural conventions, that lead us to suppose that we have an essentially independent self or ego. The task of the mystic is thus reckoned a negative task – stripping away the layers of false consciousness or ego in order to realize the fundamental unity of Self and the Absolute or Ultimate Reality. This fundamental unity has always existed; it is just that we were not aware of it previously. This important pan-cultural view of a root human mystical experience is known as the Perennial Philosophy.

The Daoist mystical experience seems to be somewhat different because it is based on the cultivation of energies in the body, rather than the sort of psychological or philosophical cultivation that is commonly associated with mystics. It is also worth noting that despite the range of opinion among scholars on what exactly is going on in these early Daoist cultivation texts, there does not seem to be a concept that is directly equivalent to the Western or Indian concept of the Soul or the Self in the sense of a disembodied storage facility for our essential personality or true nature. Rather our nature is very much understood as a dynamic, physical or energetic nature.

The noted Daoism scholar Russell Kirkland coined an important term that is very helpful in trying to make sense of these proto-Daoist practices and their accompanying experiences. Rather than having to choose whether to place them in the category of health practices for long life and physical stamina, or to place them in the category of mystical experiences, he prefers the term 'biospiritual'. This new term respects the Daoist understanding of the body as a system of vital energy that is the foundation for both physical life and spiritual life. What we in the West call matter and spirit are, in Daoist terms, both manifestations of our biospirituality.

As the traditions of biospiritual cultivation developed, the Chinese understanding of qi deepened and became more complex. By the first century CE a fairly sophisticated model of how qi functions in the body had been developed. This model serves as the basis for Daoist cultivation and traditional Chinese medicine to this day. According to this model, qi is not simply breath or air, but actually a pattern of energy that circulates throughout the body along pathways known as meridians. Just as blood physically circulates through veins and arteries, so qi circulates through these non-anatomical meridians. Anyone who has received a basic training in qi-energy practices is able to sense the qi moving through the body and it is most easily felt as a pulsating sensation in the centre of the palms.

The qi energy comes in two forms. Pre-natal qi is a fixed quantity of energy that is given to the body at conception. This energy cannot ordinarily be replaced, and throughout one's life it is slowly used up until the body eventually dies. Post-natal qi refers to the energy that sustains the body in its day-to-day life. This is the energy that is derived from food and expended through effort. People may extend their lifespan by improving the circulation of post-natal qi by eating, exercising, etc. but these practices cannot stop them from ultimately dying.

The circulation of qi in the body along the meridians is controlled by the five major organs of the body (heart, lungs, liver, spleen, kidneys) plus, in traditional Chinese medicine, a sixth non-anatomical organ known as the 'triple-heater'. These organs have the responsibility of storing and processing the qi energy as it circulates through the body. When energy circulates freely, the body is healthy. When energy is blocked, pathologies develop. Traditional Chinese medicine resolves the symptoms of illness by locating the source of the pathology and restoring the proper circulation of qi, through herbs, acupuncture, massage or a combination of various qi therapies.

The basic physiological principle at work in traditional Chinese medicine is the continuous exchange of vital energy according to the pattern of yin and yang. As we breathe in and out, and as our heart beats, so also qi pulsates through the meridians. What is important for Daoism is that this pattern of yin and yang does not just govern human physiology but in fact is 'hard-wired' into the basic constitution of the universe and thus governs all aspects of Daoist theology, ritual and practice. The treatise on yin and yang in an early medical compendium known as the *Yellow Emperor's Simple Questions* stresses the cosmic significance of the categories of yin and yang:

> The Yellow Emperor spoke: [The two categories] yin and yang are the underlying principle of heaven and earth; they are the web that holds all ten thousand things secure; they are father and mother to all transformations and alterations; they are the source and beginning of all creating and killing; they are the palace of spirit brilliance.
>
> In order to treat illnesses one must penetrate to their source. Heaven arose out of the accumulation of yang [influences]; the earth arose out of the accumulation of yin [influences]. Yin is tranquillity, yang is agitation; yang creates, yin stimulates development; yang kills, yin stores. Yang transforms influences, yin completes form. (trans. Unschuld, 1985, p. 283)

In this passage human beings are envisioned as configurations of energy that occupy a middle space between heaven and earth. The sky is composed of lighter, active yang energy that has separated out from the denser, receptive yin energy of the earth. In human beings these two modes of qi have come together, and human life is thus bound up in and constructed out of the life of heaven and earth. In the human body as well as the cosmos, the transformation of things, that is, the process of life itself, takes place in the form of a continuous dynamic, made up of the projection (yang) and reception (yin) of energy. Moreover, this dynamic, at its root, informs the cosmic diversity of the 'ten thousand things'. Thus the same binary dynamic of the energy in the body is the dynamic that governs the phases of the moon and the orbits of the stars. In this more expanded cosmic view of qi, the energy that gives life to our bodies is nothing less than the basic energy of the universe, which condenses in the form of matter to produce the tangible 'stuff' out of which all things are made. Things like rocks are composed of slow-moving dense qi. Our bodies are a complex of moderately condensed qi that forms the material parts (skin, organs, bones) and a relatively light and ethereal qi that gives us our minds and our spirits. The celestial beings who inhabit the heavens are, of course, one of the most rarefied forms of energy. But whether you are a sack of potatoes or Laozi himself you are still a form of energy and as such your qi is in the process of expanding and contracting, activating and storing.

Given that our life depends on the free circulation of qi, disease and death are brought on by interruptions to the flow of qi. These interruptions can take place within our bodies, but since the energy systems of our body are connected into the energy systems of earth and heaven it is necessary to take into account these broader contexts when diagnosing illnesses. One early medical text, the *Comprehensive Treatise on the Regulation of the Spirit in Accord with the Four Seasons* (*Siji tiaoshen dalun*) argues that the most important course of action for maintaining health within the body is to act in concert with the macrocosmic pattern of the seasons. This means that the well-being of the physiological systems at the microcosm level of the body can only be achieved by harmonizing with the broader macrocosmic dynamics of the context or environment in which they are located. In Daoist practice, the most important elements of this broader macrocosm are the sun and moon, the stars and planets, and the seasons. In medicine and in the Daoist worldview in general, the network of microcosm–macrocosm correspondences and the patterns of synchronicity between different dimensions of life are taken extremely seriously. These connections were analysed by early Chinese intellectuals using a type of analogical reasoning that is known as 'correlative thinking'.

CORRELATION, SYNCHRONICITY AND RESONANCE

Correlative thinking is a mode of thinking that is essentially different from logical thinking. The rules of logic dictate which conclusions logically follow from which premises. Logic is essentially a sequential way of thinking: if A, then B. The power of logical thinking is in isolating the relationships between causes and effects in a linear, temporal sequence. Correlative thinking is a way of mapping the relationships between things that do not exist in a linear cause-and-effect sequence. It is an analogical, spatial way of thinking: as A is to B so C is to D. Ancient Chinese thinkers developed these analogies or patterns to explain the functioning of three important dimensions of existence: the body, the state and the cosmos. These three dimensions of existence were thought to function analogously to each other, and, equally importantly, they function in relationship with each other. Furthermore, the personal body, the communal body, and the heavenly bodies in fact have been the three most important religious concerns for Daoists.

An early example of this way of correlative thinking can be found in *Mr. Lü's Springs and Autumns* (*Lüshi chunqiu*; third century BCE)

> Human beings have 360 joints, nine bodily openings, and five yin and six yang systems of function. In the flesh tightness is desirable; in the blood vessels free flow is desirable; in the sinews and bones solidity is desirable; in the operations of the heart and mind harmony is desirable; in the essential qi regular motion is desirable. When [these desiderata] are realized, illness has nowhere to abide, and there is nothing from which pathology can develop. When illness lasts and pathology develops, it is because the essential qi has become static.
>
> ...
>
> States too have their stases. When the ruler's virtue does not flow freely [i.e., if he does not appoint good officials to keep him and his subjects in touch], and the wishes of his people do not reach him, a hundred pathologies arise in concert, and a myriad catastrophes swarm in. The cruelty of those above and those below toward each other arises from this. The reason that the sage kings valued heroic retainers and faithful ministers is that they dared to speak directly, breaking through such stases. (*Lüshi chunqiu*, 20; trans. Sivin, 1995, p. 6)

In the above passage, the successful ruler is one who causes his virtue or power (*de*) to circulate freely throughout the state, in just the same way that a healthy body is sustained by the free circulation of qi. Just as the circulation of bodily energies and fluids is necessary for human survival, so also the free flow of 'virtue' is necessary in the state. This is a prime example of correlative thinking. It is also important to note that the definition of good that operates in both these cases is a medical definition, rather than a moral definition. A good body is a healthy body; a good state is a healthy state, and a virtuous ruler is one whose power circulates freely. Virtue seems to be something like a sort of moral energy that must flow freely. What follows from this 'medical' view about goodness is that the problem of the human condition is not some moral or existential problem, but rather what we do with our bodies and about how they are best harmonized with the state and with the cosmos. This is a psycho–social–energetic problem, not a problem of ethics (affect) or doctrine (intellect). Our emotions, wills and intellects are important, but they are systems of energy in the body and in the body-politic, and as such are no more or no less important than our gall bladders and our spleens.

In another medical text, the *Huangdi neijing suwen* (Simple Questions on the Yellow Emperor's Internal Classic), however, we see this analogical reasoning reversed. In this particular text the physiological functioning of the body is understood by analogy to the political hierarchy of the state:

> The cardiac system is the office of the monarch: consciousness issues from it. The pulmonary system is the office of the minister-mentors: oversight and supervision issue from it. The hepatic system is the office of the General: planning issues from it. The gall bladder system is the office of the rectifiers: decisions issue from it ... [and so on for the twelve systems of body functions associated with internal organs]. It will not do for these twelve offices to lose their co-ordination. (*Huangdi neijing suwen* 8.1; trans. Sivin, 1995, p. 7)

Here we see how the physiology of the body was correlated with the hierarchical configuration of the state, in which the emperor, like the heart, remains supreme, but cannot function without proper communication with the other administrative departments. In this case, therefore, the body is understood by analogy with the state.

Putting together these two early medical passages, we can begin to appreciate how this form of reasoning functions. From texts such as these, scholars have concluded that traditional Chinese thought displays an organic, mutually reciprocal system of 'correlative thinking' in which various dimensions of existence are understood by means of reciprocal correlation with other dimensions of existence.

The five phases

This way of making analogies or correlations between different types of things was systematized in a body of thought that still underpins Daoist theory and practice today. This system is based on the five phases or elements of traditional Chinese cosmology: earth, wood, fire, metal and water. The word 'phase' is more commonly used because the elements are grouped together in a sequence, and each element represents a phase in that sequence. In traditional Chinese medicine, there are two sequences: a cycle of generation in which one phase leads into the subsequent phase; and a cycle of control in which one phase blocks or controls the preceding phase.

The cycle of generation is: wood generates fire, which generates earth, which generates metal, which generates water, which generates wood. The cycle of control is: water controls fire, which controls metal, which controls wood, which controls earth, which controls water.

The principle behind the five phases system is that all the cyclical processes of the cosmos can in theory be divided into five major stages or phases. Moreover, the phases in one cycle (such as the cycle of the seasons) can be correlated to the phases in another cycle (such as the cycling of energy through the organs of the body). The addition of a new category of sequence is known as extension (*tui*). When an extension is made, and two different lists of items are brought into correlation, then it is possible, in traditional Chinese medicine, to make an analysis or a diagnosis by following through the sequences of the two things that are now correlated. But it is important to remember that we are not comparing 'things' or 'items' in this way; rather, we are making comparisons between the dynamics within the phases of two different categories of transformation. The person who first put this system together was Zou Yan (350–270 BCE)

Sima Qian's description of Zou's method of extension is as follows:

> First he had to examine small objects, and from these he drew conclusions about large ones, until he reached what was without limit. First he spoke about modern times, and from this went back to the time of Huang [Di] ... Moreover he followed the great events in the rise and fall of ages, and by means of their omens and (an examination into) their systems, extended [tui] his survey [still further] backwards to the time when the heavens and the earth had not yet been born, [in fact] to what was profound and abstruse and impossible to investigate. (*Shi ji*, 74: 3a; in Needham, 1956, p. 233)

This process of 'extension' resulted in a basic 'map' of the cosmos that is foundational for Daoism and Chinese medicine. The major elements of this map are summarized in the table below:

Cosmological Aspects					Physiological Aspects		
Phase	Direction	Colour	Season	Planet	Organ	Flavours	Emotion
Wood	East	Green	Spring	Jupiter	Liver	Sour	Anger
Fire	South	Red	Summer	Mars	Heart	Bitter	Joy
Earth	Centre	Yellow	Late summer	Saturn	Spleen	Sweet	Worry
Metal	West	White	Fall	Venus	Lungs	Pungent	Sadness
Water	North	Black	Winter	Mercury	Kidneys	Salty	Fear

Correlation was chiefly employed as a heuristic tool, often for the diagnosis of diseases. By combining the cycle of sequential causation (the vertical axis in the table above) with the principle of synchronic correspondences (the horizontal axis in the table above) it is possible to interpret any situation or event in relation to the multiple cosmic processes that may have an influence upon it. In terms of traditional Chinese medicine, if some excess of qi has occurred, it is either because the preceding item in the generative sequence has proved too strong, or the preceding item in the destructive or controlling sequence has proved too weak. In either case the remedy to the situation is to be sought in treating not the symptoms but the deficient or excessive cause, thus restoring the system to its natural balance. But the vertical axis on the table above only tells one part of the story. Equally important is the horizontal axis that maps the correlations between one vertical system and another. The horizontal relationships are not explained as logical 'cause' and 'effect' within a linear temporal sequence, but as a synchronic relationship of 'stimulus' and 'resonance'.

Thus, a transformation in the seasons implies a corresponding transformation in the relative strengths of the various bodily functions, which requires a corresponding transformation in diet in order to maintain a homeostatic equilibrium. From this we can see that, according to the traditional Chinese worldview, the universe is not comprised of a number of discrete elements or 'atoms', but, in broad terms, of configurations of energy or force that transform in 'phases', like the seasons, in a set sequence or repetitive cycle. Equally importantly, the principle of interconnectedness entails that there are resonances or correspondences between the phasing of one dimension of reality and another. One way of explaining this mutual resonance between things is to imagine qi as a wave-form or a string. Thus a stimulus in one area produces a corresponding resonance in all other areas, just as someone plucking a guitar string sets off harmonic vibrations through the wood and all the other strings. Some commentators even draw parallels between qi theory and the basic picture of the universe at a quantum level that has emerged in contemporary physics (see Capra, 2000).

The gods of the body

The most important way in which this system of correspondences functions in Daoism is in the way in which the organs of the body are co-ordinated with gods. Gods are said to be resident in the body, and the body is thus regarded as a cosmic entity. The text that most powerfully details this system of correspondence is the seminal work known as the *Scripture of the Yellow Court* (*Huangting jing*). In this work, each major organ of the body is correlated with a deity who is named and described.

Organ	Name of god
Heart	Cinnabar Prime, Guarding Numinous
Lungs	Luminous Florescence, Vacuity Completing
Liver	Dragon Smoke, Cherishing Brightness
Kidneys	Occult Tenebrity, Nourishing Baby
Spleen	Constantly Existing, Soul Resting
Gall	Dragon Radiance, Awesome Bright

The title of the text derives from the description of the body as a palace complex. Each organ is a palace court presided over by a deity who oversees its proper functioning. The text is extremely poetical and symbolic, and the deities are described in magnificent detail:

> The palace of the heart [is like] a lotus bursting with
>   blossom
> Under which the Lad, from the family of Cinnabar Prime,
> Governs and presides over cold and heat, and harmonizes
>   the healthy circulation [of vital essence].
> He wears flying robes of cinnabar brocade and cloaks
>   himself in jade gauze.

> With golden hand bells and a pearly sash he dwells in
> tranquillity, regulating blood, patterning my life so that
> my body will not wither.
>
> (*Huangting neijing jing*, 10:1–5, author's trans.)

As this extract suggests, the function of these deities is entirely therapeutic: they direct the healthy functioning of the body. Nearly every verse of the text ends with a line describing the practical efficacy of the body gods. The implication of this is that the life within our bodies is somehow interwoven with the lives of gods; it is as though our blood vessels and meridians are conduits of divine grace or spiritual energy. In this regard the biospirituality evident in this text is not wholly removed from that of the early Great Peace or Celestial Masters' theology. The difference, however, is that the gods in those traditions were viewed as celestial deities who could be dealt with via the ministrations of ritual masters. The *Scripture of the Yellow Court* paved the way for an altogether more introspective tradition in which the correspondence between humans and gods does not take the form of a literal written, priestly correspondence, but an internal, symbolic correspondence that was actualized through the visualization practices examined in chapter 5 and the inner alchemical systems in chapter 6.

LONGEVITY PRACTICES

Alongside these esoteric practices developed far more popular forms of qi cultivation that many people undertake simply to improve their health. In fact it is through these health practices, such as Qigong and taiji quan that Daoism is gaining a foothold throughout the world. Whether or not you consider yourself a Daoist by doing so, involves all the sorts of questions of identity that were discussed in chapter 1. Teachers of these practices do not usually refer to them as religious practices since they perceive that religion can have many pejorative connotations in the relatively secularized modern-day context.

Although health is usually thought of as a matter for science, not religion, there has always been a strong connection between religion and health in all of the world's religions. The shamans of traditional indigenous cultures function as local health care providers. Jesus is said to have healed the sick. Religious communities establish hospitals, and comfort those in distress. Scientists are now recognizing and studying the healing power of prayer in aiding, among other things, the recovery from surgery. In Daoism, the most important bridge between religion and health today is the practice of taiji quan.

Taiji quan

Taiji quan, more commonly known as Tai-Chi, is the most widespread, popular practice connected to Daoism. The modern forms of taiji quan probably go back only as far as the late Qing dynasty (nineteenth century), when they were developed as a martial art form. The name literally translates as 'supreme ultimate boxing'. Nowadays it is common not as a martial art but is practised in a slowed-down form of gentle, stylized movements. The connection with Daoism arises in the fact that it is traditionally claimed that taiji quan was invented by Zhang Sanfeng, a Daoist immortal who is alleged to have lived in the thirteenth or fourteenth century at Mount Wudang, the most important centre for Daoist martial arts. It was at centres like Mount Wudang that advanced Daoist monks developed ways of manipulating qi and even projecting it from the body that could be applied to hand-to-hand combat. Romantic stories about such figures abound in Chinese popular culture and even made it to the Oscars in the form of Ang Lee's celebrated film *Crouching Tiger, Hidden Dragon*. What we can say with historical certitude is that the invention of taiji quan, for whatever reason, came to be attributed to Zhang Sanfeng and he came to be revered as an important figure whose statue can be found in many Daoist temples including the Baiyun guan in Beijing.

The basic principle of taiji quan as it is practised today is that the individual physically embodies the interplay of yin and yang in a sequence of movements that embody assertive (yang) and receptive (yin) modes of action. Of course it is perfectly possible to practice taiji quan as a form of gentle exercise, and this is the way it is most commonly presented to newcomers. At the same time it is also possible to undertake taiji quan as a form of qi cultivation in which the individual is guiding the qi of his or her body through the various external movements. At a more cosmic level, it is possible to see taiji quan as a type of ritual dance in which one embodies and plays out the basic yin–yang complementarity of the Dao.

One of the largest taiji quan organizations in the world is the Taoist Tai-Chi Society, founded by Moy Lin-Shin. In 1970 Moy emigrated from China's Guangdong province to Canada, and established an organization for teaching taiji. The organization promotes the health benefits of taiji quan but it also maintains a religious wing that goes under the name Fung Loy Kok. The religious wing of the organization is less obvious than the health practice wing, perhaps reflecting the modern Western ambiguity towards the connection between religion and health (see Seigler, 2003). The Toronto Chinatown headquarters is a physical manifestation of this ambiguity. The building looks like an ordinary building on the outside and on the inside there is a large taiji quan practice room on the ground floor. Above it, hidden away from outside observation, is a large Daoist temple complete with shrine to Zhang Sanfeng and other Daoist and Buddhist deities. This duality to a large extent accurately mirrors the relationship between Daoist religious practices and health practices. People commonly practice taiji quan and other Daoist-inspired cultivation for no reason other than their own health and welfare. It is possible, however, to use these practices as the foundation for an engaged Daoist religious life. In this way Daoism offers a hierarchy of practices that begin with simple, exoteric physical cultivation practices, and gradually take on a more internal, meditative dimension. It is rare that people persevere on this Daoist path to the full extent of becoming radically transformed spiritual beings who wield extraordinary psycho-physical powers. Unlike Islam, where the benefits and responsibilities of the religion are enjoined upon all members equally, Daoist organizations typically present a more hierarchical or graded path for individuals to follow.

Qigong

In the nineteenth century, a variety of styles of qi-practices known as qigong (qi-skill) were popularized throughout China. The principle of qigong is that by actively guiding and circulating qi throughout the body, the overall functioning of one's physiological system will be strengthened and enhanced. The basic sensation of qi can be easily taught in a few minutes. The practices themselves range from the simple to complex and may be performed by means of physical movements akin to taiji quan, or wholly internally. In either case the purpose is to stimulate the healthy circulation of qi throughout the body. Qigong may also be performed on a person by an advanced practitioner. The practitioner uses his or her own qi to stimulate the qi of the other person.

One of the world's largest qigong organizations is known as Falun dafa, which practises a type of qigong that it calls falun gong (Dharma

Wheel Skill). Falun dafa takes Buddhist ideals of cultivating respect and compassion as the necessary corollary to qi cultivation. The method of falun gong was invented in 1992 by a Chinese qigong practitioner, Li Hongzhi. Li developed the basic doctrines and principles of the practice and controls the styles of practice that may be taught and undertaken. Since 1999, Falun dafa has been outlawed in China as a dangerous cult and Master Li lives in permanent exile in the United States. Falun gong cultivation groups exist throughout North America and Europe. The 'wheel of dharma' refers to the rotations of the cosmos, symbolized in the Buddhist swastika, and located within the body in the abdomen. The basic principle of falun gong is that the dharma wheel rotates within one's body generating a positive flow of qi energy that can be used to benefit the practitioner. In addition to practising falun gong, members of Falun dafa are also required to follow the threefold path of 'zhen-shan-ren' or truthfulness, goodness and forbearance.

Daoism and sex

Another important set of longevity practices that developed alongside Daoist cultivation practices are what are euphemistically known as the 'arts of the bedchamber'. In fact Daoism has had a complex relationship with Chinese sexual yoga, and the two are far from synonymous. The common element between the two lies in the shared worldview: the cosmos flourishes by means of the binary intercourse of yang and yin, projection and reception, active and passive, male and female. It seems, from later condemnations, that the early Celestial Masters' movement practised a sexual initiation rite that symbolized the merging of these two elemental forces. Later on, Daoist inner alchemical practices prized the cultivation of *jing*, the 'essential qi' that is physically manifest in sexual fluids. As with taiji quan, people can undertake Chinese sexual practices for no reason other than their own benefit or interest. At the same time it is clear that sexuality has been an element of Daoism that ought not to be overlooked.

The chief goal of the earliest tradition of Chinese sexual practice was to improve the health and longevity of the male practitioner. A sexual treatise found in the Mawangdui tomb excavations (dated to 168 BCE), entitled *Uniting Yin and Yang (He yinyang)*, speaks of absorbing the *jing* energy upwards in order to live forever and be equal with heaven and earth (Wile 1992, p. 78; see also Harper, 1987). This earliest fragment of sexual literature reveals the basic direction that Chinese sexology comes to take: the goal of sexual practice is not the conception of children, nor the erotic stimulation of the partners, but increasing the practitioner's vitality. Wile (1992, p. 6) explains:

> The Yellow Emperor, summarizing the lessons of his sexual initiation in the Classic of Su Nü, concludes, 'The essential teaching is to refrain from losing [jing] and to treasure one's fluids.' Because loss of semen depresses the body's entire energy economy, semen is seen as possessing a material and energetic aspect ... If the semen is retained, the sexual energy will support superior health.

Sexual arousal leads to the activation of jing (whose physical aspect is in both male and female sexual fluids) which must be absorbed and retained within the body of the male. The tenth century CE Japanese medical compendium *Ishimpo* contains a text that is far more explicit on this subject:

> According to Pengzu the Long-Lived, if a man wishes to derive the greatest benefit [from sexual techniques], it is best to find a woman who has no knowledge of them. He had also better choose young maidens for mounting, because then his complexion will become like a maiden's. When it comes to women, one should be vexed only by their not being young. It is best to obtain those between fourteen or fifteen and eighteen or nineteen. In any event they should not be older than thirty. Even those under thirty are of no benefit if they have given birth. My late master handed down these methods and himself used them to live for three thousand years. If combined with drugs they will even lead to immortality. (*Yufang bijue*, 635; trans. Kohn, 1993, p. 155)

At the heart of this sexual technique for longevity lies the notion of an intrinsic connection between sexuality and vitality: releasing sexual fluids is the way to beget offspring; conserving sexual fluids is the way to conserve one's own vitality. Clearly there are some elements that are important in a wide variety of Daoist contexts, chief among which is the quest for immortality and the idealization of youthfulness. *Daode jing* chapter 55, for instance, refers to the vitality of a child 'who does not yet know the union of male and female'.

The clearest evidence of the use of sexual practices in Daoist religion comes from the early Celestial Masters' communities. Our knowledge of this is limited to later condemnations of the ritual and to a Daoist text that documents a sexual ordination or initiation ritual known as the

Ritual of Salvation of the Yellow Book of Highest Clarity (see Schipper, 1993, pp. 148–52; Bokenkamp, 1997, pp. 43–6). This text outlines a ritual for 'harmonizing qi' that is quite different than texts such as the *Yufang bijue*, quoted above, in their 'sexual vampirism'. The ritual took place in the presence of a Daoist master and the initiates followed a precisely patterned sequence of movement and prayer that culminated in the act of penetration. In this ritual both partners had equal roles: the activity of one partner was matched by the activity of the other partner. Throughout the ritual deities were invoked, and, in keeping with the principle of correspondence, the couple's movements had to be co-ordinated with cosmological and numerological patterns. Since the religion of the Celestial Masters hinged upon establishing registers by which people were initiated into a celestial society, this ritual symbolized the merging of celestial registers and initiation of a couple into this society. The significance of this ritual lies in the fact that it incorporated the cosmological principle of the harmonizing of yin-qi and yang-qi with the social character of religious liberation in Celestial Masters' communities.

Perhaps the most important commonality of Daoist practice and Chinese sexual yoga is thus the universal Chinese cosmology of yin and yang. But again it is important to recognize that there is nothing specifically Daoist about the idea of harmonizing yin and yang, and it would be a mistake to identify texts or practices as Daoist on the basis that they focus on this idea. As esoteric sexual practices became more common in the Ming dynasty, practitioners drew upon a wide range of Daoist, Confucian, alchemical and cosmological theories in order to justify their practices. One Ming dynasty alchemical text, the *Jindan qiuzheng pian* (Seeking Instruction on the Golden Elixir) makes clear the convergence of many of these elements:

> Master Shao [a Confucian philosopher] said that the *jing* of yin and yang is concealed within each other's domain. Thus, Taiji divided into the 'two aspects', and the 'two aspects' became the 'four images', and from the 'four images', the 'eight trigrams' ... In man and woman, when yin and yang have intercourse, a material being is formed ... When male and female have intercourse, yin cannot but embrace yang, and yang cannot but be rooted in yin. (trans. Wile, 1992, p. 150)

As this text makes clear, the patterning of the cosmos according to the principles of yin and yang was correlated with the sexual reproduction of the human species. The birth of life takes place by means of the interaction of these two fundamental principles, and only in this respect does the sexual act take on a cosmic import. It should be noted that the experience of sexual desire (a major theme in Western sexual theory) is quite irrelevant to understanding the cosmic significance of reproduction. What is important is that the pattern of the universe is manifested in the pattern of human reproduction.

TRANSCENDENT BODIES

How do all these methods of qi-cultivation relate to Daoism? A clue to this question can be found in the excavations at the Mawangdui tombs. Among the artefacts found there is a beautiful gymnastics chart known as the *Daoyin tu*. This chart contains forty-four images of the human body in many different poses suggestive of a routine of gymnastic practices. Although there is no accompanying text, the chart indicates that gymnastics was a well-developed science in ancient China. The intriguing question is why was this chart put in a tomb? The extraordinary fact is that many tombs of the Han dynasty that have been excavated in modern times contain texts devoted to longevity practices. Though scholars are not certain in their conclusions, the evidence suggests that the ancient Chinese viewed death as a transitory, rather than a final, state. It was precisely this transitoriness, or instability, that made the deceased potentially dangerous people who require special attention. The discovery of these documents, moreover, suggests to scholars that people believed it was still possible for some sort of transformation to take place within the body of the dead person. The fact that Daoists are also involved in ritually liberating their ancestors from hell similarly suggests that death is not the end of everything.

Even more than liberation, Daoism holds out the possibility of transmuting one's body into a transfigured celestial being. Such celestial beings were known as *xian*, conventionally translated as 'immortals'. The word 'immortal' is problematic because it can clearly apply to people who are dead in the conventional sense; many scholars prefer to call such people 'transcendents'. Whichever word we use, the point is that Daoism clearly holds out the promise of something more than mere longevity. Whether through post-mortem rituals or a lifetime of alchemical meditation, the purpose of Daoist cultivation is to achieve a totally transformed body. The question of how longevity and transcendence are related is a major debate within the tradition, but the basic premise that joins together both the longevity and transcendence traditions is that life is more than biology.

One way that Daoists learn about the extraordinary people who have achieved the rare feat of transcendence is through hagiographies. The lives of transcendents are in fact a major genre of Daoist literature and offer inspiration to those who would seek transcendence for themselves. An example of a very brief hagiography is that of a figure called Huang Ziyang (which also indicates the high esteem given to peaches in the Daoist tradition!):

> The Lord [Pei] said: Huang Ziyang was a native of Wei. [While] young, he knew of the subtleties of prolonging the life. He learned the dao on Mount Boluo for ninety-odd years. He merely ate the peel of peaches and drank the yellow water from within the stones. Later he met with [the immortal] Sima Jizhu. Jizhu took the Eight recipes of guiding immortals (Daoxian ba fang) and gave them [to Huang]. [Huang] subsequently took [them] and transcended the world. (trans. Bumbacher, 2000, p. 386)

The literature tells us that Daoist transcendents, or 'perfected persons' (*zhenren*) possess bodies that are quite impervious to the forces of nature:

> The utmost man is daemonic [a spirit]. When the wide woodlands blaze they cannot sear him, when the Yellow River and the Han freeze they cannot chill him, when swift thunderbolts smash the mountains and whirlwinds shake the seas they cannot startle him. A man that yokes the clouds to his chariot, rides the sun and moon and roams beyond the four seas; death and life alter nothing in himself, still less the principles of benefit and harm. (Graham, 1986b, p. 58)

Transcendents, moreover, possess supernatural powers of control over spirits and humans as they are able to manipulate the qi that surrounds them as well as the qi of their own bodies:

> Immortals can control the evil or dangerous activities of animals, ghosts and mountain sprites. Through it they can inhibit bleeding, aid in the restoration of broken bones, prevent being cut by swords and cure snake bites. In addition, they can create extraordinary and indelible writing, shrink the earth, relieve drought and cover great distances in mysterious ways. (Penny, 2000, p. 125)

Of all the countless transcendent beings in the world, eight are singled out for special recognition in the Daoist tradition. Images of these 'Eight Immortals' (six men, one woman and one person who appears in either sex) adorn Daoist temples and they feature in many works of literature and drama as much as in religious texts. Of the eight perhaps the most famous is Lü Dongbin who ascended to transcendence after he famously experienced his entire life as a dream.

Daoists then have a variety of attitudes towards embodied life. There are those for whom physical longevity is an important goal, those who seek to liberate the dead from hell, and those for whom the ordinary categories of living and dead seem not to apply any more. If there is anything in common between all of this, it is that the status and functioning of our bodies (and not just souls or minds) seems to be the central focus of much of Daoist practice.

Given the possibility that the boundary between life and death is perhaps more porous than would ordinarily seem to be the case, and that death can be seen as a valuable stage in one's ascension towards heaven, it is not surprising that Daoists can adopt an unusual attitude towards our ordinary embodied life. A fitting end to this investigation of Daoist bodies is perhaps the story of Master Zhuang's reaction to his wife's death:

> Master Chuang's wife died. When Master Hui went to offer his condolences, he found Master Chuang lolling on the floor with his legs sprawled out, beating a basin and singing.
>
> 'She lived together with you,' said Master Hui, 'raised your children, grew old, and died. It's enough that you do not wail for her, but isn't it a bit much for you to be beating on a basin and singing?'
>
> 'Not so,' said Master Chuang. 'When she first died how could I of all people not be melancholy? But I reflected on her beginning and realized that originally she was unborn. Not only was she unborn, originally she had no form. Not only did she have no form, originally she had no vital breath. Intermingling with nebulousness and blurriness, a transformation occurred and there was vital breath; the vital breath was transformed and there was form; the form was transformed and there was birth; now there has been another transformation and she is dead. This is like the progression of the four seasons – from spring to autumn, from winter to summer. There she sleeps blissfully in an enormous chamber. If I were to have followed her weeping and wailing, I think it would have been out of keeping with destiny, so I stopped.' (*Zhuangzi*, 18; trans. Mair, 1994, pp. 168–9)

SUGGESTIONS FOR FURTHER READING

Kaptchuk, Ted J. 1983. *The Net that Has No Weaver: Understanding Chinese Medicine*. New York, Congdon & Weed

Roth, Harold. 1999. *Original Tao*. New York, NY, Columbia University Press

Schipper, Kristofer Marinus. 1993. *The Taoist Body*. Berkeley, University of California Press

Wile, Douglas. 1992. *Art of the Bedchamber: The Chinese Sexology Classics Including Women's Solo Meditation Texts*. Albany, State University of New York Press

4

Power

德

All too often discussions about Daoism centre on the idea of Dao, and neglect its corollary, *de*. The *de* of the *Daode jing*, as we have already seen, basically means the power, virtue or potential that is generated when one attains the Dao. In fact the term '*de*' is much older than the term 'dao' and relates to the capacity to rule the nation. If an aristocrat had the right sort of *de*, then he would be granted the mandate of heaven (tianming) and become king. To have *de* (virtue) is to have the power, the possibility of being granted the mandate (ming); and conversely the mandate (ming) is the possibility of power (*de*) (Kruykov, 1995, p. 330).

The roots of the term '*de*' go back as far as the Neolithic civilization known as the Shang Dynasty or Shang-Yin culture. Our knowledge of this ancient civilization is based in part on so-called oracle bones – the shoulder-blades of oxen or tortoise-shells that were used in a divination ritual known as scapulimancy. A question was carved into the bone in an early form of Chinese characters, the bone would be heated, and it would crack. The reader of the oracle looked for the answer to the question in the way the crack formed on the bone. Archeologists have deciphered many of these oracle bones and in so doing have learned a lot about Shang language and culture. The Shang word that eventually became the classical Chinese *de* functioned as a verb with the general meaning of 'to punish', and which referred specifically to the prerogative of the ruler to sacrifice human life in an act of ritual violence that established and maintained his power over his subjects (Kruykov, 1995, p. 326). This indicates that the basis of royal power lay in the capacity to generate the fear and respect of others (Kryukov, 1995, p. 326).

In the subsequent Zhou dynasty, which deprecated human sacrifices, *de* was not generated by spilling blood, but conferred by Heaven as a mandate to rule over the people. *De* was thus the privileged possession of the emperor, known as the Son of Heaven, and the elite clans, but it was not conferred automatically: it had to be sought through intercession with the ancestors. Through ritual means it was passed on from generation to generation. Its sociological function, as Allan points out (1998, p. 102), was to be an hereditary trait particular to each aristocratic family. This power is thus transmitted – as it were genetically – from generation to generation and reauthenticated by interaction with the ancestors.

In the disunity of the Warring States the question was naturally raised as to what sort of *de* one needed to be granted the mandate of Heaven to unite the empire and rule over 'all under heaven' (*tianxia*). Put another way, what power or what virtues does the ruler need? It was at this time that Confucius instituted a revolution in which de came no longer to be understood as a purely 'genetic' characteristic but as a moral virtue that enabled one to spread harmony throughout the world. No longer was birth a sufficient guarantee of success in bringing stability to the empire: the right quality was 'virtue'. Confucius was known for teaching all who would be taught, whether rich or poor. The later Confucian philosopher Mencius even went so far as to claim that the seeds of virtue lie within every single person. It is nearly impossible to underestimate how radical a shift this was in the development of Chinese culture, given the fact that *de* was once thought to be an aristocratic privilege.

Daoists, however, had a different understanding and based their idea of *de* on a far more naturalistic philosophy known as Huang-Lao. The Huang-Lao ideology rose to prominence during the Han dynasty, and is based on the five phases system of correspondences, according to which all phenomena are to be understood as phases in the dynamic breathing-in and breathing-out of cosmic qi energy. The earliest form of this way of thinking held that the transfer of the dynastic mandates arose *by virtue of* (*de*) a particular phase in the cyclical transformation of things. One classic text puts it this way: 'Each of the Five Virtues [*de*] is followed by the one it cannot conquer. The dynasty of Shun ruled by the virtue of Earth, the Xia ruled by the virtue of Wood, the Shang dynasty ruled by the virtue of Metal, and the Zhou dynasty ruled by the virtue of Fire' (*Wen Xuan* 59, 9b; trans. adapted from Needham, 1956, p. 238). As the system of five-phase correlations became more complex, the life of the state was thought to function in synchronic resonance with the orbits of the stars and planets, the rotation of the seasons and other natural cycles. A fully developed system of correspondences is elaborated in a Daoist text called the *Taishang Laojun jiejing* (Scripture of Precepts of the Highest Lord Lao):

> Lord Lao said: The five precepts in heaven are represented by the five planets [Jupiter, Venus, Mars, Mercury, and Saturn]. They rule the energies of the five directions, making sure they remain in harmony and maintain their constancy. As soon as the Dao of heaven loses its precepts, there are natural catastrophes.
>
> On earth, they are represented by the five sacred mountains [Mts. Tai, Heng, Hua, Heng, and Song]. They govern the energies of the earth and rule the weather, gathering and dispelling the clouds. As soon as the Dao of earth loses its precepts, the hundred grains can no longer grow.
>
> Among the seasonal patterns, they are represented by the five phases. As soon as the five cycles lose their precepts, fire and water fight each other, and metal and wood do each other harm.
>
> In government, the five precepts are represented by the five emperors. As soon as rulers lose their precepts, dynasties topple and rulers perish.
>
> In human beings, they are represented by the five inner organs. As soon as people lose their precepts, their health and inner nature goes astray.
> (trans. Kohn, 1994, p. 203)

The authority to rule was thus inscribed in the cyclical transformations of nature, and, in particular, the rotation of the planets in the heavens. This ideology was used by the Han dynasty to legitimate its own authority: if heaven itself had granted the mandate, and that mandate was part of the fabric of cosmos, to challenge the power of the emperor would be to challenge the laws of earth and heaven.

We know of course that the Han dynasty did not last for ever, and although its collapse can certainly be attributed in part to serious damage to the economic and social fabric of the country, another factor was, ironically, the very ideology that it had used to legitimate its own power. Implicit within the concept of the five phases was the notion that eventually the cycle moves on, and the mandate of heaven must be revoked and handed to another dynasty. The question was, when?

The answer to this question lay in the heavens: the political power granted by the mandate of heaven had to correspond to the various seasonal and astrological cycles. One Han dynasty intellectual, Liu Xin, is a prime exemplar of what we might term the astro-political thinking that developed in China in the Han dynasty. Liu sought a way of reconciling all the various cycles of nature, the sixty-year cycle of the Chinese calendar and the movement of the planets, all in accordance with the system of five phases (Bokenkamp, 1994, p. 64). The purpose of all these calculations was to determine the times of 'apocalypse' that occur at the conjunction of all the cycles, once every 23,639,040 years (Bokenkamp, 1994, p. 65). At this point the world was expected to undergo a radical transformation.

Not everyone, however, was willing to wait such a long time for the mandate of heaven to move on to the next phase! According to Zhang Jue, the leader of the Way of Great Peace, the year in which the mandate was going to be revoked was 184 CE, because this year was a jiazi year that marked the beginning of a new sixty-year cycle in the Chinese calendar. He organized thirty-six (a 'magic' number: $2^2 \times 3^3$) groups of followers known as 'yellow turbans' in recognition of their distinctive headdress. Yellow was chosen because it corresponds to the 'earth' phase that they sought to inaugurate. Zhang and his followers believed that the year 184 CE would usher in the dawn of a new age, an age of 'great peace' that would begin a new phase in the evolution of the Dao.

DAOIST MILLENARIANISM

The Way of Great Peace has been described as a millenarian movement, and the phenomenon of millenarianism is an important aspect in the relationship between Daoist movements and Chinese imperial power. The term 'millenarianism' derives from the Christian belief in a thousand-year period that succeeds the current world order and precedes the final apocalypse. The modern academic category of millenarianism as used in the comparative study of religion, denotes a religious belief that the world will soon come to an end and a newer and better one will take its place (Kohn, 1998).

Much of our modern understanding of millenarianism was shaped by the work of Norman Cohn (1970; 1993) who traced millenarian thought back to the Persian prophet Zoroaster. According to Cohn, one of Zoroaster's innovations was the absolute emphasis on the concept of linear time rather than cyclical time. It is this transition from a 'primitive' cyclicality to a more 'modern' linearity that Cohn views as one of the necessary conditions for the millenarian worldview to emerge. According to millenarian thought, time will not repeat itself in the usual cyclical fashion. Rather an utterly new and decisively different order will be ushered in by a heroic saviour.

Given that the idea of the mandate of heaven and the selection of 184 CE seems to be based on the idea of cycles, it is not so clear that the Way of Great Peace may properly be classified as a millenarian movement according to Cohn's definition. To investigate this question further, it is necessary to examine more carefully the ideology that the Way of Great Peace espoused. This will also help us to understand the concept of power as it applied to this early Daoist movement.

Our understanding of the worldview of the Way of Great Peace is based largely on a text known as the Scripture of Great Peace (*Taiping jing*). The extant edition of this text dates only as far back as the Ming dynasty, over a thousand years later than the original movement, and so scholars debate how much of the extant edition of the text actually corresponds to the original worldview. Any assessment of the worldview of the original Yellow Turbans must therefore remain somewhat tentative. Nonetheless, the principal ideas, as we saw in chapter 2, are that heaven, earth and humans exist in a symbiotic relationship based upon the principle of mutual communication. The text decisively rejects a laissez-faire attitude to this relationship. Rather, heaven (yang) and earth (yin) were seen as achieving a 'central harmony' (*zhonghe*) in the human realm. It was thus the task of human beings to ensure that this harmony is in fact created. The chief means of doing so was by ensuring that the heavens, the earth and human beings maintained an active communication system. However, generations of mismanagement by human beings had led to a situation in which humans, heaven and earth were no longer in communication with each other. The result of this breakdown was the constant recurrence of evil and suffering and a history that never witnessed the elimination of 'evil influences'.

This important question suggests a dissatisfaction with the status quo and the inability of imperial sacrifices to the traditional gods and ancestors to underwrite the permanent harmony of the empire. Despite the best efforts of priests and politicians, suffering and disharmony kept coming back. The Yellow Turbans sought a religious answer to this question of suffering, and came up with the doctrine of 'inherited guilt'. According to this novel theory guilt was accumulated and transmitted from generation to generation, building up in a linear fashion that was never eliminated by traditional cycles of sacrifices. The text describes this doctrine as '*cheng-fu*'.

Cheng refers to 'before' and *fu* to 'after'. *Cheng* means that the ancestors originally acted in accordance with the will of heaven, and then slowly lost it; after a long time had elapsed, [their mistakes] had amassed and those of today living afterwards, then through no guilt of their own succeed to [the formers'] mistakes and culpability and so continuously suffer from the catastrophes engendered by them. Therefore that which is before is *cheng* and that which is afterwards is *fu*. *Fu* means that the various catastrophes do not go back to the government of the one man, but to a successive lack of balance. Those who live before put a load on the back of those who come later. This is why it is called *fu*. *Fu* means that the ancestor puts a load on the descendent. (Lai, 2001, p. 106)

This continuous accumulation of guilt could only be dealt with by a revolutionary new order: the Way of Great Peace. This new order, brought in by Zhang Jue and the Yellow Turbans, was dedicated to the cult of a newly titled supreme deity, the Great One of the Central Yellow who presided over a Yellow Heaven and embodied aspects of Laozi, the mythical author of the *Daode jing*, and the Yellow Emperor, mythical patriarch of the Chinese people (Seidel, 1969, p. 58). In this respect it seems that the Yellow Turbans did not view their movement as a continuation of the traditional dynastic cycle, but as a radical innovation.

According to Livia Kohn, the Way of Great Peace decisively rejected the cyclical cosmology that dominated earlier history. She writes:

The cyclicality of the mandate of heaven was modified to allow a linear course for history; the idea of Great Peace implied a total break with the preceding age as well as the judgment and destruction of the wicked. Furthermore, the inspiring sage became a savior, a divinely appointed agent of a personal high god. This high god was not only the highest of all but also the unique creator of the world, who nevertheless communicated directly with prophetic seers ... As a result, early Daoist movements are highly similar in doctrine, literary formulation, and social organization to comparable millenarian groups in the West, but also constitute a serious break with earlier Chinese doctrines and religious practices. (Kohn, 1998)

So it was that the Yellow Turbans rose in rebellion in 184 CE, convinced that they were on the vanguard of a new age in China's political and religious history. Though ultimately unsuccessful, their rebellion greatly weakened the Han dynasty and helped speed its total collapse by 214 CE.

Like the Way of Great Peace, the Covenant of Orthodox Unity (or Way of the Celestial Masters) also originated as a religious-political movement towards the end of the Han dynasty. The important difference was that the Orthodox Unity theocracy was founded in Sichuan province in the west of China, far away from the concerns of the Han dynasty government. Although it is difficult to reconstruct how precisely this movement flourished, we do know that Zhang and his descendents shared some of the concerns of the Way of Great Peace. Before Zhang Daoling's grandson, Zhang Lu, gave up power, he too helped organize a rebellion in 184 at the same time as the Yellow Turbans. Thus we know that both these early Daoist movements were characterized by a certain strand of violent millenarian thinking in which religious ideology precipitated bloody rebellion.

The cult of Laozi

A further commonality between the Way of Great Peace and the Way of the Celestial Masters is the role played by Laozi. The supreme deity of the Way of Great Peace was thought to have manifested as Laozi, and the role of Laozi was further solidified in the Way of the Celestial Masters. The biography of Zhang Daoling contained in Ge Hong's *Biographies of Divine Transcendents* (*Shenxian zhuan*) relates that Zhang was a student of alchemy who moved to Sichuan and composed many Daoist scriptures while living on Mount Heming. While meditating one day,

> suddenly there were heavenly beings descending with a thousand chariots, ten thousand riders and golden carriages with feathery canopies drawn by countless dragons on the outside and tigers on the inside. One was called the archivist and also the child of the Eastern sea. He then gave Ling the newly emerged Way of Orthodox Unity and Awesome Covenant. After Ling had received this he was able to cure diseases, whereupon the common people respectfully revered him as their teacher and his disciples' households reached ten thousand in number. (*Biography of Zhang Daoling* in *Biographies of Divine Immortals (Shenxian zhuan)* by Ge Hong, author's trans.)

The terms 'archivist' and 'child of the Eastern sea' are allusions to the figure of Laozi, the 'Old Master', or 'Old Child' by an alternative translation, whom Sima Qian had identified as a Zhou dynasty archivist. Laozi thus became the central figure of the Celestial Masters' pantheon. The community also practised the recitation of Laozi's *Daode jing* as part of Zhang's health care programme and as an aid to meditation on the figure of Laozi as a celestial deity.

The role of Laozi in the organization of the community is further evident in the form of an important commentary on the *Daode jing* that is attributed to either Zhang himself or his grandson (see Bokenkamp, 1997). The full version of this commentary, known as *Xiang'er* (perhaps meaning 'Thinking of You'), is extant in a version found in the excavation of the Dunhuang caves and dated around 600 CE, and effectively interprets the rather enigmatic aphorisms of the *Daode jing* into a system of precepts for the members of the community. It should be noted that some scholars believe this text originated in the later southern Celestial Masters' tradition of the fifth century and not the original Han dynasty movement (see Hendrischke, 2000, p. 146; Kobayashi, 1987), however the text effectively promotes a religious ideology according to which meditation on the figure of Laozi is rewarded with good fortune and long life.

Perhaps the most important document that involves the figure of the deified Laozi with the political turmoil at the end of the Han dynasty is the *Scripture of the Transformations of Laozi* (*Laozi bianhua jing*). Although the extant version is also a seventh-century Dunhuang manuscript, the text can reliably be dated back to somewhere between the *jiazi* year of 184 and the end of the Han dynasty (Hendrischke, 2000, p. 147). It describes Laozi as the high god who created the world, and who appears from time to time to save the world from chaos. In subsequent literature the figure of Laozi became increasingly significant in the political ambitions of the Li clan who claimed to trace their lineage back to Laozi (identified as the archivist Li Er; see Seidel, 1969).

DAOIST MESSIANISM

The notion of Laozi's manifestations gave birth to a form of Daoist messianism that continued after the dispersion of the original Celestial Masters' community. Throughout the relatively turbulent centuries that followed until the reunification of China under the Sui dynasty (581–618), the fragmented Daoist movements that constituted the remnant of the original tradition sought to align themselves with the various political authorities that established themselves throughout China. In this respect the idea of a messiah figure became an important ideological tool by means of which Daoists sought to invest aspirants to or occupiers of the royal throne with religious – and therefore political – authority.

The term 'messiah' is a Hebrew word meaning 'the anointed one', and is a reference to the ancient rite of accession in which monarchs were anointed with oil. The modern meaning of the term refers to the period in Jewish history roughly coterminous with the Han dynasty (second century BCE to second century CE) during which there arose the phenomenon of 'messianic expectation' – the notion that the god of the Jews would send a leader to rid the nation of its foreign occupiers and restore once again the kingdom of Israel. Scholars of comparative religions now use this term to designate any comparable phenomenon. Although we have no direct evidence that millenarianism and messianism were imported from the West, it has been suggested that the fact that these phenomena occurred in roughly similar time periods is more than a coincidence. Livia Kohn writes:

> Given this historic coincidence in timing, it is quite conceivable that merchants travelling along the silk road, which had been opened in the second century BCE, carried ideas in addition to goods into China, that people of various cultural backgrounds migrated and settled there, and that Chinese soldiers in outlying border posts came into contact with Western ideas. (Kohn, 1998, p. 43)

The best evidence we have for this phenomenon of Daoist messianism is contained in a Daoist sectarian text that takes the form of a report of Zhang Daoling's final sermon to his lieutenant, Zhao Sheng. The *Oral Instructions Declared by the Celestial Master of Orthodox Unity to Zhao Sheng* [*Zhengyi tianshi gao Zhao Sheng koujue*] is dated around 400 CE, and bears witness to a complex apocalyptic chronology that appears to have been rewritten several times. This may well be evidence of having to readjust the chronology of the messianic expectations in accordance with changing political circumstances or as events that the text predicted did not seem to happen on schedule (see Nickerson, 2000, p. 264).

The basic cosmological principle that the text espouses is that the nature of heaven is to intervene in human history when the political situation descends into chaos. The last intervention had taken place when Laozi revealed the Way of Orthodox Unity to Zhang Daoling, and the Way of the Celestial Masters was thus established. Since then the state of the world has gone into decline again, and the text goes on to predict that another intervention will take place shortly in the form of a messianic figure known as Lord Li (Nickerson, 2000, pp. 264–5). What is important about this intervention to come is that it will be an event of cosmic redemption, and not just a shift in political authority. In common with many messianic phenomena, the text divides the people of the world into two camps: the 240,000 members of the elect or 'seed people' (*zhongmin*), and everyone else. The number 240,000 has a clear symbolic meaning, because the administration of the original Celestial Masters' movement was divided into twenty-four parishes, likely corresponding to the division of the calendar year into twenty-four solar houses. According to this new text, when the *jiazi* year arrives (probably 424 CE) terrible destruction will be wreaked on earth, and the corrupt will be consigned to one of three 'evil paths'. The elect will survive by virtue of possession of a talisman that guarantees their protection by an army of spirit warriors, and these seed people will then form the new millennial kingdom of Great Peace on earth (Nickerson, 2000, p. 265). The fusion of religious and political elements in this text is further apparent in the fact that the text lists various types of corrupt Daoist priests as being among those who will not form part of the elect and will suffer retribution when the new kingdom is inaugurated.

The northern Celestial Masters

As we have seen so far, Daoism originated in the revolutionary millennial atmosphere of the end of the Han dynasty. One Daoist movement, the Way of Great Peace, failed; another, the Way of Orthodox Unity, was temporarily successful in establishing a theocracy in the west of China. Millenarian and messianic Daoist movements thrived in the political flux that followed the collapse of the Han dynasty. At the same time as the southern Celestial Masters' movement just discussed, another Daoist called Kou Qianzhi (365–448) was instrumental in establishing another theocracy in the north. Kou based his bid for power on a revelation he received from the Supreme Lord Lao (*Taishang Laojun*; the deified Laozi) that denied the legitimacy of the original Celestial Masters and supported his own claim to the title of Celestial Master. He instituted a 'new code' of Daoism that rejected the taxation system and sexual initiation rites that were features of the original movement and formed the basis for a renewed Celestial Masters' movement known as the 'Daoist theocracy'.

The most important feature of this new movement was that it was politically successful, and Kou's new code became the ruling ideology of the northern Wei dynasty. This dynasty was not an ethnic Han Chinese dynasty but a foreign occupation by the Toba, a nomadic Central Asian people related to the Huns who invaded eastern Europe and contributed around the same time to the downfall of the Roman empire. Thus the first time that Daoism became the official ideology of a recognized Chinese dynasty, it did so under the patronage of non-Chinese foreign occupiers. Since the system of the Celestial Masters was a theocracy, in 440 the Emperor himself was invested with Daoist registers and proclaimed the Perfected Lord of Great Peace (*Taiping zhenjun*) (Mather, 1979, p. 118). In this respect Kou Qianzhi achieved what the Taiping Daoists had failed to do and what the original Celestial Masters had achieved only fragmentarily: the full integration of the Daoist precepts and practices into the governing of the state. Daoist priests were the administrators of this earthly realm, conducted Daoist rituals in co-ordination with the calendar and basically provided political and religious stability for their foreign overlords.

The most notable external influence on the Chinese religious landscape at this time was the continuing expansion of a foreign religion: Buddhism. Buddhism introduced new religious practices, most notably the idea that people might leave their families and take up a communal religious life in a monastery. One might have thought that this separation of organized religious life out of the mainstream functioning of society must have seemed very strange to Daoists like Kou, who worked so hard to integrate the functioning of Daoist religion and the state. In fact Daoism wholeheartedly embraced the trend towards monasticism, and established rival monasteries of its own. This rivalry intensified after Kou's death in 448 and both religions competed for the favour of the state. When the Daoist leadership lost the imperial favour in 450, the theocracy was dismantled, its leaders were unceremoniously turfed out of the capital Chang'an (present-day Xi'an) and decamped west to establish what became an important Daoist centre in the nearby town of Louguan.

Daoists congregated at Louguan because of its association with the myth of Laozi's journey west. According to the myth, Laozi had given the *Daode jing* to Yin Xi the keeper of the Hangu pass. One of Yin Xi's alleged descendants, Yin Tong (398–c. 499), established a Daoist centre at Louguan on the basis that it was at Louguan, in the foothills of the mountains, that the actual transmission of the *Daode jing* had taken place. Once the exiled Daoist leadership established itself in Louguan, the town became a major centre of Daoist religious and political thinking. All the while the myth of Laozi's journey west gained in importance, and enhanced scriptures were composed, including the *Scripture of the Opening of Heaven* (*Kaitian jing*), which gave Laozi an even deeper cosmic-historical role in all the major events of Chinese dynastic history (see Kohn, 1993, pp. 35–43).

As the Daoists regrouped intellectually and politically, they grew in strength. In 520 they engaged the Buddhists in the first of a series of formal debates at the court. At stake was the official patronage of the dynasty, on which depended the economic well-being of the monasteries. The first debate of 520 took the form of an argument over the relative status of Laozi and the Buddha. In a brilliant theological manoeuvre, the myth of Laozi's journey was extended further west and the Daoists now claimed that the Buddha was none other than Laozi himself in Indian guise (see Kohn, 1995). The value of this claim was that it not only asserted the superiority of Laozi over the Buddha, but also of Daoist religious leadership over Buddhist religious leadership, since Buddhism was interpreted as nothing more than an improperly transmitted form of Daoism. At the same time it represented a significant step in the universalization of the idea of the Dao, thus lending at least some legitimacy to foreign religions. If the Dao truly was a universal cosmic force then it followed that the teachings of foreign religions are not absolutely wrong, merely relatively imperfect. The consequence of this was that the future relationship between Daoists and Chinese Buddhists, though shot through with bitter rivalry and theological acrimony, took place by means of each attempting to incorporate and assimilate many of the other's ideas and practices and to claim them as part of the original Dao or Dharma. In this way both Laozi and the Buddha emerged in Chinese religion as cosmic beings who take a multiplicity of forms for the expedient salvation of living beings – and who will reappear soon either as the manifestation of Laozi or as the Buddha Maitreya to bring order and peace to the state.

Perhaps by virtue of the fact that Daoism was a Chinese religion and Buddhism a foreign religion, the former tended to have the upper hand over the latter until the advent of the ethnically Manchu Qing dynasty in 1644, who tended to favour Buddhism. However, from the founding of the Tang dynasty (618) onwards, many emperors sought Daoist legitimation of their reign, and, consequently, a close relationship between Daoists and the court came to develop, particularly during the Tang and the Ming dynasties. Under this alliance, Daoist priests confirmed that the mandate of heaven had been properly transmitted to the new emperor, and invested him with Daoist registers, effectively ordaining him as a priest into a covenant relationship with the heavenly powers. In this way the official cult of the state and the life of Daoist religion were blended together, in stark contrast to the time when Daoist movements first began organizing against the Han dynasty government.

Official state sanction, particularly as existed in Tang and Ming times, meant that Daoism was part of the official fabric of society; the trade-off was that Daoism was also effectively regulated by the court. Given Daoism's turbulent political history the authorities made sure they were quick to put down religious movements that showed tendencies of challenging imperial power, a trend that continues to this day. We may concur with Pierre-Henry de Bruyn (2000, p. 616) that the Daoist religion was 'both worshipped and feared by the rulers, a testimony to its great popular influence and religious power'.

DAOISM IN CONTEMPORARY CHINA

The situation of Daoism in contemporary China is problematical given that the ideology of the Chinese Communist Party is officially atheist. After the establishment of the People's Republic of China it was relatively easy to identify and expel the foreign Christian missionaries and to close down churches, but it was not until the Cultural Revolution that the state apparatus sanctioned the destruction of China's own religious heritage. Since 1980, however, the overt functioning of religion in China has been somewhat tolerated provided that it conforms with the official government theology that attempts to distinguish between 'true religion' and 'popular superstition'. In 1979 the *People's Daily*, the official newspaper of the Chinese Communist Party, contained an article on the freedom of religion in China that has been much discussed. The article says that 'by religion, we chiefly mean worldwide religions, such as Christianity, Islam, Buddhism and the like. They have scriptures, creeds, religious ceremonies, organizations, and so on ... Religious freedom, first of all, refers to those religions' (trans. in MacInnis, 1989, p. 33). The article then distinguishes legal religions from popular practices, which it defined as superstition (*mixin*): 'activities conducted by shamans and sorcerers, such as magic medicine, magic water divinations, fortune telling ... praying for rain, praying for pregnancy, exorcising demons'. Ironically this distinction between 'higher religion' and 'popular religion' is precisely the sort of elite definition of religion that operated in the minds of Christian missionaries who also sought to save the Chinese people from their own 'backward superstitions'. Nonetheless, official, organized Daoism is beginning to thrive in a limited way in China, under the auspices of the government's Religious Affairs Bureau, which regulates the activities of five officially recognized religions: Daoism, Buddhism, Protestantism, Chinese Catholicism and Islam. Temples have been reopened and new priests and monks have been ordained, but nothing happens without the official sanction of the government. Popular cultivation movements such as Falun dafa that attempt to operate outside state authority are ruthlessly persecuted as 'deviant sects'. State control over religion, as we have seen, is nothing new in China, nor is it a concept that is in any way alien to Daoism. But the result of this historic and continued linkage between Daoism and political authority has been that Daoism has thrived whenever it has been in favour and has suffered whenever it has been out of favour.

In an attempt to gain an indication into the current status of Daoism, the author recently visited Chengdu, the capital of Sichuan province. Chengdu's most famous Daoist temple Qingyang gong is open and thriving and home to some twenty or thirty monks. Its precincts are filled every day with people burning incense and bowing before the gods, acts that presumably had been considered popular superstition of the worst kind until recently. Nonetheless it must be remembered that this is the only Daoist temple in a city of some eleven million people, and very few people maintain shrines in public places such as shops or street corners, as are common in Chinese communities around the world. Religion is functioning but only in the spaces where it can be officially authorized.

In interpreting the significance of the historical circumstances outlined above, two extremes should be avoided. The first extreme is to view religion solely as a tool used by the elite for the legitimation of power. The reason why religion looks like this in past historical periods is in part to do with the fact that we only have historical documents dealing with the way in which religion functioned in elite society and consequently our knowledge of the religious life of ordinary people is limited. This is certainly true of Daoism: the texts on which we base our knowledge of Daoism in this classical period were written by the elite for the elite, and so we ought not construe the relations between Daoist leaders and the imperial courts as the only form of Daoism of that time. The second extreme is to view 'true religion' as personal spirituality and to dismiss or condemn the ways in which religion exerts political power or is constrained by political power. This view is largely a cultural by-product of modern individualism and the myth of the separation of church and state in Western countries such as the United States. Rather, since human beings are social beings, and religion is a social phenomenon, religious organizations necessarily have some role to play within the networks of power and authority that constitute the social fabric regardless of whether society cares to admit it publicly.

NEGOTIATING WITH DESTINY

Since the time of the *Daode jing* forward, it is clear that one of the chief inspirations for the historical popular success of the Daoist religion has been the desire of people to create a better society for themselves. In Daoism this took the form of establishing a harmony between the state as the body of the society with the heavens. Based on this interpretation, an important question is how the close connection between elite Daoist theology and imperial power affected Daoist spirituality. At a popular level it is perhaps difficult for us to know exactly what was going on, but it must not be forgotten that during this classical period Daoist cultivation was developing methods of meditation and alchemy that are discussed in the next two chapters. In fact one way of interpreting the evolution of Daoism as a whole is to view it as the continuing quest for harmony between the three most important dimensions of being: the cosmos, the state and the body. According to this view, the body of the individual practitioner, the body of the community as a whole, and the body of the Dao are hologrammatically related to each other. Each contains the others within itself; each is a reflection of the other and functions in sympathetic resonance with the others.

A powerful way of interpreting the relationship between Daoist interest in political authority and Daoist personal religion was developed by Julia Ching in her book *Mysticism and Kingship in China: The Heart of Chinese Wisdom* (1997). This book presents an interpretation of the whole of Chinese religion, not just Daoism, in the light of the paradigm of the sage–king. Ching's thesis is that the model of the perfect ruler who fuses together spiritual wisdom with political power was extended to, and appropriated by, Chinese religious traditions as a model for the ordinary person's religious life. In Daoism the way this works is fairly simple to explain. The original theory of the Mandate of Heaven was that the person who had the right *de* would receive the mandate. During the Axial Age period, when the notion of *de* came to acquire the notion of virtue, there was an accompanying transformation in the notion of a mandate. The Chinese term for 'mandate' is *ming* which now has the general meaning of 'command', 'fate', 'life' and 'destiny'. In the earlier aristocratic culture, it was primarily the emperor whose *ming* was important. By virtue of being conferred with the 'mandate' he was able to rule over the people. In fact the emperor was in the unique position of being at the apex of the social hierarchy and being the person who alone stood before Heaven as the representative of the people. In a sense, religion was the privilege of the emperor and the aristocratic families who venerated their ancestors and who received authority from them to rule over the common people.

The revolution in the Axial Age meant that ordinary people came to understand themselves in terms of a relationship with Heaven. Since people from a non-aristocratic background had no famous ancestors whom they could venerate, Heaven (or Sky) came to be understood as an impersonal Principle that governed the affairs of humankind. Of course the most important activity of Heaven was still to confer the mandate (*ming*) upon the ruler, and to take it away from him when it was necessary to do so. But ordinary people too began to see their lives as being circumscribed by the dictates of a Heaven over which they had little control. In an agricultural society Heaven was seen as controlling the rotation of the seasons, the times of rain and sun, and the orbits of the stars in the sky. The importance of this naturalistic aspect of Heaven has led some interpreters to argue that it should be translated simply as the 'sky', which is its basic meaning in Chinese. But the most important way in which Sky/Heaven rules over human lives is in determining the times of our birth and death. In this way ming came to be understood as the fate or lot that applied to everyone from the Emperor down to the common masses.

It is possible to understand this fate in an existential way as the 'givenness' of human existence, thus acknowledging the fact that much in our lives lies beyond our control. A stoical way of looking at this is that the human task is to make the best out of what one is given and to resign oneself to those things over which one can have no control. Daoism, however, developed a wholly different way of viewing one's ultimate destiny or fate as something that could in principle be influenced or negotiated with. The way in which this is possible is that in the Chinese worldview one's fate or destiny (*ming*) is bound up with one's nature (*xing*). Of course it is easy to imagine that part of the givenness of our life is that we have been given a particular nature with which we must make do. But, as we saw in chapter 2, the intriguing possibility that presented itself to ancient Chinese thinkers was that our nature was something that could be cultivated and that the cultivation of our nature would, conversely, have some influence over our destiny. Mediating between our nature and our destiny is the Way that encompasses both and is the path of communication between the two.

One of the problems in studying Daoism is that there exists throughout Daoist history a multitude of conceptions of where one's destiny lies and a corresponding multitude of methods for negotiating with this destiny. For the Way of Great Peace, negotiating with destiny took the form of a revolutionary social movement that aimed to precipitate the transfer of the mandate of Heaven and the overthrow of the ruling Han dynasty. The more common Daoist form of negotiating with destiny is evident in the preoccupation with death and immortality. Thus many Daoist movements take seriously the goal of extending one's life as much as possible even to the extent of vaulting over the horizon of life and death itself and transforming oneself into an immortal or perfected person.

Thus from the perspective of personal negotiations with destiny, the covenantal relationship executed between Zhang Daoling and Laozi did not only provide for the establishment of a theocracy in Western China, but the healing of the sick through confession and the submission of petitions for pardon to the appropriate celestial authorities. In this way the bodies of ordinary people are a vital constituent of the body of the community, and the destiny of the Celestial Master is bound up with the destiny of the people under his authority. Thus all Daoist leaders urged that the ordinary people engage in the proper cultivation of their own bodies, not out of a sense of altruism, but because of the inherently reciprocal or recursive nature of the cosmos.

In the next two chapters we look at the primary means that developed in Daoist movements by means of which individuals are able to negotiate their destinies. In the Way of Highest Clarity (Shangqing dao), Daoist adepts visualized themselves in journeys to the stars, and practised a form of insight meditation in which the constellated powers of the night sky were visualized in the organs of the body, transforming them and revitalizing the energies within the body. In the monastic Way of Complete Perfection (Quanzhen dao) fate is negotiated with by means of an 'internal alchemy' in which the energies of the body are circulated and refined to produce an elixir of immortality. All these widely-differing Daoist practices have in common the transformation of one's fate, life or destiny. The theory is that by shifting the destiny (*ming*) towards which the course of the adept's path (*dao*) aims, his or her life, its virtues and powers (*de*) will be subtly and slowly transformed in the here and now.

SUGGESTIONS FOR FURTHER READING

Ching, Julia. 1997. *Mysticism and Kingship: The Heart of Chinese Wisdom.* Cambridge, Cambridge University Press

5
Light

光

This chapter focuses mostly on the Daoist movement known as the Way of Highest Clarity (Shangqing dao). This movement no longer exists as an independent lineage today, as all forms of Daoism were officially consolidated into two branches, the way of Complete Perfection and the Way of Orthodox Unity in the Ming period. Its influence, however, is deep and can be seen in Daoist cultivation to this day. Its hallmark is a devotion to the qualities of light – transparency, radiance and colour – that suffuse its worldview and practices.

THE DEVELOPMENT OF SHANGQING DAOISM

Shangqing Daoism developed in the medieval period following the collapse of the original Celestial Masters' movement. During this time, China experienced a period of political disunity that lasted approximately four centuries until the reunification under the Sui dynasty and then the establishment of the next truly great dynasty, the Tang, in 618. During these four centuries of disunity two important Daoist movements emerged: Highest Clarity (Shangqing) and Numinous Treasure (Lingbao). Of these two movements, the latter was strongly influenced by the arrival of Buddhism in China but the Shangqing movement developed relatively free from Buddhist influence in the south-east of China. It did, however, incorporate the religious phenomenon of shamanism that was discussed in chapter 2. Not only is shamanism evident in religious practices that involve the adept journeying to the stars to encounter various deities, but also mediumism is evident in the origin of the movement.

The Way of Highest Clarity can be traced back to a series of revelations from a transcendent being known as Lady Wei to a medium or visionary known as Yang Xi. These revelations began in 364 and lasted approximately three years. The revelations took the form of sacred texts and talismans that were then passed on from generation to generation. Like the registers of the Celestial Masters, the texts and the talismans are in effect contracts between humans and spiritual powers. The main difference from the Celestial Masters' tradition is that Highest Clarity texts also revealed esoteric techniques for the individual to encounter the deities of the stars, the planets, the sun and the moon. The greatest Western interpreter of Shangqing religion was Isabelle Robinet, who taught at the University of Aix-en-Provence. According to her, the impact of Shangqing Daoism was that it transformed the formal bureaucratic religion of the Celestial Masters into a personal quest for transcendence (Robinet, 2000, p. 200). The religious transactions between the celestial powers and the community that take place through the ritual submission of petitions by priests were transformed into an internal, mystical encounter between the individual and the gods.

Our present knowledge of the origins of Shangqing Daoism depend upon the Shangqing Patriarch Tao Hongjing (456–536) who collected and edited many of the original texts. Writing in the year 499, he states: 'The scriptures of Highest Clarity appeared in 364 in the East Jin dynasty. Lady Wei of Southern Marchmount, known as the Purple-Vacuity Primal Lord, descended from Heaven and bestowed these texts upon Yang Xi [330–386], a secretary in the household of Situ Wang. Yang Xi wrote down these scriptures in the Li script. He later gave them to Officer Xu Mi [303–373] and Xu's son, Hui [341–c. 370]' (Yu, 2000, p. 306).

Thus began one of the most important movements in Daoist history. From his visionary meetings with Lady Wei, Yang Xi recorded dozens of sacred texts that were passed down through the Xu household. The Xu family bestowed texts upon their friends and within two or three generations the original texts were dispersed throughout a wide area. Those who were the guardians of the most important texts styled themselves as 'Patriarchs', and although the revelations themselves can be dated back to 364, the Way of Shangqing only came into being in a formal Daoist lineage thanks to the efforts of those who propagated the texts, especially Lu Xiujing and Tao Hongjing. Lu, the great Lingbao reformer and classifier of Daoist texts, passed on the original revelations to his student Sun Youyue, who passed them on to Tao, the ninth patriarch.

Tao attempted to collect the original texts back together and developed a technique of handwriting analysis to distinguish between original texts and forgeries, an account of which is contained in his *Declarations of the Perfected (Zhen'gao)*. Tao also established Mount Mao (Maoshan, the original place of revelation, south east of Nanjing) as the centre of the Shangqing tradition (Strickmann, 1979). As a result Mount Mao attracted the interest of many influential literati who were fascinated by the prospect of self-cultivation and the quest for mystical self-realization. For this reason Shangqing Daoism is sometimes referred to as Maoshan Daoism, but the two terms are not quite synonymous. Maoshan Daoism can be used to refer to the entire tradition of Daoism that grew up around Mount Mao, including the Daoism that flourished after the Shangqing lineage was absorbed into the Zhengyi (Orthodox Daoism) lineage under the Ming. The term Shangqing, by contrast, can refer to the original revelation that took place in the 360s and also the tradition of those who claimed to be ordained into the lineage of that original transmission.

The Shangqing lineage reached its high point during the Tang under the twelfth patriarch, Sima Chengzhen (647–735). Sima became one of the most renowned and influential Daoists of all time. In 721 he ordained the Xuanzong Emperor (713–56) into a lay Daoist lineage and initiated him into some Daoist texts (Kohn and Kirkland, 2000, p. 347). The Highest Clarity deities were granted authority over the civic deities, and thus the Highest Clarity lineage effectively supplanted the lineage of the Celestial Masters as the 'Daoism of record' at the court. The emperor established Sima in a monastery near the capital, where he devoted himself to a life of scholarship. As the principles and techniques of Highest Clarity Daoism came to be absorbed into the Daoist mainstream, so also the Way of Highest Clarity came to be eclipsed by other forms of Daoist tradition. The thirty-fifth Celestial Master was given authority over the ordination of Highest Clarity priests under the reign of the Lizong Emperor of the Southern Song dynasty (r. 1225–64), effectively ending the power of the lineage to maintain control over the transmission of its own teachings and practices (Davis, 2002, p. 38). One of the last important Shangqing patriarchs was Liu Dabin (fl. 1317–28) who wrote a history of Maoshan Daoism.

LIGHT PRACTICES

The term 'Shangqing' itself refers to the heaven of Highest Clarity populated by celestial immortals of the highest rank. It was thought that through the methods revealed by these transcendent beings and recorded in the Shangqing scriptures, the adept could transform his or her earthly body into a celestial body of pure light and ascend to the highest heaven. The texts detail three types of practice that enable this transfiguration to take place: astral journeys to the stellar deities of the big dipper to present petitions to the deities who govern the destiny (*ming*) of human lives; absorbing the spiritual essence of the sun and the moon to refine the body into an ever more diaphanous and spiritual body; and the internal visualization of gods of the big dipper in correlation with the various organs or energy systems of the body. The goal of all these practices is to become a perfected person (*zhenren*). This term was first encountered in the *Zhuangzi*, and referred to the Daoist sage who has transcended the boundaries between self and world. In the Shangqing tradition, the term '*zhenren*' came to be used as a formal title that could be granted to an immortal by the highest deities of heaven in the same way that members of the nobility are invested with titles by monarchs. This preoccupation with ranks and titles is thought to reflect the aristocratic milieu of the recipients of the Shangqing revelations.

As an encouragement to undertake the arduous quest for transformation, hagiographies were circulated of those who were revered by the transmitters of the Shangqing corpus. The hagiography of a famous immortal known by his formal title as the Perfected Purple Yang was cherished by the Xu family who were the original recipients of the Shangqing transmission. The Perfected Purple Yang, was born Zhou Yishan in 80 BCE, during the Han period. According to the hagiography, he practised a technique known as the salutation of the sun and would get up early to soak up the dawn light, that is to say, energy radiated at the time of perfect balance between night and day, yin and yang. Zhou's father caught him in the act one day and asked him what he was doing. Zhou is said to have replied, 'I, Yishan, from the bottom of my heart love the sunlight and the splendour of its eternal radiance' (Porkert, 1979, p. 26). The hagiography goes on to relate that after five years' practice Zhou's body became so luminous and transparent that one could see his internal organs. It seems from this text and from others that the Shangqing Dao is devoted to themes of light, luminosity and transparency. This is the reason why I translate the term 'Shangqing' as Highest Clarity rather than Supreme or Upper Purity as it is sometimes known.

Absorption of cosmic light

The 'spiritual technology' that centres on the practice of absorbing the light was not invented by the Shangqing. Traces of this practice can be seen in the early shamanic journeys documented poetically in the *Chu ci*:

> My face, like jade, is flushed with radiant color;
> My pure essence is starting to grow strong,
> My solid body dissolving into softness,
> My spirit's ever subtler and more unrestrained.
> ...
> Holding to my sparkling soul, I climb to the empyrean;
> Clinging to the floating clouds, I ride up further high.
>
> (trans. Kohn, 1993, p. 254)

As the adept journeys to the sky, his or her body takes on the characteristics of light itself: it becomes sparkling, radiant and ethereal.

In the Shangqing tradition this practice was more clearly articulated as the absorption of qi (*fuqi*) and the absorption of light (*fuguang*). The theory behind this is based on the understanding of the body as a vehicle for the dynamic processing of energy. Ordinarily humans feed off solid energy, summed up in Chinese tradition as the 'five grains': rice, two types of millet, sorghum and wheat. A central goal of Daoist cultivation is to reduce one's dependence on these relatively gross forms of energy and instead to convert one's body to running on more refined forms of energy. It is thought that gross forms of energy are difficult for the body to process, and hasten its decay. This notion is thematized mythologically in the form of three parasitical death worms who are said to inhabit the body, feeding off the grains that we take in through our mouths, all the while growing stronger until they eventually cause the body to die. Korean Daoists used to stay up drinking through the night once a year to ward off these worms, until the ritual was banned under King Yŏngjo (r. 1742–76; Jung, 2000, p. 815). A more common Daoist practice is known as bigu, conventionally translated as 'fasting' or 'abstention from grains' during which time Daoists effectively go into a form of hibernation consuming almost imperceptible amounts of food, but feasting on energy that they absorb in other forms (see Eskildsen, 1998).

Chiefly this is done through advanced forms of breath meditation that take a lifetime to master. In the Shangqing tradition, however, it was thought that the energy of light was of an even subtler and more refined form of energy than breath or vital energy (qi). The celestial immortals are therefore said to feed off light itself, and consequently their bodies are ethereal and radiant, as opposed to the ponderous fleshly bodies that ordinary humans are burdened with. All these qualities are summed up in the description of the celestial being, Lady Wei Huacun, who revealed the original Shangqing corpus. In her hagiography, she is described as a radiant being from outer space:

> Empyreal phosphor, glistening high;
> Round eye-lenses doubly lit;
> Phoenix frame and dragon bone;
> Brain coloured as jewel-planetoids;
> Five viscera of purple webbings;
> Heart holding feathered scripts.
> (*Sandong zhu'nang* 8. 22b; trans. Schafer, 1977, p. 230)

Astral voyages

The Shangqing preoccupation with light also fits in with the religious importance of stars, chief among which were thought to be the stars of the constellation known in Chinese as the Northern Bushel (beidou), in English as the Big Dipper or Great Bear, or by the Latin name Ursa Major. The reason the Big Dipper was chosen is that it points towards the pole star which, in Chinese cosmology signalled the location of the supreme ridgepole (*taiji*) from which the fabric of the heavens were thought to be suspended and around which all the other heavenly bodies are seen to rotate. In neo-Confucian philosophy the taiji was understood as a metaphysical principle, usually translated into English as the Supreme Ultimate, but in Daoist religion the term has a more basic astrological significance.

Stars were not considered to be deities themselves, but rather symbols of deities or residences for them. Either way, they represented constellated spiritual powers, and as such were thought to exact powerful influences over human life. In keeping with the principle of correspondence between the heavenly bodies and the body of the state, the stars of the dipper were correlated with the emperor himself (Schafer, 1977, p. 49), and in keeping with the principle of yin–yang complementarity, the stars of the dipper corresponded to the administration of the underworld, known as Fengdu. Although the Shangqing tradition relied less on the memorializing of celestial officials than the Celestial Masters, it was still important to submit petitions on behalf of one's deceased ancestors. The innovation of Shangqing ritual was that the ordained adept presented the memorials to the relevant officials by means of an astral journey through the stars of the dipper to the Gate of Heaven. This gate, located at zenith point in the night sky, corresponded with the entrance to the underworld, whose officials governed over the fates of those who had died. From this it is evident that the Shangqing adepts were not so much concerned with their own physical immortality on earth, but rather the possibility of ascending into the heavens in a transfigured state after death.

To understand these important concepts correctly, we must refer to the Shangqing notion of the 'embryonic knots'. When a human embryo is formed in the womb, twelve 'knots' bind the viscera together. Since these knots constrict the energy pathways in the body they eventually cause our vital physiological processes to shut down completely:

> When man receives life inside the womb,
> he receives the breaths of the Nine Heavens,
> which coagulate their essence [jing] and spontaneously
>   form a man.
> When a man is born [i.e. conceived], there are in the womb
>   twelve knots and nodules
>   which keep the five innards [the five viscera] tightly twisted
>   together.
> The five innards are then hindered and obstructed.
> When the knots are not untied,
> when the nodules do not disappear,
> [this] is the cause of human maladies;
> it is because the nodules create obstacles;
> when human fate [ming] is cut off,
> it is because the knots are tightened.
>
> (*Jiudan shanghua taijing zhong jijing*, 3a; trans. Robinet, 1993, p. 140)

As Robinet notes, the eventuality of death is actually implicit in the conception of an embryo (1993, p. 141). Thus the fact that we are born means that we will die at some point, and there is no escaping this physiological fact. The point was to prepare for it correctly so that death did not result in one's languishing in the underworld, but rather was the first stage in a process of transformation that would eventually lead to the adept's becoming a transfigured celestial being in the heaven of Highest Clarity. Thus the transcendence sought by the Shangqing Daoists was not the negation of some future death; in fact it was the embracing of one's eventual death in such a way as to take advantage of the possibilities for transformation that death represents. One's ultimate destiny or fate (*ming*) can thus become the power (*de*) for transformation.

The Shangqing text entitled *Three Ways to Cross the Heavenly Pass* (*Tianguan santu*) contains an excellent example of the way in which the adept makes the journey to the stars of the dipper. One prayer within this text goes:

> Let my eyes be bright and of penetrating vision!
> Let them mirror everything without end!
> Let me communicate with the truth of the mystery!
> Let its essence flow into my body!
>
> Let me reach out to the august Dipper's handle!
> Let me fly all the way across its seven stars!
> Let me stride on light and ride on air!
> Let me end only in time with heaven itself!
>
> (*Tianguan santu*, 4a; trans. Kohn, 1993, p. 261)

The successful adept is then de-listed from the registers of the underworld, and invested with a high rank in the heavenly realms. As such the adept becomes a powerful official with supernatural powers:

> I am a minister of the Lord Emperor of Heaven.
> My name is registered in Jade Clarity.
> From there on down to the Six Heavens,
> To all the demon palaces of the Northern Emperor,
> All realms are under my control.
> They are part of my jurisdiction –
> How would any demon dare to go on living there?
>
> Watch out!
> On the right of my belt, I carry the talisman Easy Fall.
> On the left, I have the talisman Fire Bell!
> I can throw fire as far as ten thousand miles!
> I can awe and control as many as ten thousand souls!
>
> Any criminal will at once be executed!
> Any offender will at once be punished!
> Whenever the Lord Emperor has an order,
> I will immediately hasten to carry it out!
>
> (*Tianguan santu*, 11b; trans. Kohn, 1993, p. 266)

In this instance the adept has successfully attained the rank of minister, and been registered in the heaven of Jade Clarity, the first of the three supreme heavens. Once this initiation is complete, the adept is then able to arrange for the liberation of his or her ancestors. This is important because the sense of self-identity in the Daoist world is different than in the modern West: human beings are not lonely individuals, but the midpoint in an ongoing process of conception, birth and death that stretches back and forth to the horizons of time. We are who we are not because of some innate quality that belongs to us individually but by virtue of our location in this genealogical matrix. Thus the liberation of the self can only be achieved as part of the liberation of one's ancestors and descendants.

Journeys to the stars, then, were an important way in which this liberation could take place in the Shangqing tradition. Such journeys were ways of communicating between the human and the celestial worlds, and they were the means by which humans had the possibility of negotiating with their fate or destiny.

Visualization of body gods

A key feature of the Shangqing revelation is the idea that gods inhabit the body. Thus the journey to the stars of the dipper was not something that had to take place in the form of an ecstatic journey in which the practitioners, like the shaman, as it were step outside their ordinary bodies. Rather, the Shangqing tradition proposed that all of this journeying could take place internally through a meditative process of visualization. In fact the notion that our bodies are residences for gods is the reason why this visualization is possible. One Shangqing text describes how human beings come into existence:

> The Supreme [Lord] said: Now, people are only concentrated essence and accumulated energy. When someone conceives an embryo, blood accumulates, joining yellow and white, ethereal and solidified, cinnabar and purple, melding and vaporizing. In this way one's bones solidify, saliva spews forth, and bodily fluids scatter, diffuse and circulate.
>
> The four limits converge and combine; the nine palaces joining together as one; the five spirits are incarnated in bodily form [i.e. in the five viscera]. The Supreme Unity fixes the tally and register. Suddenly it is established. Indistinct, yet it has form. Vague, yet whole. Cast away, yet being born. Thereupon the nine spirits come to stay in their palaces. The five viscera mysteriously grow and the five spirits take residence there.

> Fathers and mothers only know the beginning of giving oneself life and nurture, and are unaware that the Imperial Lord and the five spirits come between them. (*Jiuzhen zhongjing*, 2a–b, author's trans.)

As this text makes clear, conception is not simply a physiological matter that takes place between one's father and mother, but in fact it is also a spiritual activity that incorporates, literally, the activity of the gods. In this text the five spirits that correspond to the five directions of the cosmos are correlated with the five viscera or organs of the body according to the system of five-phase correspondence that we saw in chapter 3.

Thus in the Shangqing tradition, the journey to the stars could be made by sitting in one's quiet chamber and visualizing the deities associated with the stars of the dipper descending into the various organs or energy-systems of the body. In this way one achieves internally the same effect as described above in the journey to the heavenly pass. In these texts, visualizing the correspondences between the gods and the body has the effect of actualizing them, that is, making the connections stronger and deeper. In this way the Shangqing adept knits him- or herself ever more deeply into the fabric of the cosmos.

An example of a Shangqing visualization text is the *Central Scripture of the Nine Perfected*. This text contains a technique known as the Method of the Nine Perfected which consists of a systematic programme for correlating the organs of the body with the stellar deities. The idea is that the energy of the bodies that is processed by the various organs will be as it were irradiated by the potent light energy of the stars. The method consists of visualizing the five spirits that correspond to the five major organs of the body merge with the deity known as the Imperial Lord of Great Unity on each of nine separate occasions over the period of a year. These nine spirits produce an energy of a particular colour in nine layers around a particular organ or energy system of the body. The organ is thus regenerated or transformed by the visualization process.

The First Method of the Nine Perfected

> In the first month, on your birthday, the *jiazi* day, or the *jiaxu* day, at dawn, the five spirits and the Imperial Lord of Great Unity merge together into one great spirit which rests in your heart. The spirit is called the Lord of Celestial Essence, his style is Highest Hero of Soaring Birth, his appearance is like an infant immediately after birth. On

that day at dawn, enter your oratory, place your hands on
your knees, control your breathing, close your eyes. Look
inside and visualize the Lord of Celestial Essence sitting in
your heart. His name is called Great Spirit. Make him spew
forth purple energy to coil thickly around your heart in
nine layers. Let the energy rush up into the *niwan*. Inner
and outer [dimensions] are as one. When this is done,
clench your teeth nine times, swallow saliva nine times,
then recite this prayer:

Great Lord of Celestial Essence,
Highest Hero of Soaring Birth,
Imperial Lord, transform inside me,
Come into vision in my heart.

Your body is wrapped in vermilion garb,
Your head is covered with a crimson cap.
On your left you wear the dragon script;
On your right you carry the tiger writing.

Harmonize my essence with the threefold path,
Unite my spirit with the Upper Prime.
To the Five Numinous Powers I present a talisman,
With the Imperial Lord may I be wholly identical.

Your mouth spits out purple florescence,
To nourish my heart and concentrate my spirit.
As my crimson organ spontaneously becomes alive
May I become a soaring immortal.

(*Jiuzhen zhongjing*, 1.3a–4a, author's trans.)

As this meditation makes clear, the deity in question is described in
precise detail so that the adept knows that he is visualizing the correct
deity. The ceremonial garb including the cap and the talismans indicates
that the deity is of a high rank, as is only fitting for a deity who is
associated with the heart – the most regal of all the bodily organs. The
visualization has to take place at a certain date, which is also indicative
of the network of cosmic correspondences that have an effect upon the
spiritual life of the Daoist. Not only does the Shangqing Daoist occupy a
moment in the continuing evolution of his family, he or she is also
implicated in the fabric of the cosmic environment. It is for this reason
that envisioning the gods in the body is not so much a supernatural
process as one that makes clear the connections that are already there.
The body of the Daoist adept is already the body of the universe, and, as
the text on the conception of the individual indicated, it is not an

unnatural thing for gods to dwell in one's organs, rather it is what they do for a living. It is always good to remember that within the overall Chinese cosmological system human beings occupy a privileged position as the mediators between heaven and earth.

CONTEMPORARY VISUALIZATION PRACTICES

The Shangqing revelations represent a decisive moment in the transformation of Chinese Daoism that set the tone for the later flourishing of methods of internal alchemy and meditation. Whereas the previous chapter examined the ways in which patterns of correspondence were established between the heavens and the whole body of people as a community, the Shangqing scriptures downplay the importance of the state and the community and view the individuals (incorporating their ancestors) who possess the talismans and the scriptures as the most important religious actors. The Way of Highest Clarity thus demonstrates a process of interiorization by means of which the overt ritual activities of the Celestial Masters could take place internally, within the body of the practitioner. This process of interiorization culminated in the methods of internal alchemy that are discussed in the next chapter.

The relationship of the person to the stars of the dipper is one of the central features of Daoist cosmology that continues to this day in both ritual and meditation. The ritual of 'pacing the dipper' or 'pacing the net' (bugang) stretches back to before the Shangqing period, and is evident in an ancient ritual in which priests perform liturgical movements based on the pattern of the dipper. As they ritually enact this celestial choreography they simultaneously invoke the corresponding astral deities. The more internal, meditative visualization process also continues in the teaching of contemporary Daoist energy-practitioners. One such practitioner, a Thai Daoist called Mantak Chia, has become well known in the Western world through his Healing Tao organization. One set of practices that his organization has developed is called 'Dark Room Enlightenment'. The title itself reflects the essence of the Shangqing cosmology in which the stars in the night sky function as the clearest possible indication of the complementarity of dark and light, yin and yang. In this modern practice the visualization of the stars of the dipper plays a central role, but instead of being co-ordinated with the organs of the body, it is co-ordinated with areas of the brain.

1. The first exercise, the Big Dipper, should be practiced only during night time and sleep. Practice the Big Dipper only in the brain. Each star three times with each breath.

a. The first star is located in the Jade Palace, the power of cerebellum. Visualize it as the purple light, inhale, gather the purple light into the cerebellum. Hold the breath, condense the light inside the cerebrum, and exhale, relax and observe the energy circulation in the cerebrum.

b. Then concentrate on the memory centre in the brain by inviting the second star. Visualizing it with dark-blue light during inhalation. Hold the breath, let the light circulate around the memory centre. Exhale, observe the Chi circulation.

c. Then concentrate on the pineal gland by inviting the third star with the light-blue light.

d. Fourthly, concentrate on the thalamus glands by inviting the fourth star and green light. This star is the division between the left-brain and right-brain, or animal brain and human cortex.

e. Then concentrate on the hypothalamus and pituitary glands by inviting the fifth star and yellow light. This star connects to human smell and balance.

f. The sixth star connects to the olfactory gland and orange light and temples above the [?] and in front of ears. Hearing-palace and Ear Gate pressure points are located here connecting the Small Intestine and Triple Warmer.

g. The seventh star gives ultimately the birth of red fire, the solar light, and passion of sixth sense to mystic awareness. It is located on the yang third eye, or Spirit-hall pressure point.

h. After meditating on each star three times, then visualize all the rainbow colours/lights showing into the brain. Above the rainbow colours is the mystic black light, and below is the white.

i. This star exercise connects to the Spleen and planet Saturn, in a sense that the brain becomes the cosmic soil. (Healing Tao, 2002, pp. 37–8)

From this extract from the guidelines for Dark Room Enlightenment, published on the Healing Tao website, it is easy to discern the continuing influence of the Shangqing tradition. What has changed is that the traditional Chinese view of the qi flowing throughout the whole body has been replaced with a focus on the brain, and thus the various organs of the body have been replaced by specific areas of the brain. In this way an ancient Daoist tradition is Westernized in that it reflects the contemporary Western emphasis on the brain as the most important organ of the body. This reflects an attempt on the part of many contemporary practitioners to explain their practice and experience in the terms of modern medical science as well as the traditional Chinese view of the body. It also reflects a trend in the study of religions to forge connections between the language of mystical experience and the language of neurobiology. It is not surprising to see that Daoism is expanding most throughout the West where it presents itself as a 'spiritual technology', that is, a collection of scientifically explainable psycho-energetic practices rather than as a religious tradition.

SUGGESTIONS FOR FURTHER READING

Robinet, Isabelle. 1993. *The Mao-shan Tradition of Great Purity.* Berkeley, University of California Press

Schafer, Edward. 1977. *Pacing the Void: Tang Approaches to the Stars.* Berkeley, University of California Press

6

Alchemy

丹

In many religions, it would be accurate to say that time is of the essence. The Abrahamic religions (Judaism, Christianity and Islam) provide a mythic metanarrative of creation and redemption that gives a linear structure to the concept of time. The story of creation in the book of Genesis provides a mythic explanation of the creation of the world out of the void by divine fiat. The Christian book of Revelation, or Apocalypse, offers a view of the end of time as a cosmic battle between the forces of good and evil. Christians view themselves as located in a middle time between creation and final judgement. Similarly, the Jewish myths of slavery and exodus, land and exile provide the foundations of the theological narrative upon which Jewish identity is constructed. These myths serve to locate individual experience and self-understanding within some overarching temporal framework.

As we have seen in Shangqing Daoism, one of the most important foundations for a Daoist understanding of the world lies not so much in some mythic metanarrative, but in having a correct perception of the correlations between the organs of the body and the stars in the sky. The spatial aspect of Daoist cosmology cannot be underestimated. Many Daoist texts place great importance on achieving the correct alignment of various phases of cosmic energy, and many texts contain maps or diagrams of the individual in relation to the important features of the religious landscape, notably the stars and the mountains. It would be an accurate assessment to say that Shangqing Daoism is at heart concerned with locations, images, visualization, talismans and maps. Space seems to be of the essence, not time; cosmography its concern, not cosmogony.

The final purpose, however, of all this religious 'mapping' is to enable some form of transformation to take place. It is at this level that the Daoist adept is concerned with the passage of time and the myriad processes that take place within it.

ALCHEMY AND THE QUEST FOR IMMORTALITY

The relation of human beings to time is most clearly thematized in the quest for immortality and transcendence. As we have seen in the various Daoist traditions thus far, Daoism emphasizes both the cyclical and the linear aspects of time. The cyclical aspect is important in co-ordinating the body and the community with the passage of the seasons and the rotations of the heavenly bodies. The linear aspect is evident in the quest for a utopian civilization and in negotiating with one's personal destiny (death) so as to be ultimately and irrevocably liberated and transformed. There is no notion in classical Daoism that one will be reincarnated as some other life form.

An example of the way in which Daoism draws on this linear view of life can be seen in the quest for immortality that was evident long before the formation of organized Daoist religious movements in the late Han period. The First Emperor of the Qin dynasty (Qin shi huangdi) bankrupted the state with his obsession for what can only be described as a post-mortem immortality, and spent most of his life preparing for this afterlife by constructing an extraordinary mausoleum filled with 6000 unique, life-sized terracotta warriors.

The Wu Emperor of the Han dynasty (r. 141–87 BCE) is also said to have been fascinated by immortality, and invited a collection of 'doctors, diviners and magicians' (De Woskin, 1983) or 'magico-technicians' (*fangshi*) to court. By 60 BCE we have the first record of the ingestion of an alchemical elixir of immortality, and a developing interest in the properties of various minerals (Pregadio, 2000, p. 166). Gongsong Qing, one of the Wu Emperor's most senior advisers on the subject of immortality, persuaded the Emperor to hold sacrifices on Mount Tai 'and after that he will ascend to heaven and become an immortal' (Liu Feng, 1998, p. 47). Although the alchemical tradition was from the beginning linked into the religious culture of the time, the development of the alchemical tradition in China took place to a certain extent independently of Daoism. Rather, it is more accurate to say that Daoist traditions made use of and contributed to the development of alchemy and immortality in their own religious contexts. As Benjamin Penny points out, 'the language and lore of immortality have so thoroughly pervaded the common stock of Chinese ideas that they are no longer thought of as belonging specifically to Daoism, or even to religion in general' (Penny, 2000, p. 109).

So far as the Daoist traditions of alchemy are concerned, there are two basic styles of alchemy. The one that is historically the earliest can be translated literally as 'outer alchemy' (*waidan*) and refers to the concoction of an elixir of immortality that takes place using physical ingredients in a laboratory. The reason why this became a Daoist religious endeavour was that the alchemical process could be conducted as a Daoist ritual activity. The second form of alchemy is known as 'internal alchemy' (*neidan*) and uses the energies of the body as the ingredients for the alchemical reaction. This internal alchemy came to prominence as part of the Shangqing drive to interiorize Daoist practices.

LABORATORY ALCHEMY

The basic principles of laboratory alchemy only make sense in reference to an important Chinese cosmogonic scheme that has not yet been explained. This linear cosmogony explains that in the beginning there was simply a nothingness, an ultimate non-being (wuji) or pregnant chaos (hundun). Out of this nothingness emerged the Yang phase. This Yang was not the ordinary sort of yang that is complemented by yin, but a pure Yang with no trace of yin whatsoever. This pure Yang then began to move and the yin phase was born within it. From the interaction of yin and yang came the second phase of creation, comprising four subdivisions, yang–yin, yin–yin, yin–yang, and yang–yang. In the third phase of evolution these four then subdivided again into eight phases, and again into sixteen and so on. This cosmogonic scheme came to be represented in diagram form: the solid line represents yang, and the broken line represents yin.

The Eight Trigrams

Before Time	Nonbeing	○
Stage 0	Pure Yang	●
Stage 1	yang and yin	— - -
Stage 2	four combinations	☰ ☱ ☲ ☳
Stage 3	eight trigrams	☰ ☱ ☲ ☳ ☴ ☵ ☶ ☷

This ancient cosmogonic scheme was the basis of the *Book of Changes* (*Yijing* or *Zhouyi*), an ancient divination manual that was used in the Zhou dynasty and has been widely studied and translated in the West. The eight combinations reached at stage three are represented by eight trigrams (*bagua*), and the *Yijing* itself uses sixty-four six-line hexagrams.

The basic process of the cosmos, according to this worldview, is one of gradual evolution and complexification away from a primordial purity and simplicity. This original purity is found in the element of pure Yang. The goal of the alchemist is literally to reverse time and, by a process of reversion (*fan*), to restore an element to its purest form. It was thought that the element that consists of pure Yang exists in a state before the birth of the cosmos itself. If one could appropriate this property of pristine perfection by ingesting the pure element, then one's body would be restored to the same pristine state.

Two methods were devised for this process of reversion or 'decoction'. The first was to refine mercury from cinnabar (*dan*), a reddish mineral that is a compound of mercury and sulphur. Mercury was thought to be a pure yin element, and by adding this again to the sulphur (yang), an element of pure Yang would be created. The process of refining the cinnabar takes seven, or in some cases nine, stages of heating in a crucible. The pure Yang element that is produced by this process thus represents the primordial Oneness out of which the world has evolved (Pregadio, 2000, p. 180; Robinet, 1995, p. 194). The second method involves a similar refining process using mercury (yin) and lead (yang) to create the same pure Yang element.

An example of the way in which this alchemy was carried out as a religious endeavour is to be found in the Daoist movement known as Taiqing (Great Clarity) that was active around the third to fifth centuries. The alchemical recipes were said to be revealed from the heaven of Great Clarity (Taiqing) and the process of concocting the elixir took place under the protection of various Daoist immortals. Fabrizio Pregadio (2000, p. 188) has noted eight ritual features of the Taiqing tradition that clearly distinguish its alchemy as a religious activity. Firstly the would-be alchemist must ritually prepare for the process by undergoing a rite of purification (zhai). He then undergoes a type of ordination process in which he is formally presented with the recipes that have come from the heaven of Great Clarity. The alchemist wears talismans about his person to protect him from evil influences, and constructs a Daoist altar (*tan*) within his laboratory. The ingredients for the elixir must be procured on auspicious days, and before the alchemical process begins, invocations are made to Daoist divinities requesting their assistance in the endeavour. Talismans protect the elixir as it is being compounded, and finally, the elixir is ingested 'at dawn, facing the rising sun, after another invocation to the gods' (Pregadio, 2000, p. 188; Ware, 1966, pp. 80–1).

Perhaps the greatest exponent of the alchemical tradition was Ge Hong (283–343). Ge was an aristocrat who grew up near present-day Nanjing in the south of China. He lived during a period when the north had been invaded, and the empire had moved its capital south. He devoted his life to researching alchemy and the lives of those who had successfully undergone alchemical transformation. He firmly believed that immortality was a reality and spent much of his life amassing the ingredients and constructing laboratories. He died on Mount Luofu in today's Guangdong province, though tradition has it that he merely feigned death and in fact ascended to immortality himself. His two main works are his autobiography *The Master who Embraces Simplicity* (*Baopuzi*), and a collection of hagiographies of those who had achieved the rare status of immortals, the *Biographies of the Divine Transcendents* (*Shenxian zhuan*; Campany, 2002). It was Ge's belief that the alchemical quest and Daoist religion were firmly related, though as we have seen it is more accurate to say that these were two independent traditions that overlapped in places. An example of Ge's outlook can be found in his biography of Zhang Daoling, the first Celestial Master. Ge portrays Zhang as an alchemist from a poor family who does not have the necessary financial means to concoct an elixir of immortality. For this reason Zhang moves west and, following his revelation from Laozi, sets up his Way of Orthodox Unity. Because of Zhang's success in healing the sick, he attracts many people to his community and in this way he becomes financially successful and is finally able to amass the ingredients that he needs. Ge's intention seems to be to place the emergence of Daoism within this broader alchemical tradition, which indicates his own view of their relative importance.

The main problem with the process of laboratory alchemy is that ingesting mercury can be fatal. Early Chinese alchemists were well aware of this and yet pursued the dream of immortality against all odds. One explanation for this could be that they possessed a sincere religious conviction that the risk of mercury poisoning was outweighed by the reward of getting the formula right. Another explanation is that death is not seen as the final state, and that the purpose of alchemy was not to prevent the body from dying but rather to ensure that, after death, the corpse was adequately prepared to ascend to heaven.

INTERNAL ALCHEMY

As the self-cultivation movements of Shangqing Daoism focused on the internal disposition of the individual in relation to the cosmos, alchemy also began its own transmutation into an internal religious science. This 'inner alchemy' (*neidan*) draws heavily on the view of the body that was explained in chapter 3 and seeks to undertake the alchemical process of reversion within the body itself. A hint as to how this came into being is found as far back as the *Daode jing*. Chapter 55 of this text advocates a return to the potency of a child who is full of energy and yet has no sexual experience. The implication is that as we grow up energy slowly dissipates from our bodies. Children grow quickly because they are sexually immature and do not lose their vitality through sexual activity; after the onset of puberty, however, we do not so much grow up as grow old. One branch of Chinese sexology based itself on the notion that our primordial qi energy is particularly dissipated when it is converted into semen in men and menstrual fluid in women. This *jing* energy, when expelled from the body, is lost forever. Eventually so much of the adult's energy is dissipated that our bodies can no longer function and we die. Jing is physically present in men as semen, and in women as menstrual blood. For this reason women's bodies go through menopause as a way of conserving energy in their advanced years.

On an altogether more transcendent plane, Shangqing Daoists were practising their own form of internal alchemy that we saw in chapter 5. Through the process of visualizing gods in the body, the energy systems were irradiated with celestial light, and the body of the adept was transformed gradually into that of an ethereal light-being.

As the tradition of inner alchemy developed it combined the elements of sexology, laboratory chemistry and meditation into its own highly complex and symbolic vocabulary for transmuting the energies of the subtle body. The basis of this practice is that the jing energy of the body can be refined back into qi energy which can itself be used to create an immortal embryo composed entirely out of non-decaying spirit energy (shen). The embryo is then nurtured until it is strong enough to exit the body through the crown of the skull.

Despite the obvious differences with the laboratory alchemy discussed above, there are some important commonalities that deserve mentioning. Firstly, both inner and outer alchemy are based on a cosmogony based on the interaction of yin and yang and the corresponding evolution towards greater complexity. Both traditions similarly believe that it is possible to reverse or invert (*ni*) this process in order to attain a state of original, transcendent purity. This original state is, furthermore, the natural state of things. The apparent complexity of the process to arrive at this natural state only goes to show how far away we are from that primordial state, usually referred to as the 'before-heaven' state. Conversely our ordinary reality is known as the 'post-heaven' state. The language of outer alchemy is also preserved in inner alchemy. Lead and mercury (yang and yin) are now understood allegorically as the energy of the lungs and kidneys. The main points in the body where the alchemy takes place are known as 'cinnabar fields' (*dantian*) of which there are three: the *niwan* (mud-pill) in the head; the *zigong* (purple palace) in the chest; and the *dantian* in the abdomen, about an inch below the navel.

The first stage of inner alchemy involves refining *jing* into qi. Given that *jing* manifests in men and women differently, men and women have different practices to get access to this energy. In men this involves becoming sexually aroused to the point of ejaculation, but then, by applying pressure to the base of the penis, they guide the energy up the dumai meridian that runs up the spine to the niwan cinnabar field in the head, and then guiding it down again through the renmai meridian back to the lower cinnabar field in the abdomen. This 'microcosmic orbit' inverts the normal flow of jing through the body and through this reversal the jing is refined back into an 'outer medicine' or 'pearl of dew' in the lower cinnabar field (Skar and Pregadio, 2000, p. 489). When men successfully stop themselves from ejaculating this is known euphemistically as 'subduing the white tiger'. The equivalent for women is 'decapitating the red dragon' and involves a combination of breast massage and diet, combined with visualizing the blood rising through the body instead of flowing out. Women already contain the 'pearl of dew' inside their bodies; they do not have to go to all the trouble of creating one. Rather through the practice of massage and diet they refine and nurture what is already there.

If the practitioner is successful then he or she will have created the first stage of the immortal embryo that is to grow inside them. This is the equivalent of going out to amass the ingredients in laboratory alchemy.

The next stage involves transmuting the pearl of dew into the immortal embryo, and is equivalent to the refining process that takes place in the tripod. At this point the practitioner circulates energy through the lungs and kidneys (yang and yin) in order to change the pearl of dew into a 'golden flower' or 'inner medicine' made out of a refined or pure energy. The energy is circulated through the body this time in a 'macrocosmic' orbit that goes all the way down to the feet, and after ten months the immortal embryo is fully developed. The embryo is composed of pure spirit energy (shen), the most refined form of qi available.

The final stage of inner alchemy involves nurturing the embryo until it is ready to leave the body. This typically takes nine years of practice and is known as 'reverting spirit into emptiness'. When this process is complete, the embryo of pure Yang, in a complete inversion of the physical process, is born through the crown of the head at a point known as the 'Heavenly Gate', a term we first encountered as the gateway to the highest point of the cosmos in the Shangqing astrological system. When this 'birth' occurs, the adept has successfully reversed time, and reverted to a 'pre-heaven' state of primordial unity, and is merged fully with the Dao. What this actually entails is, of course, difficult to explain and is symbolized in various ways in the literature. A trivial example would be the attainment of seemingly magical powers that permit the practitioner to exist in several locations at the same time. A more serious example would be the total abdication of the physical body, which is now, to all intents and purposes, a corpse. One contemporary practitioner of inner alchemy explained immortality to me as freedom, that is, by identifying more and more with the subtle body or network of sub-molecular energies, one becomes less and less constrained by the limits to which ordinary physical bodies are subject.

THE WAY OF COMPLETE PERFECTION

In the Daoist tradition, the most important successful practitioners of inner alchemy were two immortals known as Zhongli Quan and Lü Dongbin. These two were legendarily instrumental in the founding of the Way of Complete Perfection, the monastic form of Daoism that is one of the two major forms of Daoism today. According to tradition, Zhongli and Lü appeared to an educated landowner by the name of Wang Zhe (1112–70), and instructed him in the methods of Daoist cultivation. At the age of forty-eight, Wang adopted the Daoist name Wang Chongyang, left his family, and engaged in a period of extreme asceticism and intense cultivation. He dug himself a pit in the ground that he named 'the Tomb of the Living Dead' where he lived for three years, before building a hut where he lived for another four years. After seven years of solitude Wang set his hut on fire, began dancing madly and left his neighbours to put the fire out. He then headed east and began his career as a teacher, founding five congregations in present-day Shandong province (Yao, 2000, p. 568).

His successors were seven Daoists known collectively as the 'seven perfected'. These seven were instrumental in establishing what became the most important Daoist monastic organization, the Way of Complete Perfection. The first disciple, Ma Yu, was a rich landowner who permitted Wang to establish a 'Complete Perfection Hut' on his grounds. Ma's wife, Sun Bu'er became the seventh disciple and the most famous woman Daoist. The Ma residence effectively became the first monastic centre of the Way of Complete Perfection, and they received visitors who sought out Wang and his teaching. Each of the seven disciples eventually established their own lineages based on their own religious experiences and practice of internal alchemy. Of the seven, the most important is Qiu Chuji, the third disciple, who is famous in Chinese history for his meeting with the Mongolian ruler Chinggis Khan. During this time war ravaged the north of China. The Song court had fled south after being defeated by the Jurchen, a north Asian nomadic people. The Jurchen Jin dynasty ruled in the north from 1115–1234, while the Southern Song dynasty occupied the south. Then throughout the thirteenth century the Mongol Khans were active in central and northern Asia, steadily increasing their control until they successfully established the Yuan dynasty in 1271 under Chinggis's grandson, Kublai. In the middle of all this Qiu was sought out on three occasions by three different rulers, the Xuanzong Emperor of the Jin, the Ningzong Emperor of the Southern Song, and Chinggis the Khan of the Mongols (Yao, 2000, p. 571). Of the three, Qiu accepted only Chinggis's invitation and selected eighteen disciples to set out on a three-year journey to central Asia. The account of this journey was written by Li Zhichang and has been translated as *Travels of an Alchemist* (Waley, 1931). Just before Qiu left the court, the Khan issued an edict putting Qiu in charge of all those who 'leave their families' (chujia) and granting Qiu's religion tax-exempt status in return for prayers for the Khan's long life. The Way of Complete Perfection thus soared in popularity attracting thousands of recruits who sought to escape the ravages of war and poverty in the sanctuary of the monasteries

(Yao, 2000, p. 372). Moreover, Qiu's branch of the Way of Complete Perfection, known as the Dragon Gate (Longmen) branch, is the one that continues as the main form of monastic Daoism today.

Monasticism was first brought to China by Buddhists, but Quanzhen Daoists discovered that monasteries were an ideal space in which they could devote their attention to the long and arduous process of self-cultivation. The basic prerequisite for Daoist cultivation, according to Wang, was that the aspirant should be as free from emotional anxieties as possible. Monastic communities aim to ensure this typically by following a highly regimented routine based on a hierarchical system in which senior members transmit their teachings to junior members. They are thus an excellent way of consolidating and perpetuating the transmission of religious teachings and practices.

Wang's basic guidelines for Daoist cultivation are contained in his *Fifteen Discourses*. Before beginning the process of inner alchemical transformation, it is necessary that individuals first engage in an external physical cultivation, training their bodies and minds to function in a balanced state. Only when this physical, emotional and psychological stability is reached can the monastic begin the process of inner alchemy. The Way of Complete Perfection thus sought to integrate or harmonize the three teachings of Daoism, Buddhism and Confucianism. From Confucianism came the basic rules of morality and emotional balance; from Buddhism came the focus on one's psychological and mental clarity; and from Daoism came the internal cultivation of the body and the quest for self-transformation. In this respect it can be said that Wang did not so much harmonize the three teachings but assimilate them within his own understanding of cultivation.

One of the most important innovations was the emphasis on the cultivation of the mind as well as the body, which Wang styled the dual cultivation of nature (xing) and life or destiny (ming). By nature he meant one's inner psychological constitution, and by life he meant the physiology of the body. The goal of the cultivation is to attain a state of 'purity and tranquillity' (qingjing), and the Scripture of Purity and Tranquillity (Qingjing jing) is one of the main Complete Perfection scriptures (Wong, 1992; Kohn, 1993). The ideals of purity and tranquillity are again construed in both a psychological and a physiological sense, and a common metaphor that is employed in Complete Perfection texts is 'subduing the monkey-mind and controlling the horse-will' (Yao, 2000, p. 583). The genius of this system is that it attempts to overcome the common dualism between mind and body, recognizing that the cultivation of the mind can only take place if one pays attention to one's physical condition, and vice versa. Perhaps the most important area where this is evident is in the attempt to minimize the effect of desires, for desires are what bridge our mental and physical natures. For this reason monks and nuns generally follow an ascetic lifestyle: they must practice celibacy and should generally avoid wine and meat, though there is no hard and fast rule about this. Given the fact that one can only achieve transcendence for oneself, individuals must be allowed a certain degree of latitude. On the other hand individuals require the expert guidance of a master and for this reason must generally obey the rules.

The daily practice that takes place in Quanzhen monasteries thus typically has two components: one is a fairly extensive amount of time to allow for individual cultivation; the other is communal activities such as group meditation, morning and evening worship, as well as chores to keep the monastery functioning. In many ways Quanzhen monasteries adapted some of the routines of Chan (Zen) Buddhism, whose practitioners had perfected the discipline of group meditation. Just as in Chan monasteries, it was the task of one monk to beat other monks with a stick if he should fall asleep. A further commonality between Buddhist and Daoist practice is the notion of the middle way or the avoidance of extremes. One reason why Wang established the monastic system was that he recognized that it was valuable for people to engage in individual cultivation, but people also needed to have companions. His *Fifteen Discourses* state that a seeker of the way should have a companion but not someone that he or she is overly attached to. Friends should provide emotional stability rather than evoke passionate sentiments (*Chongyang shiwu lun*, ch. 6; trans. Kohn, 1993, p. 89).

Despite (or because of) this accommodation between Daoism and Buddhism, relations deteriorated rapidly in the thirteenth century. Part of the problem was economic: rather than building monasteries of their own, Daoists had begun to take over monasteries that Buddhists had abandoned during the wars. As China settled down into a reasonable degree of political stability, the Buddhists wanted their monasteries back. The other reason for the disputes was that Qiu's journey west to meet with Chinggis had given new impetus to the myth of Laozi's journey west and the relative inferiority of Buddhism to Daoism. Daoists published a new version of this story, entitled the *Picture Book of Lord Lao's Eighty-*

one Transformations (Laojun bashiyi hua tushu), to the outrage of many Buddhists. Unfortunately for the Daoists, one of those Buddhists happened to be Chinggis's successor, Kublai. A series of debates were held at the Khan's court in 1258, which the Daoists lost resoundingly. Daoists were ordered to convert to Buddhism, Daoist texts and printing blocks were burned and two hundred monasteries returned to the Buddhists (Liu Feng, 1998, p. 279). It is clear, however, that Daoism merely suffered a temporary setback, and the Way of Complete Perfection survived and prospered.

The Way of Complete Perfection thus established and maintains to this day a system that permits people to dedicate themselves to the pursuit of psychological and physical transformation. Quanzhen Daoism is now one of the main forms of Daoism in mainland China. Although few people are willing to engage in a spiritual journey of such dedication, monks offer advice to lay Daoists who visit temples and engage in various types of meditation and energy practices. Perhaps they do not hope to become immortal, but they do hope to embody the Dao to some small degree and thus lead pure and tranquil lives that enable them to withstand the rigorous challenges and pressures of modern life.

In this way, the lives of Quanzhen Daoists are not best seen as correlations with the stars and visualizing the body in relation to the cosmos. Rather their lives are 'lifetimes' that embody the transformative powers of the Dao with an intensity that is not ordinarily seen in human beings. Through the inner alchemical cultivation of purity and simplicity, they aim to reverse time itself and emerge from the 'living graves' of their bodies as transfigured beings for whom time and space pose no bounds. Thus they can fulfil Zhuangzi's ideal of free and easy wandering in a life of perfect simplicity and harmonious spontaneity.

TRANSFORMATION

The Daoist experience with alchemy bears witness to the theme of transformation that has been at the heart of Daoism since its origins. So far in our survey of Daoism we have witnessed three main ways in which this process of transformation has manifested itself: the transformations of the cosmos; the transformation of the gods; and the transformations of the body.

Going right back to the proto-Daoist philosophy of the *Daode jing* and the *Zhuangzi*, we see that the fact of transformation is built into the constitution of the universe. Such transformation is held to be natural or spontaneous (*ziran*); what is unnatural is to persist in the state to which one has become accustomed. The *Zhuangzi* expresses this idea best in its numerous stories of people who, by a conventional standard, are disabled or physically abnormal in some way. Chapter 5, in particular, contains stories of people known as 'Nag the Hump', 'Toeless Nuncle Hill' and 'Lipless Clubfoot Scattered' (see Mair, 1994, pp. 42–50).

This idea reaches its philosophical apex in the famous story of Zhuangzi's dream. Zhuangzi dreamt that he was a butterfly, but when he awoke he did not know whether he was Zhuangzi who had been dreaming that he was a butterfly, or whether he was now a butterfly who was dreaming of Zhuangzi (*Zhuangzi*, 2; see Mair, 1994, p. 24). Zhuangzi's reason for adopting this attitude is presumably rooted in his experience of the possibility for radical transformation that is inherent within things. For Zhuangzi, this possibility engendered a mystical attitude towards the Dao and a sceptical attitude with respect to the value of conventional philosophy and logic (see Kjellberg and Ivanhoe, 1996).

In the alchemical tradition, the transformation within the universe is expressed using the model of the sixty-four hexagrams and the notion that it is possible to cycle back through the transformations to arrive at a pristine state. This suggests that the experience of transformation is not always a good one for human beings, but the alchemists made use of the possibility of transformation to transform the way in which transformation takes place. In so doing they live out the Daoist maxim that 'my destiny is my own and does not lie with others' (Robinet, 2000, p. 212).

The second type of transformation is the transformation of deities. It is hardly surprising that the Complete Perfection monks should have returned to the myth of Laozi's transformations in their debates with Buddhists. The myth of a wise and immortal cosmic teacher who can take many forms throughout history precisely cohered with their own experience of personal self-transformation, and represented the ideal towards which they aspired. In some respects this myth permitted them to absorb Buddhist practices where it was convenient for them to do so; in other respects it was used, as before, to assert the superiority of Daoism over Buddhism.

Arguing that Daoism is better than Buddhism because Laozi is older than the Buddha points to another feature of the transformations of the alchemical process, namely that earlier stages of transformation are better that later. Here the cycles of transformation within the natural world must be placed in the firmly linear context of cosmic history. This attitude reflects the worldview that emerged during the period of the Warring States, when all philosophers looked back to a golden era in the past. It reflects the attitude of the *Daode jing* in which power that is unexpended is better than power that is actually used. It reflects the worldview articulated in Buddhist-influenced Numinous Treasure tradition that the universe goes through a process of decay until finally the Heavenly Worthy is moved to issue the law or dharma to save living beings (see chapter 7). But perhaps even more basic than all of these, the 'earlier is better' attitude attests to the universal human experience of physical decay in one's body.

In this regard, the inner alchemy tradition represents the possibility of not simply reversing the process of aging, but actually transforming the process itself. This is the most radical possibility that the Daoist tradition holds out, and is dependent on the persistent Daoist view that human beings stand at the apex of the creativity of the Dao and are in the position of directing the continuing evolution of heaven and earth. This is not to say that we are gods, but that we have a deep potential for transformation that lies, like the immortal embryo, pregnant within ourselves. Transformation takes place when one unlocks this pregnancy or potential (de) within oneself, so as to transform one's life or ultimate destiny (ming).

If the Daoist view of transformation is correct, it requires us to reconsider our conventional Western distinctions between what is natural, unnatural and supernatural, for clearly nature is not something that is fixed, but something with a rather more porous identity, capable of radical shifts and evolutions. This perhaps unsettling view sits surprisingly well with our postmodern condition. Genetic engineering is currently stretching the limits of what exactly is natural, unnatural and supernatural. Here the human technological capacity – a capacity that originated naturally in the evolution of opposable thumbs – has reached its apotheosis, and we have entered the age of the superman. The superman, according to Gilles Deleuze, is 'the man who is in charge of the animals. It is a man in charge of the very rocks or inorganic matter. It is man in charge of the being of language ... It is the advent of a new form that is neither God nor man and which it is hoped will not prove worse than its two previous forms' (Deleuze, 1988, p. 132; quoted in Surin, 1998, p. 183). In the development of technologies of in vitro fertilization, cloning, genetic engineering, artificial intelligence, nano-technology, cyborgism and in the re-engineering of our planetary atmosphere we are in the process of changing the very conditions of life itself. In this respect we are not only transforming ourselves, but we are transforming the way transformation has hitherto taken place. In so doing we are fulfilling the very same alchemical ambitions that motivated the early Daoists. The alchemical quest for transformation is alive and well in university laboratories.

SUGGESTIONS FOR FURTHER READING

Campany, Robert Ford. 2002. *To Live as Long as Heaven and Earth: A Translation and Study of Ge Hong's* Traditions of Divine Transcendents. Berkeley, University of California Press

Cleary, Thomas. 1987. *Understanding Reality: A Taoist Alchemical Classic by Chang Po-tuan.* Honolulu, University of Hawai'i Press

Porter, Bill. 1993. *The Road To Heaven: Encounters with Chinese Hermits.* San Francisco, Mercury House

7
Text

經

Although we are accustomed to seeing the printed word as a feature of
ordinary life, it is important to remember that written texts were at one
time extraordinary works of human culture, and the use of these rare and
precious texts is one of the most important features of the Daoist
religion. The spirits communicate with humans by revealing texts, and
Daoist priests communicate with the spirits by submitting written
memorials to them. Texts are not only a means of communication, but
also have a talismanic function as the guarantee of the relationship
between the Daoist and the celestial powers. Thus it is just as important
to study the way texts are used in Daoist ritual as it is to understand the
words that are on the page. To give one contemporary example of this,
the Fung Loy Kok Daoist temple in Toronto holds services where people
can come and chant scriptures. The scriptures are chanted in Cantonese,
and yet many of the worshippers are Euro-Canadians who do not
understand a word of what they are saying. To them the meaning of the
words is not the point. The significance lies in the ritual chanting of the
text by the community. It is this ritual activity that unlocks the potential
contained within the sounds.

Any investigation of Daoist texts must, however, begin with the
important role played by Chinese characters. One theory about the origin
of Chinese writing has to do with the ancient divinatory practice of
scapulimancy that was practised in the Neolithic Shang dynasty culture.
The earliest examples we have of Chinese characters are the questions
and answers recorded on these bones and shells (see chapter 4).
According to this theory, Chinese characters thus originate in the

possibility of communication between humans and the heavens. Writing is thus a special form of communicating with the divine. Whether or not this hypothesis is true, it does reveal an important fact about the written word in the Daoist texts: Chinese characters encode the interaction of heaven and earth just as the oracle writing did. Moreover although it would be an inaccurate oversimplification to suggest that Chinese characters are essentially stylized pictures, the pictorial quality of Chinese writing was extremely important in Daoist scriptures, many of which contain talismans in the form of highly stylized Chinese characters.

THE RELIGIOUS ORIGINS AND FUNCTIONS OF DAOIST TEXTS

Cosmic revelation

The notion of revelation is a key to understanding how scriptures facilitate the communication between humans and spirits. As we have already seen, Ge Hong's biography of Zhang Daoling shows how Laozi appeared in a vision to Ge and revealed the Way of Orthodox Unity to him. By the sixth century it was claimed that Zhang had received as many as 1502 fascicles of text, which, according to Benn (2000, p. 313) was probably an exaggeration designed to increase the importance of the Orthodox Unity priesthood. As the Daoist tradition developed more and more revelations took place and it was only thanks to the efforts of Lu Xiujing and others, who collected and sorted through this mass of texts, that some systematic description and understanding of this ongoing revelation could take place. It was this process of sorting into 'grottos' (see chapter 2) that led to the formation of the two catalogues of Daoist scripture that we know as Highest Clarity and Numinous Treasure. Each of these traditions contain its own theories about how the revelation of Daoist texts takes place: the Shangqing texts opted for a cosmological theory, and the Lingbao tradition supplemented this with a theory of revelation based on the mythology of the various incarnations of the cosmic being known as the Heavenly Worthy of Primordial Beginning (Yuanshi tianzun).

The revelation of the Shangqing scriptures that began in 364 CE continued, and extended, the notion that texts of Chinese characters somehow disclose – and facilitate – the real interaction between humans and their cosmic environment. The texts of the revelation were said to have pre-existed in heaven, and, indeed, predate time itself. This notion is based on the Chinese term for scripture (jing) which also means the weft of a piece of fabric. The cosmos was envisioned as a piece of cloth – the fabric of the Dao – which revolved around the Supreme Ridgepole, whose location is marked by the Pole Star. The revealed scriptures – those designated by the title 'jing' are nothing less than the weft of this celestial fabric. Given the cosmological view of the text, it becomes clear that texts are not only to be understood in an intellectual sense, but also in some sense activated. Isabelle Robinet has pointed out that the Shangqing texts revealed by the immortal Lady Wei to the medium Yang Xi 'are only the material aspect of texts that were formed from the primordial breath that existed before the origin of the world' (1993, p. 23). As humans recite the texts which are traces of the originals in the heavens, deities echo in response. Thus revealed texts are tokens of divine power that mediate the cosmic Dao to the people. They thus have a talismanic quality as they function as a covenantal seal between the privileged one who possesses the text and the radiant one who revealed it.

This reciprocity, a persistent feature of the Daoist worldview, is explained in the *Scripture of the Salvation of Humankind (Duren jing)*, a Numinous Treasure text that begins the Ming dynasty Daoist Canon: 'It is by leaning upon the Tao that the *ching* [*jing*; scriptures] have been constituted; it is by leaning upon the *ching* that the Tao manifests itself. Tao is substance and the *ching* are function' (Robinet 1993, p. 23). The terms 'substance' and 'function' are standard terms in Chinese philosophy and indicate that texts function in a reciprocal relationship to the Dao. Without one there would not be the other, for the substantive nature of the Dao is that it manifests itself in the form of textual communications.

The Lingbao tradition, under the heavy influence of Buddhism, presents an alternative explanation for the revelation of texts. In the Lingbao text, *The Roots of Sins (Zuigen pin)*, the Heavenly Worthy of Primordial Beginning relates how the law and the texts of Numinous Treasure were made available to the world during various stages of its evolution, known by the Sanskrit term 'kalpa'.

When heaven and earth were established once more, I emerged into the world and was called Nameless Lord. I brought forth the Law, to educate and transform, to save [people as] heavenly beings. In this age the actions of men and women were [both] refined and coarse; there was inequality in the same heart. Some believed [in the Dao]; they all obtained long life. Some gave rise to jealousy and hurt, and were evil, rebellious and disloyal; they all died early deaths. At this time there were the roots of karmic retribution of good and evil. After I had passed through, the entire kalpa came full circle. Heaven and earth were again destroyed; there was no more light; dismal and dark it was. After a period of five kalpas came Opening Sovereign, the first year.

The true texts of the Numinous Treasure were opened and made accessible by the three original energies. Heaven and earth were again in correct order; the five writings were blazing and radiant. I became manifest in the Heaven of Beginning Green Energy under the name of the Heavenly Worthy of Primordial Beginning to send down broadly the Law, to educate and transform, and save [them as] heavenly beings. At the time when this first began, the people were simple and pure; they lived a life of 'knotted cords', and their minds were free from rigid conventions. They were in harmony with spontaneity, and all attained long life to the extent of 36,000 years. (*Zuigen pin*, ch. 1, author's trans.)

Here the Heavenly Worthy graciously appears to save living beings and to restore them to the simple life when people used knotted cords to keep track of their accounts. Coincident with this plan to save the world is the appearance of the true texts of Numinous Treasure, and as a result of the texts being revealed, the salvific function of the Heavenly Worthy was fulfilled. Significantly, Daoists claimed that the Numinous Treasure texts were revealed directly from the highest deities to Daoist masters of sufficient virtue. This was thought to make them superior to the Shangqing revelations, which took place via a transcendent spirit (Lady Wei) and a medium (Yang Xi) (Yamada, 2000, p. 231). Thus in the Numinous Treasure tradition, the process of revealing the texts is itself to be understood as an act of compassion or grace by means of which people are able once again to live a life of divine simplicity.

Spirit-writing cults

Unlike many religions that fixed their scriptures at a particular time and allow no more additions, Daoism continues to generate revelations. The vast quantity of revealed texts within Daoism is testimony to the widespread phenomenon of mediumism, in which women can play an important role either as the revealing spirit (for example Lady Wei Huacun in the Shangqing revelations) or as the medium who transmits the communication (Despeux, 2000b). Although the transmission of the

Shangqing texts was clearly an elite affair for the educated few, we know that by the Song dynasty the phenomenon of spirit-mediums cut across religious and social boundaries (Davis, 2002, p. 54). Spirit-mediums were used not only for the production of religious texts, but also for conducting exorcisms to heal the sick. Such exorcisms were performed by 'ritual masters' (fashi) who could be Daoist priests operating at an elite level, or could simply be undertaken by village mediums for a local clientele.

It was during the nineteenth century, however, that the phenomenon of spirit-writing cults became extraordinarily widespread throughout southern China, and continues this day in south-east China, Hong Kong and Taiwan. A séance is typically held in a special hall located within the precincts of a Daoist temple. The people attending the session make offerings to the spirit who is invited to descend into a stick that is wielded by two mediums. The stick moves automatically and traces Chinese characters on a planchette covered with sand or incense ashes. A third person calls the characters out as they appear and a fourth person copies them down onto paper. The fact that the Qing government attempted unsuccessfully to ban these cults suggests that they were widespread among the common people and looked down upon by the elite. It is perfectly possible for these séances to have nothing to do with the elite Daoist deities that are typically invoked by Daoist priests, but there are many ways in which these cults became part and parcel of the Daoist religion, especially in southern China. Firstly, many people who officiated at these ceremonies, not as the mediums but as the persons who invoked the spirits, were Daoist priests or were regarded as Daoist priests. Secondly, these ceremonies frequently, but not always, take place in Daoist temples. A third reason can be seen in the rise of a specific type of spirit-writing cult centred on Lü Dongbin, the most famous of the eight Daoist immortals.

These Lüzu (Patriarch Lü) cults were influenced by the spread of Complete Perfection teachings, though they are not a part of Complete Perfection Daoism (Shiga, 2002, p. 189; Tsui, 1991). Like the ritual masters of the Song dynasty who healed the sick through exorcism, the Lüzu cult also had an important role in healing, for some of the main clientele are Chinese herbalists who obtain recipes for compounding drugs from Patriarch Lü himself (Shiga, 2002, p. 195). Again this aspect of the spirit-writing phenomenon fits in well with the rest of the Daoist tradition as a whole, for the Daoist Canon contains many recipes for the concoction of drugs and elixirs. Lü's reputation as an alchemist and a healer made him an obvious person from whom to seek advice on these matters.

The other main product of the spirit-writing cults in general was morality books (*shanshu*). Unlike the elite Daoist precepts that are transmitted in Daoist ordination rituals, these books are aimed squarely at a popular audience, and bear witness to the increased spread of printing, reading and writing in the Qing dynasty. The system of morality is basically a traditional Confucian ethic combined with the Buddhist notion of karmic rewards and punishments and a Daoist quest for longevity and immortality (Esposito, 2000, p. 645). The books offer a type of moral calculus that specify so many merit or demerit points for good and bad actions. Good deeds are rewarded with long life and prosperity; bad deeds are met with sickness and suffering. Such books were widely printed and distributed by the Qing court in order to promote social stability.

Morality books are also an important feature of the Daoism that was propagated in Korean and Japanese religion. Koreans translated Chinese morality texts into the vernacular script with the same aim of promoting a harmonious society. The *Complete Writings of Patriarch Lü* (*Lüzu quanshu*) were also introduced to eighteenth-century Japan, combining morality texts and devotional literature side by side (Masuo, 2000, p. 838).

Text and lineage

Returning to the elite Daoist revealed texts, it is important to note that simply to possess one of these revealed texts is thus to have a clue to the fabric of the Dao itself. Given this fact, it is not surprising that they were jealously guarded and passed down only to those who were properly initiated in their use. The adept, being initiated into the use of a sacred document, is placed not only in a historical lineage of transmission, but also in the cosmological 'space' that the scripture represents, the communicative possibility (dao) that mediates between heaven and humankind. Transmission rituals are thus an important part of the function of a Daoist priest. The priest typically selects one of his sons whom he will train, initiating him into the use of the scriptures, and eventually ordaining him in his place.

In the earliest Daoist community of the Celestial Masters, everyone in the community over the age of six was ordained with a register (*lu*) that contained the names of the celestial functionaries and warriors that were at his or her command. The register would be worn on the belt so as to protect the children from malevolent spirits and assist in their development. As the children grew older they would receive a longer register of deities. At the same time that the person was ordained into this spiritual power, he or she also received a text of written precepts (*jie*) (Benn, 2000, p. 313). Thus with increasing power came increasing responsibility.

Since the dissolution of the original community, texts are transmitted only at formal rituals of ordination in which ordinands receive a variety of texts including liturgies, precepts, registers and talismans. By receiving a liturgical text in ordination, one is authorized to perform the liturgies and practises that the text describes and to petition the spirits listed on the register. The priesthood, like the original community, is a hierarchical institution; the higher one climbs, the more liturgies one is authorized to perform, the more spirits one may petition and the more powerful talismans one can use for protection. The model for the ordination rituals is basically legalistic. Ordinands swear that they will faithfully perform the liturgies into which they are initiated, but also that they will never sell or reveal the contents of the texts to outsiders. This secrecy clearly indicates that the power and authority of the lineage-holder is based exclusively on the texts that are transmitted to him. Were those texts to become widely available, then others could potentially have the same access to the spirit world that he does. This would be bad for the authority of the priests, but it could also be dangerous for the untrained person for such texts are 'powerful esoteric writs that could inflict great harm if they fell into the wrong hands or passed on to the ignorant who had not received oral instructions for their use from a preceptor' (Benn, 2000, p. 329). Moreover, as we saw in chapter 4, Daoist texts could also function as powerful political weapons. Thus those who controlled the scriptures and the talismans controlled the means of legitimating dynastic authority.

Despite the necessarily secretive nature of Daoist ordinations, many texts were collected and published in several compendia. The greatest of these is known as the Daoist Canon (*Daozang*), which is a vast treasury of texts that was put together in 1445 under the reign of the Ming dynasty Zhengtong Emperor. It contains nearly 1500 Daoist texts and the current small print version published in China occupies thirty-six large volumes, or four CD-ROMs. The Canon contains a wide variety of

Daoist literature, including charts, talismans, registers, precepts, liturgies, methods and hagiographies, but only a fragment of the texts has been translated into English. Even though many texts are published now in the Daoist Canon and are relatively accessible to those who can read classical Chinese, there is a large and probably undeterminable number of texts that scholars have no knowledge of because they are still transmitted in secret. Furthermore, many texts are deliberately cryptic and use a highly symbolic language so that if they were to fall in the hands of someone who had not been properly instructed in their use, they would make no sense. In this regard it is quite remarkable that we have as much knowledge of the Daoist tradition as we do.

Once ordained into a lineage of textual transmission, a Daoist priest is then able to perform the most important liturgical functions. Of these the most ancient is the submission of petitions to the celestial functionaries. The submission of petitions was incorporated into the zhai ritual in the Lingbao tradition, and is now an integral part of the main jiao offering that Daoist priests perform today. The main function of the zhai ritual is to expunge all records of a person's sins from the official database kept by the relevant celestial bureaucrats. The ritual is frequently performed for the deceased so that they will be released from the punishments of hell. Petitions are also made to the gods to confer merit points on those who assist the priest (Benn, 2000, p. 335). The form that petitions take is largely based on the form of memoranda used in the imperial state administration. The Daoist priest thus functions similarly to an official in government service, except for the fact that the administration that he deals with is comprised of spirits, not bodies.

Talismans and diagrams

In addition to the liturgical function of texts outlined above, Daoist texts contain a wealth of talismans, sacred charts and other diagrams. Such diagrams may be understood as maps of the sacred space to which the Daoist priest seeks access. They permit him to find his way within the spirit world and as such are valuable indications of the way the Dao functions.

Of these non-verbal materials, perhaps the most important genre is the talisman (*fu*). The principle of the talisman is derived from the ancient Chinese security system of the tally. A tally is any object that has been divided in two, with one half going to each person. Whenever the two halves are rejoined, and they tally with each other, the identity of the two parties is thus assured. The Shangqing view of texts as cosmic emanations by definition gives them a talismanic quality, as they are copies of some original that is said to pre-exist in the heavens. The person who performs a Shangqing liturgy thus authenticates himself to the relevant spirits by offering up the correct talisman, and similarly verifies that the deity is carrying a talisman. Talismans are thus like royal seals (yin) for they 'seal' a pathway between humans and deities, and can be compared to the sacred treasures that were used in the imperial court to signify the possession of the mandate of heaven by the emperor. Foundational to the idea of the talisman is thus the principle of reciprocity or duality, and this can also be observed in that sacred talismans are often stylized forms of Chinese characters written in duplicate, as mirror images or in two colours (Robinet, 1993, pp. 27–8).

Talismans did not originate with Daoism nor are they used exclusively within Daoism. Some of the earliest records of talismans are associated with the 'magico-technicians' of the Han period who used them to exert authority over demons and spirits (Despeux, 2000a, p. 500; De Woskin, 1983). Alchemists also wore talismans for protection when searching in the mountains for rare herbs and minerals. Talismans do, however, form a major part of the rituals performed by Daoist priests. Most are written on paper and can be presented to the spirits by burning, but they can also be executed in thin air by the priest using the appropriate hand gestures (Despeux, 2000a, p. 529; Chenivesse, 1996, p. 72).

The use of talismans was instrumental in the founding of the Numinous Treasure tradition on which much Daoist ritual today is based. The basis of the Numinous Treasure scriptures is the *Perfect Text of Numinous Treasure in Five Tablets* and the corresponding *Five Talismans*. These five texts and five talismans correspond to the five directions, five cosmic emperors, and five organs of the body (see chapter 2). The Perfect Texts are said to have coagulated from primordial essence when the five directions of the cosmos were being born. Possession of these talismans thus puts the priest in the ritual centre of the cosmos, which enables him to offer petitions to the right spirit functionaries and obtain the release of spirits from hell. When Daoist priests erect an altar today, they thus place the five talismans around it in order to demarcate the ritual space they are creating (Dean, 2000, p. 659).

Daoist ordination rituals also make use of talismans to cement the bond between an ordinand and his teacher. The ordinand takes a knife and divides a paper talisman in two, keeping one half and giving the other half to the teacher. This did not mean that the two people were equal, but rather that the ordinand was now formally accepted as his master's subordinate (Benn, 2000, p. 300). Once ordained, however, the new priest is able to make use of the talismanic authority that has been given to him.

Less common than talismans, but also an important genre of Daoist text is the diagram or chart. Unlike talismans, these documents do not necessarily imply any contractual authority, rather they aim to represent the true nature of some dimension of reality (Despeux, 2000a, p. 499). The most basic Daoist symbol is the yin–yang symbol on the front of this book, but the diagrams contained in Daoist revealed texts are typically far more complex. Among these documents we find diagrams of the cosmos, images of sacred mountains and other features of religious landscape, and diagrams of the body. Such diagrams predate the development of Daoism in China, but became an important form of Daoist expression. The *Map of the True form of the Five Peaks*, for instance, depicts in stylized form the five sacred mountains of China that correspond to the five directions of the cosmos (Despeux, 2000a, p. 505). Maps of the underworld (Mount Fengdu) also assisted adepts in their visualization practices. Without such a map it would be impossible for practitioners to journey to the underworld to liberate their ancestors. Similarly, maps of the constellations, especially the Big Dipper, assist in journeys to the heavens.

The prevalence of such charts suggests that the correct representation of cosmic space was an important Daoist concern, perhaps even equal in importance to the mythic narratives of Laozi's transformations. Given that the most basic meaning of the word 'Dao' is a 'path' or a 'way', it is not surprising that representations of the Dao should take on a visual or spatial form. This spatial aspect of Daoism can also be correlated with the visualization practices discussed in chapter 5. It seems that, for many Daoists, having a correct mental image of the true nature of things was an important method for following the Dao. This suggests that our ordinary perceptions are somehow deficient and as a result the Way is not obvious to us. Revealed charts and maps thus help us to remedy the deficiency in our ordinary perception of the world, and permit us to find the true Way. This points to another recurrent feature of the Dao, namely the priority of internal forms over external forms, and the notion that truth and salvific power are hidden deep within the cosmos and must somehow be revealed or exposed to us. When such an act of communication takes place, we have a pathway, a Dao for us to follow. Sacred charts and diagrams are thus representations of those ways and permit Daoists to make their own journeys along the Way, following in the footsteps of those who have gone before.

TRANSFORMATIONS OF MEANING IN DAOIST TEXTS

Since transformation is an essential feature of the Dao it is not surprising that Daoist texts are not static documents, but bear witness to a continuing process of redaction and commentary. Nowhere is this more true than for the most ancient and influential Daoist text, the *Daode jing* (*Scripture of the Way and its Power*), which has been subject to countless interpretations and applications throughout its 2400-year history. The section above focused mostly on the ritual function of texts, but Daoist texts were also valuable to Daoist literati who sought to reshape Daoist culture and values by reinterpreting the ideas of its most fundamental documents. In order to give an example of how this process of commentary and editing continues to take place in Daoism, this section examines some of the most influential interpretations of the *Daode jing*.

The way in which any text is interpreted of course develops largely out of the relationship that obtains between concerns of the interpreter and the words that he or she encounters on the page. The range of interpretive possibility is particularly broad in the case of the *Daode jing* because its language is extremely terse and underdetermined (see LaFargue, 1994). Extraordinarily, it contains no references to people, places or events, and its messages resemble brief notes, or distilled maxims, whose meaning, scholars hypothesize, could once upon a time have been expounded upon by reference to a body of oral tradition to which we no longer have access. The fact that this oral knowledge was lost in effect freed the text from the bondage of the particularity of time and place, and it thus became even more capable of being interpreted and used in a whole variety of ways. The thirteenth-century commentator Dong Sijing aimed to synthesize all the various ways of interpreting the text in order to arrive at a definitive understanding. Having consulted a whole range of commentaries to produce his 'Collected Interpretations', he declared that the *Daode jing* 'centres around nonaction, serenity, and spontaneity, and advises people to live in weakness and softness and respond in emptiness or receptivity; they should be free from strife and competition, forget their self, the world and all opposites' (Robinet, 1998, p. 122). What exactly this means, of course, has varied tremendously throughout history.

The standard version of the *Daode jing* is a short text of some 5000 Chinese characters that was put together in the form of rhyming aphorisms probably some time in the fourth century BCE. The oldest version of the text that we possess was discovered in the archeological excavations in Guodian, and dates back to the third century BCE. The discovery consists of fragments of text written on bamboo slips which were originally bound together. The binding has decayed and all that remains is a jumble of slips that archeologists have been painstakingly putting back together. Another version of the *Daode jing* was found in the Mawangdui tombs, dated to 168 BCE. Here the text is preserved on silk, but the order of the chapters is different. This version begins with the *Scripture of the Power* (*Dejing*; usually chapters 38–81 of the traditional arrangement); and puts the *Scripture of the Way* (*Daojing*; chapters 1–37) second.

The Wang Bi commentary

The standard version of the *Daode jing* that is used today was put together by the astonishingly brilliant philosopher Wang Bi (226–49 CE), who tragically died at the age of twenty-three (see Chan, 1991). Wang belonged to a school of intellectuals known as 'Dark Learning' (Xuanxue). He aimed to explore the fundamentally dark and mysterious principles of creation and then translate them into a programme of political philosophy. His exploration of the *Daode jing* centred upon the notion of 'nothing' or 'non-being' out of which the ten thousand things in the universe arise. This nothing is imaged in two important ways in the *Daode jing*: as the hub of a wheel where the spokes meet, and as the emptiness that gives a vase its usefulness. Wang Bi recognized that the text was pointing at a deeply mysterious fact of nature – that space or emptiness or nothingness is precisely the place where power and life are generated. The *Daode jing* advises the reader to emulate this nothing-ness, to become weak and empty, and to return to a child-like state that is paradoxically full of potential and life.

Wang Bi interpreted this by reference to the account of creation in the *Daode jing* in which the Dao gives birth to One, One gives birth to two, two to three and three to the ten thousand things. The One is the central place of unity, like the hub of the wheel; but the One is not a thing 'out there' like a deity but, like the emptiness in the vase, is the mysterious centre of things. The things of the world originate out of nothing and return to nothing. Wang Bi thus interpreted the One (or transcendental unity of the world) by reference to the nothing from which all things originate. This nothing or non-being is the transcendent ground of all things, deeply mysterious and hidden. For Wang Bi, it is the task of the ruler to be this One for his people, their point of unity, their deep, abiding wellspring of life and harmony. In order to be like the One, then, the ruler must be like nothing, emulating as far as possible the naturalness of the world and refusing to intervene with programmes of good works and education. For Wang Bi, the feudal, hierarchical structure of society is naturally ordained and thus should not be tampered with. For the system to work properly only requires the ruler to be as though he were not at all.

Wang Bi's commentary on the *Daode jing* is not only a profound work of mystical philosophy, but also evidence of a deeply engaged political mind. His interpretation of the *Daode jing* takes absolutely seriously the notion, present in the original text, that the Daoist sage is a powerful ruler figure who stands as the root of his people. As we have already seen in chapter 4, the Daoist tradition maintained this important connection between what we would term religion and politics.

The Heshang Gong commentary

Heshang Gong literally means the 'Master [who lives] on the river' and refers to a figure who was said to have lived by the banks of the Yellow River during the reign of the Han dynasty Wendi Emperor (179–157 BCE). The text that bears his name is a commentary on the *Daode jing* that scholars believe dates to about the second century CE (see Chan, 1991). Instead of dwelling on the notion of the One as the empty centre of things, the Heshang Gong commentary explains the One by reference to the essential energy (*jingqi*) that is the foundation for all life. This One essential energy generates the two, the three and the ten thousand things. The two is understood as yin (receptive, dark, female) and yang (active, light, male) modes of qi energy, which interact to form the three principal lifeforms in the universe: heaven, earth and humankind. From these three develop the ten thousand things. The natural Way, therefore, is to generate vitality in a recursively multiplying florescence of life. The destiny of human beings (ming) is thus to be imbued with an innate power (de). This innate power is nothing other than the One, that is, the essential energy (jingqi) of the universe.

Like Wang Bi's commentary, Heshang Gong's metaphysical inter- pretation of the *Daode jing* leads to some very important practical conclusions. These conclusions, however, are very different than Wang Bi because Heshang Gong views the One basically as life-energy rather than non-being. What is natural for human beings then is to conserve this energy as much as possible so as to prolong the vitality with which we have been endowed. This does not mean for Heshang Gong pursuing wild quests for an elixir of immortality, since it is also natural that life comes to an end. Rather he seems to advocate a type of longevity practice that is rooted in the sorts of cultivation practices that we saw in the *Neiye*. These practices are centred upon nourishing the energy associated with the five inner organs of the body (liver, heart, spleen, lungs and kidneys), not just the heart-mind. Moreover in the Heshang Gong commentary, the five organs are governed by five spirits (shen) who function as energy fields, controlling the flow of energy in the body. The human body is thus seen as a repository or receptacle for essential energy (jingqi) that is controlled by five spirits that direct the flow of energy through the five inner organs. The best way to protect these five spirits and 'guard the One' is by diminishing one's desires. Reduced desires lead to reduced stress upon the body because fewer external demands are placed upon it.

In addition to this practical concern with the life-force of the human body, the Heshang Gong commentary also views the Daoist sage as a ruler. In the case of the ruler, his body is his country. To 'guard the One' as it relates to the country means to diminish the desires of the people, and avoid placing excessive demands upon them, whether in the form of taxation or military service. The Daoist state is thus a peaceable, secure and tranquil state that has the potential to endure for a long time without experiencing disaster, violence or military incursions.

The Xiang'er commentary

The Xiang'er commentary dates from about 200 CE and originated in the milieu of the first formal Daoist religious organization, the Celestial Masters. It is generally attributed to the first Celestial Master, Zhang

Daoling, or his grandson, Zhang Lu. No one is quite sure what the title means, but one interpretation takes the title literally as meaning '[the Dao is] thinking of you' (Bokenkamp, 1997, p. 61). The commentary basically describes precepts or rules by which individual members of the Celestial Masters' community should live their lives. Following these rules not only ensures the vitality of the individual, but also the vitality of the community as a whole. The commentary thoroughly accepts the divine status of Laozi, the *Daode jing*'s mythical author.

Since the founding covenant of the Celestial Masters was executed between Zhang Daoling and Laozi, the text of the *Daode jing* that Laozi allegedly composed must have played a key role in the running of the Celestial Masters' community. From the original text's vague aphorisms comes the ethics, precepts and admonitions that are necessary for the organization of any human society. Thus from a short phrase such as 'Blunt its sharp edges; release its vexations' comes the following more lengthy interpretation:

> The 'sharp edge' refers to the heart as it is plotting evil. 'Vexations' means anger. Both of these are things in which the Dao takes no delight. When your heart wishes to do evil, blunt and divert it; when anger is about to emerge, forgive and release it. Do not allow your five viscera to harbor anger and vexation. Strictly control yourself by means of the precepts of the Dao; urge yourself on with the [hope of] long life. By these means you will reach the desired state. The stirring of vexations is like the rapid vibrations of lute strings; this is why it leads to excess. You should strive to be slow to anger, for death and injury result from these violent urges. If the five viscera are injured by anger, the Dao is not able to govern. This is why the Dao has issued such heavy injunctions against anger and why the Dao teaches about it so diligently. (*Xiang'er zhu* 20; trans. Bokenkamp, 1997, p. 80)

In this example, an extremely vague aphorism has been interpreted in terms of the personal morality that is required to attain the Dao and therefore long life. In this way the commentary shapes the original text of the *Daode jing* in a way that is useful for the original Celestial Masters' community.

Influential Western interpretations

Since the *Daode jing* was first translated into English, it has also enjoyed a life of its own in the Western imagination. Below are two contending twentieth-century interpretations of the text.

One of the most influential scholars of Chinese thought in the twentieth century was Joseph Needham, a British biochemist who devoted his life to the publication of a monumental multi-volume history of 'Science and Civilization in China'. His Needham Research Institute, based at Cambridge University, is still continuing his work after his death in 1995. Needham advocated a hypothesis of an affinity between Daoism and science in China. This affinity he claimed was based on an understanding of the Dao not as some transcendent Absolute or godlike metaphysical Principle, but simply as the self-generating 'colossal pattern' of the operation of nature. For Needham, then, the Dao of the *Daode jing* represents a kind of utopian organic naturalism. He viewed this organic philosophy as the antidote to the feudal hierarchies of ancient China, but, as a socialist, he also saw them as the antidote to Western dualisms of spirit and body and what he saw as the unscientific view of nature and politics that they generate. Julia Hardy (1998, p. 173) writes that

> more than any other scholarly interpreter, Needham appropriated the *Tao-te-ching* in service of his own agenda – his interpretation was shaped by his perceptions of the situation and needs of the modern West ... His understanding of ancient Taoism and Chinese history was skewed by this agenda, but he struck a chord in Western consciousness and his work elicited considerable popular response.

Further connections between Daoism and ideas of nature are explored in chapter 8.

Another line of popular Western interpretations has been almost exactly the opposite to this one, and integrates the *Daode jing* and Western individualism into a sort of personal life philosophy centred upon the principle of non-action (wuwei). According to these interpretative perspectives, individuals can find happiness and success if they practise a kind of live-and-let-live Dao in which they do not interfere in the lives of others and do not expect others to interfere in their own lives. A particularly popular book of this genre is the *Tao of Pooh* (Hoff, 1982) in which Winnie-the-Pooh is seen as the archetypal Daoist sage who finds a perennial peace and happiness in just letting the world go by and trying not to understand too much about it. This type of New-Age Daoism can readily be understood as the spiritual handmaid to a laissez-faire free-market capitalism in which the natural operation (or Dao) of the market must never be interfered with by taxation, government regulation or trade tariffs.

Texts and contexts

The reauthentication and reinterpretation of scriptures is common in the development of all religions and serves as a way of manufacturing and legitimating authority in the present. Daoists, like many religious people, look to the past to legitimate what they do in the present. Daoist priests derive their authority from the formal, ritual transmission of ancient texts. Daoist intellectuals stake their claim to authority by framing their own agendas in the terms of ancient texts such as the *Daode jing*. What is particularly true of the Daoist tradition is that the *Daode jing* admits a wide range of interpretations and can be applied to an even wider variety of contexts. Thus Daoism, from the beginning, has not had any strict boundaries that have limited the way the tradition develops. This fluidity has been one of the tradition's greatest assets, for it has come to appeal to a wide range of people in a wide range of circumstances, but it is also a liability, in that Daoism's boundaries have been very porous, absorbing and being absorbed into Buddhism, popular religion, and now the Western intellectual tradition.

The greatest danger posed by the absorption of the Dao into the Western tradition is that the text becomes subject to reinterpretation in a purely individualistic and intellectual way. In contrast, within the Chinese Daoist tradition, the *Daode jing* has always been interpreted by reference to the functioning of the body, whether construed as the body of the individual or the body of the community. The continuous process of reinterpretation of the *Daode jing* has up to now been a somatic, as well as intellectual process. It remains to be seen whether this traditional emphasis on the body will be continued in modern Western interpretations (see Clarke, 2000; Miller, 2002).

SUGGESTIONS FOR FURTHER READING

Boltz, Judith. 1983. *A Survey of Taoist Literature: Tenth to Seventeenth Centuries*. Berkeley, University of California Institute of East Asian Studies

Kohn, Livia and Michael LaFargue, eds. 1998. *Lao-tzu and the Tao-Te-Ching*. Albany, State University of New York Press

8
Nature 自然

So far we have seen how Daoists have managed and transformed their relationships with history and text, the stars of the sky, the ancestral spirits, and the gods of the body. The most important 'space' in which Daoism functions that has not been examined so far is the natural environment. Daoists have long had a deep and abiding affinity with nature, but the ways in which they deal with the natural environment on a religious level are perhaps quite different than one would expect. As the Canadian sinologist and environmentalist Jordan Paper has noted, many Western environmentalists have latched on to a certain way of interpreting the *Daode jing* and the *Zhuangzi* as being prototypical of contemporary environmentalism. Paper gives the example of Doris LaChapelle's 'extended rhapsody', *Sacred Land, Sacred Sex – Rapture of the Deep*:

> Now after all these years of gradual, deepening understanding of the Taoist way, I can state categorically that all these frantic last-minute efforts of our Western world to latch on to some 'new idea' for saving the earth are unnecessary. It's been done for us already – thousands of years ago – by the Taoists. We can drop all that frantic effort and begin following the way of Lao Tzu [Laozi] and Chuang Tzu [Zhuangzi]. (LaChapelle, 1988, p. 90, cited in Paper, 2001, p. 10)

Although LaChapelle is clearly not as well informed about Daoism as the reader of this book ought to be by now, the fact is that the natural environment has functioned as a kind of sacred space for Daoists. It does not follow from this, however, that Daoists are necessarily good environmentalists by a modern Western definition.

The connection between Daoism and nature begins with the Chinese term '*ziran*', translated literally as 'self-so' and meaning 'natural' or 'spontaneous'. In modern Chinese, the term '*ziranjie*' or 'natural world' is the general term for nature. Chapter 25 of the *Daode jing* states that ziran is the model for the Dao. Since the nature of the Dao is to be self-actualizing, creative and spontaneous, so also these values have come to be identified as core-values of the Daoist tradition. According to the *Daode jing*, the way in which one arrives at this state of naturalness is through the principle of 'wuwei'. Wuwei can be translated literally as non-action, but in fact means 'action as non-action', that is, 'actions that appear or are felt as almost nothing' (Liu, 2001, p. 317). It is through this type of action that the work of human beings is carried out, and the Dao is enabled to flourish in the world. As we have seen, the flourishing of the Dao came to be understood in reference to a state of creative harmony that emerges between humans, the heavens and the earth, a harmony that has implications for the way we manage our societies, and the way we take care of our bodies. All too often this type of action is misunderstood as 'letting be' whereas in fact this 'action as non-action' is really a form of spiritual technology by means of which humans cultivate their own natures and the nature around them.

Nature functions as the context for and environment within which this cultivation can take place. Thus the principal Daoist activities of running the state and cultivating the body self-consciously take place in reference to nature. In both cases nature is the space within which these vital religious functions take place and also the means by which these functions can occur. The consequence is that nature is not something to be preserved in the state of pristine wilderness, but rather employed in the service of larger religious goals. Nature thus functions as a constituent part of Daoist religious culture and is defined and interpreted by it. In other words, there is no getting around the fact that nature is a cultural construct. Daoists, like everyone else, do not value nature for its own intrinsic worth, but rather for the value it has for them and their communities (LaFargue, 2001, p. 55).

NATURAL SPACE AS SACRED SPACE

The most fundamental way in which nature functioned as a repository of meaning for Daoism can be seen in the way that early Chinese thought is deeply embedded in the natural world. Sarah Allan (1997) persuasively explains how the root metaphors of Chinese culture are derived from images of nature or explained in terms of natural phenomena. The term Dao, for instance, is explained by reference to natural phenomena such as the flowing of water. It provides irrigation – life for the ten thousand things (*Daode jing*, ch. 62) – and like water it is soft, weak, pliable, yielding, and ultimately unstoppable. Classical Confucian philosophy also sought to explain its understanding of morality by analogy with the natural environment. In an argument between the philosophers Mencius and Gaozi over the moral status of human nature, both argue over the way human nature functions like water. On the one hand water has a natural tendency to flow in a certain direction (downwards), but on the other hand water can be channelled in other directions. So also human nature has its own in-built tendencies but can, to a certain extent, be shaped through moral education (Allan, 1998, p. 42).

So far as organized Daoist religious movements are concerned, we do have some knowledge of how the early Celestial Masters' community functioned based on a collection of precepts that were transmitted as part of ordination rituals. In his study of the text known as the *One Hundred and Eighty Precepts (Yibaibashi jie)*, Kristofer Schipper notes that

> not less than twenty [of the precepts] are directly concerned with the preservation of the natural environment, and many others indirectly:
>
> 14. You should not burn [the vegetation] of uncultivated or cultivated fields, nor of mountains and forests.
> 18. You should not wantonly fell trees.
> 19. You should not wantonly pick herbs or flowers.
> 36. You should not throw poisonous substances into lakes, rivers, and seas.
> 47. You should not wantonly dig holes in the ground and thereby destroy the earth.
> 53. You should not dry up wet marshes.
> 79. You should not fish or hunt and thereby harm and kill living beings.
> 95. You should not in winter dig up hibernating animals and insects.
> 97. You should not wantonly climb in trees to look for nests and destroy eggs.
> 98. You should not use cages to trap birds and [other] animals.
> 100. You should not throw dirty things in wells.
> 101. You should not seal off pools and wells.
> 109. You should not light fires in the plains.
> 116. You should not defecate or urinate on living plants or in water that people will drink.

121. You should not wantonly or lightly take baths in rivers or seas.
125. You should not fabricate poisons and keep them in vessels.
132. You should not disturb birds and [other] animals.
134. You should not wantonly make lakes. (Schipper, 2001, pp. 82–3).

In answer to the question of why the earliest Daoist communities were concerned with the state of the natural environment, Schipper draws the conclusion that the natural environment functioned as a kind of sanctuary, in the sense of a sacred space, and in the sense of a place of refuge from the human world. Schipper, furthermore, speculates as to the consequences of doing the things that 'you should not'. The reformer Lu Xiujing wrote, 'When a Daoist master has not received Laojun's One Hundred and Eighty Precepts, then his body will have no virtue, and he cannot be deemed to be a Daoist master and receive the homage of the people, nor can he rally and administrate the gods and ancestors' (Schipper, 2001, p. 91). Thus the purpose of Daoist priests' observing this code of conduct is that they will be able to perform their religious tasks correctly and be exemplary leaders to their congregations. The implication is that by radically disturbing the ecology in which the community is situated the ability of the priest to carry out his ritual duties will be hindered.

This theory is clearly based on the broadly 'ecological' theory, first encountered in the Way of Great Peace, of the interdependent functioning of the human, heavenly and earthly realms. Thus human prosperity is not only a function of divine blessing but also natural prosperity. The *Declaration of the Chinese Daoist Association* on the topic of environmental protection contains the following quotation from the *Scripture of Great Peace*:

> [In antiquity], in the Higher August Period, because 12,000 species of living things grow and flourish, it is called the era of Wealth. In the Middle August Period, because the living things are less than 12,000 species, it is called the era of Small Poverty. In the Lower August Period, because the number of living species was less than that in the Middle August Period, it is called the era of Great Poverty; if the august breath keeps producing fewer species of things, and if no good omens are seen to assure the growth of good things, the next era will be called Extreme Poverty. (Zhang, 2001, p. 368)

In this passage the decline in human prosperity through the four ages that precipitated the revolutionary Way of Great Peace occurs in concert with a reduction in biodiversity. The flourishing of human civilization thus depends on the way we make use of our environmental context and geographic space, a theme pursued in the context of world civilizations by the Oxford historian Felipe Fernández-Armesto (2000). Given this at least theoretical respect for nature, it is important to look at the ways in which Daoists actually functioned in regard to their environments and natural contexts.

The category of sacred space is of supreme importance in the comparative study of religions (Eliade, 1961) and commonly denotes a space that is set aside and marked off in some way to distinguish it from the profane space around it. A typical example of sacred space is the way the holiest areas of temples are shielded by curtains or railings, raised on steps, and signalled with candles or incense. This sort of sacred space is humanly constructed; it is in a sense an artificial demarcation by means of which we accord a high status to some things and not to others. Daoist temples and monasteries fit into this pattern very well, being constructed so as to create a sense of distance, a definite gap between the sacred elements on the inside and the everyday life of the outside world. In addition to these formal ritual spaces, Daoists also maintain the notion of the sacred landscape, and in Daoism, as in many religions, there are clearly instances of the way in which natural space functions as sacred space.

The most important type of natural sacred space in Daoism is the mountain. As early as the Han dynasty, China had designated five sacred mountains or marchmounts (*wuyue*) to protect the five directions of the empire (the four cardinal points, plus the centre). These mountains were the focus of the state religion, and it was the duty of emperors to organize religious ceremonies at these sites (Landt, 1994; Geil, 1926).

The Taizong Emperor of the Tang was inspired by his presence at these mountains to write the following prayer, dated to 645 CE:

> The sacred mountains contain fine soaring peaks and fields of wilderness with special markers where strange animals roar and dragons rise to heaven, and the spots where wind and rain are generated, rainbows stored and cranes beautifully dressed. These are the places where divine immortals keep moving in and out. The countless peaks overlap each other; thick vapour wraps green vegetation, layers of ranges move into each other, and thus sunlight is divided into numerous shining rays. The steep cliffs fall one thousand leagues into the bottom and the lone peaks soar to ten thousand leagues high. The moon with laurel flowers blooming in it sheds veiled light. The clouds hang over the pine trees with clinging vines. The deep gorges sound loud in winter and the flying springs

are cool in summer ... Its rugged mass is forever solid, together with the Heaven and the Earth. Its great energy is eternally potent, in the span from the ancient to the future. (Munakata, 1991, p. 2; quoted in Meyer, 2001, pp. 228–9)

Direction	Sacred Mountain	Location
Northern Peak (Beiyue)	Hengshan	Shanxi
Southern Peak (Nanyue)	Hengshan	Hunan
Eastern Peak (Dongue)	Taishan	Shandong
Western Peak (Xiyue)	Huashan	Shaanxi
Central Peak (Zhongyue)	Songshan	Henan

During those times when Daoist religion and the state cult were fairly closely merged together, these five mountains functioned as sacred Daoist mountains, but as James Robson (1995) has pointed out, no one sectarian lineage or religion can claim a monopoly on Chinese sacred mountain space. A visitor to these mountains today would discover that Buddhists and Daoists and local popular cults have added their own layers of symbolism and meaning to these natural spaces (Robson, 1995; Naquin and Yü, 1992). In addition to these five imperially sponsored mountains, there are numerous other mountains that are of particular importance to Daoism, including especially Mount Wudang and Mount Qingcheng.

In keeping with the principle of the interconnectedness of human and natural environments, mountains were not simply left alone, but designated as sacred spaces by the construction of Daoist temples (*guan*), or by erecting an altar (*tan*). As Thomas Hahn has explained, the altar

was conceived as a cave and a mountain at the same time. It had depth through roads that led both inside its entrails and into the inner self of the adept, as well as height, structure and mass through which Daoists could govern the qi (vital energy) of themselves and the world. The altar would be constructed, invested and armed – or deconstructed and moved along – wherever spatial and spiritual reformation or transformation was thought necessary. (Hahn, 2000, p. 685)

This quotation excellently encapsulates the way in which Daoist religious life is woven firmly into the fabric of nature, but at the same time recognizes that the ways in which religion and nature are related shift throughout history and are reconfigured from time to time. Nature and religion are thus seen as living creatures who adapt to each other as they evolve. Hahn also emphasizes the multiple levels at which Daoist religious symbolism operates. The altar thus connects the internal energy pathways of the priest with the twisting mountain roads, thereby integrating the natural flow of qi in the environment with the natural flow of qi within the body of the priest. As we saw in the previous chapter, this correlation of external physical space and internal physiological space is typical of the Daoist representation of religious spaces and contexts, in which natural images are replicated and reformulated across a multitude of dimensions and categories of life. Layers of meaning are mapped over and against each other with the aim of comprehending the polymorphic, transfigurative character of the natural world, a world of continuous transformation (*bianhua*).

It is not surprising, then, that many Daoists should choose to live on mountains so as to improve the possibility of communicating with spirits, but this communication does not need to take place in the formal sacred spaces of monasteries and temples. Daoism maintains a strong eremitical tradition of people who wander through the mountains living on inaccessible cliffs or in caves. Such 'strange people' (yiren), as they are commonly called, continue to be drawn to China's mountains as documented in Bill Porter's fascinating travelogue, *The Road to Heaven* (1993). It is tempting to place such hermits in a tradition of religious asceticism – people who discipline their bodies so as to achieve spiritual ecstasy – or in the well-documented Chinese tradition of disenchanted scholar-officials who retire to the hills in order to pursue personal cultivation instead of public service (see Eskildsen, 1998). A more Daoist way of understanding this seemingly austere lifestyle would be to recognize that such people 'dwell on a given mountaintop solely because it is believed to be a place of spiritual potency which offers optimal conditions for the attainment of their particular goal [immortality]' (Vervoorn, 1990, p.14; quoted in Hahn, 2000, p. 694). The peaks of mountains and the hollows of caves thus form the complementary natural spaces, the yangs and the yins, in which Daoist cultivation can best take place.

The Daoist tradition of locating suitable spaces for the practice of religion is related to the traditional Chinese art of fengshui or geomancy. Fengshui literally means 'wind and water', a reference to the two important fluids of the natural environment, and has been popularized in its most trivial form as the means of enhancing one's prosperity through the arrangement of the rooms in one's house or office. The origins of fengshui, however, lie in the art of divining a suitable place for a grave, and the Form school of fengshui does this by interpreting the geophysical features of the natural environment, taking into account the streams, the ridges, the swamps and the trees. The principle behind this is that qi, being essentially a fluid – like water and wind – flows along certain natural contours and collects in certain areas. The ancient *Book of Burial (Zangshu)* states:

> [Qi] rides the wind and scatters, but is retained when encountering water. The ancients collected it to prevent its dissipation, and guided it to assure its retention. Thus it was called fengshui (wind/water). According to the laws of fengshui, the site that attracts water is optimal, followed by the site that catches wind. (Field, 2001b, p. 190)

Since Daoists recognize that their bodies are microcosmic images of the macrocosmic nature that enfolds them, it is hardly surprising that they should seek out natural spaces that they sense resonate with or amplify the body's own energy systems. This does not mean that Daoists cannot function in villages or cities, but rather the tradition is clear that some advanced practitioners seem to share an affinity for mountain spaces and the caves they enfold (see below for a discussion of the symbolism of caves).

This Daoist experience of nature was thematized religiously, that is to say, nature became a vehicle through which people could attain the realms of highest transcendence (Campany, 2001). Nowhere is this theme more clearly articulated than in the alchemist's quest (see chapter 6). To those who would argue that such alchemical quests are 'unnatural' the famous alchemist Ge Hong replied that the properties of 'unnatural' transformation are already present within nature. The alchemist's task is simply to amplify and compound what is already given to us. As the American scholar of Daoism Robert Ford Campany pithily summarizes: 'All of the tracks leading beyond this world are to be found in this world; the only way to get There is from Here' (2001, p. 137).

Two main ways emerged in Daoism of symbolizing the connections between 'There' and 'Here'. The first was to conceive of natural spaces as the dwellings for a whole range of marvellous substances and mythical and non-mythical animals. The second can be seen in the connection between texts and grottos. Below I examine these two types of connection in greater detail.

MARVELLOUS NATURE

One of the most important types of nature symbolism in Daoist mythology can be observed in traditional Chinese images of the dwellings of the immortals. Conceived either as an eastern island paradise known as Penglai, or as a western mountain known as Kunlun, these dwellings of the immortals supplied clues as to the relationship between nature and heaven. The Penglai islands, for instance, are commonly depicted as resting on the backs of turtles, covered with lush vegetation and populated with immortals and animals (Penny, 2000, p. 111). Since the immortals are traditionally associated with these rare creatures and numinous vegetation, so also Daoists took an interest in certain flora and fauna.

Evidence of this interest in vegetation can be seen in the particularly strong relationship, for instance, between Daoism and traditional Chinese herbalism. Ge Hong, for instance, saw great value in herbs, but did not think that they were as effective as elixirs: 'Through breathing exercises and gymnastics, by taking herbs and plant medicines, you may extend your years, but you will not avoid death in the end. Only taking the divine elixir will give you long life without end and allow you to live as long as heaven and earth' (Kohn, 1993, p. 308). Nevertheless, alchemists sought out plants and fungi with 'supernatural' properties, and Daoists who practise the abstention from grains replace their diet with herbs and pure qi. Tao Hongjing, the great Shangqing patriarch, compiled one of China's great classics of pharmacology, *Shennong's Materia Medica (Shennnong bencao jing)* around the year 500. In this work he sorts out over seven hundred drugs into three classes, giving the highest status to those which promote longevity with no toxic side-effects (Engelhardt, 2000, p. 78). Also associated with the traditions of immortality are peaches and a 'numinous fungus' (*lingzhi*). The immortals are thought to live off these substances, which are commonly featured in Daoist art and literature. Two other flora deserve mentioning: pine trees are commonly taken as symbols of immortality because they do not shed their leaves in winter; the gourd or calabash came to symbolize the pregnant emptiness associated with the origins of the cosmos and also the empty space of grottos (Girardot, 1983). Gourds are also the receptacle of choice for elixirs of immortality (Field, 2001a, p. lxxiii; see also Field, 1997). These natural objects thus function as a way for Daoists to gain access to the transcendent world, either figuratively in terms of religious symbolism, or literally through the ingestion of the various marvellous substances (Campany, 2001).

Animals were also important bearers of transcendence. Like plants, animals were first connected with longevity practices. The *Zhuangzi* mentions techniques known as 'bird stretches and bear strides' (*Zhuangzi*, ch. 15; Graham, 1986, p. 265; Engelhardt, 2000, p. 75). Although we do not know what exactly they were, they seem to suggest a form of gymnastic practice perhaps modelled on the shapes of animals. As the Daoist religious tradition developed, the role of animals became quite noticeable. Unlike flora, however, animals are rarely the subject of Daoist texts, yet it is quite clear animals play a significant supporting role in the Daoist imagination. Ge Hong's biography of Zhang Daoling tells how the divine Laozi met him in a chariot pulled by teams of dragons and tigers. Moreover, the preferred method of becoming a celestial immortal is to be assumed bodily into the heavens on a chariot pulled by dragons. The celestial nature of immortals can also be depicted with feathers or feathery costumes, and birds, especially cranes, are traditional Chinese symbols of longevity.

A more textual connection between animals and religion can be found in the *Chart of Being in Accord with Good Fortune (Ruiying tu)*. This manuscript, found in the Dunhuang caves, describes mythical animals whose function is to carry sacred diagrams; maps depicting the sacred spaces of the cosmos (Despeux, 2000a, p. 499). Here it can be seen that animals play a role in the continuing textual transmission of the Dao and function as intermediaries between humans and gods.

CAVERNS AND TEXTS

The second way of getting 'There' from 'Here' is to be found in the concept of a cave or grotto. As first explained in chapter 2, the cavern is both a natural space within a mountain, an image for the viscera of the Daoist's body, and also a repository for sacred texts. The Daoist literatus Ge Hong explains that

> all noted mountains and the Five Marchmounts harbour books of this sort, but they are hidden in stone chambers and inaccessible places. When one who is fit to receive the Dao enters the mountain and meditates on them with utmost sincerity, the mountain spirits will respond by opening the mountain, allowing him to see them. (*Baopuzi neipian* 19/336, cited in Campany, 2001, p. 134)

An example of the way in which the revelation of texts takes place in grottos can be seen in the two mythic explanations for the revelation of the *Scriptures of the Cavern-Divine*. One legend tells of how a Daoist named Bo He was instructed by his master to stare at the north wall of a cave in Mount Emei. Three years later he was able to see writings form on the rock-face. According to the second explanation, the texts carved themselves on the wall of a grotto in Mount Song while a Daoist was meditating there (Benn, 2000, p. 316).

Eventually the lore surrounding the various grottos in China's mountains was systematized into a scheme of ten greater and thirty-six lesser grotto-heavens (*dongtian*). These are subterranean networks of caverns that are thought to exist inside important mountains and, simultaneously in the heavens. Of these the most important is Mount Fengdu whose subterranean passageways serve as the dwelling places for the souls of the departed (Hahn, 2000, p. 698; Chenivesse, 1997; 1998). Since the grottos of the underworld are mapped onto the spaces of heaven, it is not necessary to physically ascend to the heavens to attain transcendence; this can take place perfectly well inside the cavern of a sacred mountain. Equally importantly, the grottos of the mountains are mapped onto the spaces within the body, especially the grotto-chamber (dongfang) located in the head. Thus for the perfected Daoist sage, the repositories of qi in the body, the hollows of the mountains and the vast reaches of interstellar space are each reflections of the other.

An example of how this mythological 'cross-referencing' plays out in Daoist literature can be found in the biography of the Perfected Purple Yang, Zhou Ziyang, whom we first encountered in chapter 5. In his quest for the transcendence, Zhou travelled around China making pilgrimages to China's famous mountains. According to his biography, the result of all his travels from mountain to mountain was that he amassed a vast treasury of Daoist revealed scriptures, recipes and talismans. Here it can be seen that the journey through the natural world corresponds with a journey through the thoroughly textual world of Daoist religion. The more Zhou progresses in his pilgrimage through nature, the more he clothes himself in the 'natural fibres', the textuality of the Dao. The climax of Zhou's journey is reached when he finally climbs the 'Empty Mountain' and in a cave there has a vision of three Daoist deities, the Huanglao Lord flanked by the Lord of Infinite Lustre and the White Prime Lord. The Huanglao Lord tells Zhou he 'should look back in his own grotto chamber'. At this point Zhou closes his eyes and receives a vision of the White Prime Lord and the Lord of Infinite Lustre in the inner cave of his own corporeal imagination.

It is impossible to interpret such a story in an unequivocal, literal manner. The mountains referred to are both physical mountains and metaphors for the pinnacle of religious experience and meditative transformation. The cave or grotto chamber can refer both to a physical space in which meditation is practised and also the inner-body space in which Zhou's internal vision takes place. The Daoist religious imagination draws upon a wealth of natural imagery, and in so doing reveals the deep mystery of nature's self-transformative power. In this way nature is like a text whose mysteries are waiting to be revealed to the properly initiated.

A DAOIST AESTHETIC OF SPONTANEITY

Given the importance of text and nature in Daoism, it is not surprising that Daoism had a strong influence on the development of Chinese art, particularly calligraphy and landscape painting. Many of China's most famous calligraphers were Daoist priests or lay Daoists, and the highest expression of calligraphic art was thought to occur when the brush became the vehicle for the dynamism of qi itself. In terms of painting, the aim was similarly to capture the inner, dynamic reality of the subject and not merely its outward form. The Song dynasty treatise on landscape painting *Lofty Message of Streams and Mountains* (*Linquan gaozhi ji*) by Guo Xi, for instance, counsels that artists must gain an organic intuition of the scene they are about to paint (Little, 2000, p. 719). Once this internal reality has been grasped, the artists may go back to their studios and paint the scene based on the understanding they have acquired. In this way the internal reality is the clue to realizing the external form. External appearance and outward form are thus secondary to the true nature of things, which is always internal and always communicated in an intuitive and, to a certain extent, mysterious or obscure way. The best Chinese landscape paintings are profound depictions of this internal mystery, welling up onto the surface of the scroll in swirls of ink and colour.

A further example of the spirituality of nature can be found in the Daoist gardens that were created in the homes of wealthy merchants and scholars in the Ming and Qing periods. Such gardens are described as 'eccentric' that is, asymmetrical, in contrast to the rigid symmetries of traditional Chinese courtyard architecture (Meyer, 2001, p. 224). This asymmetry indicates one reason why the Daoist natural aesthetic is also a transcendent, spiritual aesthetic. Whereas the human realm is one of order, structure and formula, the natural world is chaotic, unstructured and spontaneous. It is this aesthetic of wild, natural spontaneity to which Daoists aspire, and in which they perceive the traces of transcendence. That which is wild is uncontained and gives the sense of infinity, in contrast to the domesticated, finite spaces that are required for ordinary human flourishing (Hahn, 2001, p. 214).

The key, however, is that this wilderness exists only in relation to the familiar spaces of home. Wilderness and domestic space are thus the complements of each other and the Daoist tradition seeks out this contrast by sacralizing the hidden spaces that both enfold and lurk within: mountain grottos, bodily organs and the emptiness of interstellar space. Daoists build paths through these natural – and therefore sacred – spaces, weaving together the seemingly disparate elements of their existence into a seamless whole: the fabric of the Dao.

SUGGESTIONS FOR FURTHER READING

Girardot, N.J., James Miller and Liu Xiaogan, eds. 2001. *Daoism and Ecology*. Cambridge, MA, Harvard University Center for the Study of World Religions/Harvard University Press

Little, Stephen *et al.* 2001. *Taoism and the Arts of China*. Chicago, Art Institute of Chicago

Glossary of Chinese terms

Pinyin	Wade–Giles	Chinese	English
bagua	pa-kua	八卦	The eight trigrams; the basis of divination scheme in the Book of Changes
beidou	pei-tou	北斗	Lit. 'northern bushel'; the constellation of the Big Dipper or Great Bear
bianhua	pien-hua	變化	Transformation; the underlying principle of change within the world
bigu	pi-ku	避穀	Abstention from grains; a Daoist longevity practice based on the notion that immortals live off the air and 'soak up the dew'
bugang	pu-kang	步綱	Pacing the net; a Daoist ritual whose choreography is based on the Big Dipper
chujia	ch'u-chia	出家	Lit. 'leave home'; the process of becoming a Daoist monk
dan	tan	丹	Cinnabar; a mineral formed of Mercury Sulphide used in alchemy
dantian	tan-t'ien	丹田	Cinnabar field; one of three principal locations in the body used in the practice of inner alchemy
dao	tao	道	Lit. 'way' or 'speak'; the ultimate cosmic principle in Daoism

Pinyin	Wade–Giles	Chinese	English
daojia	tao-chia	道家	Lit. 'Dao-school'; a bibliographical classification used for proto-Daoist texts
daojiao	tao-chiao	道教	Lit. 'Dao-tradition'; the Daoist religion
daoshu	tao-shu	道術	Daoist arts; energy practices that may bear only a tenuous connection with Daoist religion
daotan	tao-t'an	道壇	Daoist altar; often erected temporarily to perform a ritual and then disassembled
daozang	tao-tsang	道藏	Lit. 'Daoist treasury'; the Daoist Canon compiled in 1445
de	te	德	Lit. 'power' or 'virtue'; what one obtains by attaining the Dao
dong	tung	洞	Cave, grotto
dongtian	tung-t'ien	洞天	Grotto-heavens; the network of caves connecting China's sacred mountains
falun gong	fa-lun kung	法論功	Lit. 'Dharma-wheel skill'; the form of qi-cultivation practised by Falu Dafa, banned in China
fangshi	fang-shih	方士	'Magico-technicians'; Han dynasty practitioners of alchemy and immortality whose methods influenced the later flourishing of Daoism
fuguang	fu-kuang	服光	Absorb the light; a Daoist energy practice
fuqi	fu-ch'i	服氣	Absorb qi; a Daoist energy practice
hun	hun	魂	Heavenly soul; the soul that ascends to heaven and is venerated in the form of ancestral tablets
hundun	hun-tun	混蛋	Chaos; the state of pregnant non-being from which everything arises, and to which Daoists aim to return
jiao	chiao	醮	Daoist ritual of renewal; the main ritual performed by Daoist priests today
jiazi	chia-tzu	甲子	The first year of the sixty-year cycle

Pinyin	Wade–Giles	Chinese	English
jing	ching	精	Essence; a form of qi manifested in sexual fluids
jing	ching	經	Scripture; weft of a piece of fabric
Laozi	Lao-tzu	老子	Old Master or Old Child; the traditional author of the *Daode jing*
li	li	禮	Ceremony, ritual
lingbao	ling-pao	靈寶	Numinous Treasure or Numinous Jewel; a classical Daoist religious movement
lu	lu	籙	Register; a listing of the names of spirits possessed by those initiated into the Way of the Celestial Masters
ming	ming	命	Fate, destiny, life; the physiological element of one's person in Complete Perfection cultivation
mixin	mi-hsin	迷信	Superstition; a theological category applied by some religious people to denigrate other religious people
neidan	nei-dan	內丹	Inner alchemy
niwan	ni-wan	泥丸	Mud-pill; the cinnabar field in the head
po	p'o	魄	Earthly soul; the soul that descends into the earth
qi	ch'i	氣	Breath, vital energy, pneuma; life-force
qigong	ch'i-kung	氣功	Qi-skill; an energy practice that became popular in the nineteenth century
qingjing	ch'ing-ching	清净	Purity and stillness; the aims of meditation in the Way of Complete Perfection
quanzhen	ch'üan-chen	全真	Complete Perfection; Total Reality; the monastic Daoist movement founded by Wang Zhe
shangqing	shang-ch'ing	上清	Highest Clarity, Supreme Purity; the classical Daoist movement
shen	shen	神	Spirit; spirits; divine; the most refined form of qi

Pinyin	Wade–Giles	Chinese	English
taiji	t'ai-chi	太極	Supreme Ridgepole; the centre of the heavens; Supreme Ultimate the foundational metaphysical principle
taiji quan	t'ai-chi ch'üan	太極拳	Supreme Ultimate Fist; Tai-Chi
taiqing	t'ai-ching	太清	Great Clarity; a Daoist alchemical movement
tianming	t'ien-ming	天命	Mandate of Heaven, conferred upon the Emperor, giving him authority to rule
tianshi	t'ien-shih	天師	Celestial Master, Heavenly Teacher; a title bestowed upon Zhang Daoling and his descendants; the first Daoist religious community
tianxia	t'ien-hsia	天下	All under Heaven; the empire
tong	t'ung	通	Communicate; go through; used as a synonym for *dong*
tui	t'uei	推	Extend; the process of bringing things into correlation with each other
waidan	wai-tan	外丹	Lit. 'outer alchemy'; laboratory or operative alchemy
wang	wang	王	King; the one who unifies the three realms of heaven, earth and humankind
wuwei	wu-wei	無為	Lit. 'non-action'; actionless-action; non-assertive action; action as though non-action
xianren	hsien-jen	仙人	Immortal, transcendent being; sometimes translated in popular literature as 'fairy' or 'wizard'
xin	hsin	心	Heart, mind; the seat of the personality and the object of Confucian self-cultivation
xing	hsing	性	Inner nature; the psychological element of one's person in Complete Perfection cultivation

Pinyin	Wade–Giles	Chinese	English
yang	yang	陽	Sunny; the complement of yin
yin	yin	陰	Shady; the complement of yang
yiren	i-jen	異人	Strange people; a name given to mountain recluses
zhai	chai	齋	Ritual of purification; a retreat or fast that was the main Numinous Treasure ritual, and became incorporated into the present-day jiao ritual
zhengyi	cheng-i	正一	Orthodox Unity; the branch of Daoism founded by the Celestial Master; one of two branches officially recognized in China today
zhenren	chen-jen	真人	Perfected person; a Daoist sage
zhonghe	chung-ho	中和	Central harmony; the ideal state attained in the Way of Great Peace
zhongmin	chung-min	種民	Seed-people; the name given to those who would survive the impending apocalypse foretold in the southern Celestial Masters' tradition
ziran	tzu-jan	自然	Self-so, spontaneous, natural; the basic principle that the Dao follows in its evolution; and the core value of Daoism

Bibliography

Addiss, M. Stephen and Stanley Lombardo, trans. 1993. *Tao Te Ching*. Indianapolis, Hackett Publishing Company

Allan, Sarah. 1998. *The Way of Water and Sprouts of Virtue*. Albany, State University of New York Press

Aslaksen, Helmer. 2002. *The Mathematics of the Chinese Calendar*. Internet: http://www.math.nus.edu.sg/aslaksen/calendar/chinese.shtml

Benn, Charles. Daoist Ordinations and Zhai Rituals. In *Daoism Handbook*, ed. Livia Kohn, pp. 309–38. Liden, E.J. Brill

Bokenkamp, Stephen. 1994. Time After Time: Taoist Apocalyptic History and the Founding of the T'ang Dynasty. *Asia Major* 3rd series, 7:59–88

Bokenkamp, Stephen, with a contribution by Peter Nickerson. 1997. *Early Daoist Scriptures*. Berkeley, University of California Press

Boltz, Judith. 1983. *A Survey of Taoist Literature: Tenth to Seventeenth Centuries*. Berkeley, University of California Institute of East Asian Studies

Bumbacher, Stephan Peter. 2000. *The Fragments of the* Daoxue Zhuan. Frankfurt am Main, Peter Lang

Campany, Robert Ford. 2001. Ingesting the Marvelous: The Practitioner's Relationship to Nature According to Ge Hong. In *Daoism and Ecology*, ed. N.J. Girardot, James Miller and Liu Xiaogan, pp. 125–48. Cambridge, MA, Harvard University Center for the Study of World Religions/Harvard University Press

—— 2002. *To Live as Long as Heaven and Earth: A Translation and Study of Ge Hong's* Traditions of Divine Transcendents. Berkeley, University of California Press

Capra, Fritjof. 2000. *The Tao of Physics*, 4th edn. Boston, Shambhala Publications

Chan, Alan K.L. 1991. *Two Visions of the Way*. Albany, State University of New York Press

Chenivesse, Sandrine. 1996. Écrit démonfuge et territorialité de la mort en Chine. Étude anthropologique du lien. *L'Homme*, 137:61–86

—— 1997. A Journey to the Depths of a Labyrinth Landscape: The Mount Fengdu, Taoist Holy Site and Infernal Abyss. In *Mandala and Landscape*, ed. A.W. MacDonald, pp. 41–75. New Delhi, D.K. Printworld

—— 1998. Fengdu: cité de l'abondance, cité de la mort. *Cahiers d'Extrême-Asie*, 10:287–339

Ching, Julia. 1997. *Mysticism and Kingship: The Heart of Chinese Wisdom.* Cambridge, Cambridge University Press

Clarke, John James. 2000. *The Tao of the West.* New York, Routledge

Cleary, Thomas. 1987. *Understanding Reality: A Taoist Alchemical Classic by Chang Po-tuan.* Honolulu, University of Hawai'i Press

Cohn, Norman. 1970. *The Pursuit of the Millennium: Revolutionary Millenarians and Mystical Anarchists of the Middle Ages,* revised and expanded edn. Oxford, Oxford University Press

—— 1993. *Cosmos, Chaos and the World to Come: The Ancient Roots of Apocalyptic Faith.* New Haven, Yale University Press

Davis, Edward L. 2002. *Society and the Supernatural in Song China.* Honolulu University of Hawai'i Press

De Bruyn, Pierre-Henry. 2000. Daoism in the Ming. In *Daoism Handbook*, ed. Livia Kohn, pp. 594–622. Leiden, E.J. Brill

De Groot, J.J.M. 1910. *The Religion of the Chinese.* New York, Macmillan

De Woskin, Kenneth J. 1983. *Doctors, Diviners, and Magicians of Ancient China: Biographies of* Fang-Shih. New York, Columbia University Press

Dean, Kenneth. 2000. Daoist Ritual Today. In *Daoism Handbook* ed. Livia Kohn, pp. 659–82. Leiden, E.J. Brill

Deleuze, Gilles. 1988. *Foucault,* trans. Sean Hand. Minneapolis, University of Minnesota Press

Despeux, Catherine. 2000a. Talismans and Sacred Diagrams. In *Daoism Handbook*, ed. Livia Kohn, pp. 498–540. Leiden, E.J. Brill

—— 2000b. Women in Daoism. In *Daoism Handbook*, ed. Livia Kohn, pp. 384–412. Leiden, E.J. Brill

Dikötter, Frank, ed. 1997. *The Construction of Racial Identities in China and Japan: Historical and Contemporary Perspectives.* Honolulu, University of Hawai'i Press

Eliade, Mircea. 1961. *The Sacred and the Profane: The Nature of Religion.* New York, Harper & Row.

Engelhardt, Ute. 2000. Longevity Techniques and Chinese Medicine. In *Daoism Handbook*, ed. Livia Kohn, pp. 74–108. Leiden, E.J. Brill

Eskildsen, Stephen. 1998. *Early Taoist Asceticism.* Albany, State University of New York Press

Esposito, Monica. 2000. Daoism in the Qing (1644–1911). In *Daoism Handbook*, ed. Livia Kohn, pp. 623–58. Leiden, E.J. Brill

Fernández-Armesto, Felipe. 2000. *Civilizations.* Toronto, Key Porter Books

Field, Stephen L. 1997. In a Calabash: A Chinese Myth of Origins. *Talus*, 9/10:52–97

—— 2001a. Prologue: The Calabash Scrolls. In *Daoism and Ecology*, ed. N.J. Girardot, James Miller and Liu Xiaogan, pp. lxv–lxxiii. Cambridge, MA, Harvard University Center for the Study of World Religions/ Harvard University Press

—— 2001b. In Search of Dragons: The Folk Ecology of Fengshui. In *Daoism and Ecology*, ed. N.J. Girardot, James Miller and Liu Xiaogan, pp. 185–200. Cambridge, MA, Harvard University Center for the Study of World Religions/Harvard University Press

Foucault, Michel. 1995. *Discipline and Punish*, trans. Alan Sheridan. New York, Vintage Books

Geil, William E. 1926. *The Sacred Five of China*. London, Houghton Mifflin.

Girardot, N.J. 1983. *Myth and Meaning in Early Taoism*. Berkeley, University of California Press

Girardot, N.J., James Miller and Liu Xiaogan, eds. 2001. *Daoism and Ecology*. Cambridge, MA, Harvard University Center for the Study of World Religions/Harvard University Press

Graham, Angus Charles. 1986a. *Disputers of the Tao*. La Salle, Open Court

—— 1986b. *Chuang-tzu: The Seven Inner Chapters and Other Writings from the Book of Chuang-tzu*. London, Allan & Unwin

Granet, Marcel. 1975 [1922]. *The Religion of the Chinese People*. Oxford, Basil Blackwell

Hahn, Thomas. 2000. Daoist Sacred Sites. In *Daoism Handbook*, ed. Livia Kohn, pp. 683–708. Leiden, E.J. Brill

—— 2001. Daoist Notions of Wilderness. In *Daoism and Ecology*, ed. N.J. Girardot, James Miller and Liu Xiaogan, pp. 201–16. Cambridge, MA, Harvard University Center for the Study of World Religions/Harvard University Press

Hardy, Julia M. 1998. Influential Western Interpretations of the *Tao-te-ching*. In *Lao-tzu and the Tao-te-ching*, ed. Livia Kohn and Michael LaFargue, pp. 165–88. Albany, NY, State University of New York Press

Harper, Donald. 1987. The Sexual Arts of Ancient China as Described in a Manuscript of the Second Century BC. *Harvard Journal of Asiatic Studies*, 47:539–93

Hawkes, David. 1959. *Ch'u Tz'u: The Songs of the South*. Oxford, Oxford University Press

Healing Tao. 2002. *Dark Room Enlightenment: Lesser, Greater and Greatest Kan and Li*. Thailand, Universal Tao Center. Internet: http://www.universal-tao.com/dark_room/DarkRoomTaoist.pdf

Hendrischke, Barbara. 2000. Early Daoist Movements. In *Daoism Handbook*, ed. Livia Kohn, pp. 134–64. Leiden, E.J. Brill

Hoff, Benjamin. 1982. *The Tao of Pooh*. New York, E P. Dutton

James, William. 1999 [1902]. *The Varieties of Religious Experience*. New York, Random House

Jung Jae-Seo. 2000. Daoism in Korea, trans. James Miller. In *Daoism Handbook*, ed. Livia Kohn, pp. 792–830. Leiden, E.J. Brill

Kaptchuk, Ted J. 1983. *The Net that Has No Weaver: Understanding Chinese Medicine.* New York, Congdon & Weed

Kjellberg, Paul and Philip J. Ivanhoe, eds. 1996. *Essays on Skepticism, Relativism and Ethics in the Zhuangzi.* Albany, State University of New York Press

Kleeman, Terry F. 1998. *Great Perfection: Religion and Ethnicity in a Chinese Millennial Kingdom.* Honolulu, University of Hawai'I Press

―― 2002. Ethnic Identity and Daoist Identity in Traditional China. In *Daoist Identity: History, Lineage and Ritual,* ed. Livia Kohn and Harold D. Roth, pp. 23–38. Honolulu: University of Hawai'i Press

Kobayashi Masayoshi. 1987. *Rikuchō Dōkyōshi kenkyū.* Tokyo, Sōbunsha

Kohn, Livia. 1992. *Early Chinese Mysticism.* Princeton, Princeton University Press

―― 1993. *The Taoist Experience.* Albany, State University of New York Press

―― 1994. The Five Precepts of the Venerable Lord. *Monumenta Serica,* 42:171–215

―― 1995. *Laughing at the Dao.* Princeton, Princeton University Press

―― 1998. The Beginnings and Cultural Characteristics of East Asian Millenarianism. *Japanese Religions,* 23:1 and 2:29–51

Kohn, Livia, ed. 2000. *Daoism Handbook.* Leiden, E.J. Brill

Kohn, Livia. 2001. *Daoism and Chinese Culture.* Cambridge, MA, Three Pines Press

Kohn, Livia and Michael LaFargue, eds. 1998. *Lao-tzu and the Tao-Te-Ching.* Albany, State University of New York Press

Kohn, Livia and Russell Kirkland. 2000. Daoism in the Tang (618–907). In *Daoism Handbook,* ed. Livia Kohn. Leiden, E.J. Brill

Kohn, Livia and Harold Roth, eds. 2002. *Daoist Identity: History, Lineage and Ritual.* Honolulu, University of Hawai'i Press

Kryukov, Vassili. 1995. Symbols of Power and Communication in Pre-Confucian China (On the Anthropology of *De*): Preliminary Assumptions. *Bulletin of the School of Oriental and African Studies,* 58:314–33

LaChapelle, Doris. 1988. *Sacred Land, Sacred Sex – Rapture of the Deep: Concerning Deep Ecology and Celebrating Life.* Silverton, CO, Fine Hill Arts

LaFargue, Michael. 1994. *Tao and Method.* Albany, State University of New York Press

―― 2001. Nature as Part of Human Culture in Daoism. In *Daoism and Ecology,* ed. N.J. Girardot, James Miller and Liu Xiaogan, pp. 45–60. Cambridge, MA, Harvard University Center for the Study of World Religions/Harvard University Press

Lai Chi-tim. 2001. The Daoist Concept of Central Harmony. In *Daoism and Ecology,* ed. N.J. Girardot, James Miller and Liu Xiaogan, pp. 95–111. Cambridge, MA, Harvard University Center for the Study of World Religions/Harvard University Press

Landt, Frank A. 1994. *Die fünfheiligen Berge Chinas. Ihre Bedeutung und Bewertung in der Ch'ing-Dynastie.* Berlin, Köster

Little, Stephen, *et al.* 2001. *Taoism and the Arts of China.* Chicago, Art Institute of Chicago

Liu Feng.1998. *Taoism as an Indigenous Chinese Religion,* trans. Lao An, *et al.,* revised An Zengcai. Jinan, Shandong Friendship Publishing House

Liu Xiaogan. 2001. Non-Action and the Environment Today: A Conceptual and Applied Study of Laozi's Philosophy. In *Daoism and Ecology,* ed. N.J. Girardot, James Miller and Liu Xiaogan, pp. 315–39. Cambridge, MA, Harvard University Center for the Study of World Religions/Harvard University Press

MacInnis, Donald E. 1989. *Religion in China Today: Policy and Practice.* Maryknoll, Orbis Books

Mair, Victor. 1994. *Wandering on the Way: Early Taoist Tales and Parables of Chuang Tzu.* New York, Bantam Books

Masuo Shin'ichirō. 2000. Daoism in Japan trans. Livia Kohn. In *Daoism Handbook,* ed. Livia Kohn, pp. 821–42. Leiden, E.J. Brill

Mather, Richard B. 1979. K'ou Ch'ien-chih and the Taoist Theocracy at the Northern Wei Court, 425–51. In *Facets of Taoism,* ed. Holmes Welch and Anna Seidel, pp. 103–22. New Haven, Yale University Press

Meyer, Jeffrey F. 2001. Salvation in the Garden. In *Daoism and Ecology,* ed. N.J. Girardot, James Miller and Liu Xiaogan, pp. 219–36. Cambridge, MA, Harvard University Center for the Study of World Religions/Harvard University Press

Miller, James. 2002. J.J. Clarke's 'The Tao of the West' and the Emerging Discipline of Daoist Studies. *Religious Studies Review,* forthcoming

Munakata Kiyohiko. 1991. *Sacred Mountains in Chinese Art.* Urbana, University of Illinois Press

Naquin, Susan, and Chun-Fang Yü, eds. 1992. *Pilgrims and Sacred Sites in China.* Berkeley, University of California Press

Needham, Joseph. 1956. *Science and Civilisation in China,* vol. 2. Cambridge, Cambridge University Press

Nickerson, Peter. 2000. The Southern Celestial Masters. In *Daoism Handbook,* ed. Livia Kohn. Leiden, E.J. Brill

—— 2002. 'Opening the Way': Exorcism, Travel, and Soteriology in Early Daoist Mortuary Practice and Its Antecedents. In *Daoist Identity: History, Lineage and Ritual,* ed. Livia Kohn and Harold D. Roth, pp. 58–80. Honolulu, University of Hawai'i Press

Paper, Jordan. 1995. *The Spirits are Drunk: Comparative Approaches to Chinese Religion.* Albany, State University of New York Press

—— 2001. 'Daoism' and 'Deep Ecology': Fantasy and Potentiality. In *Daoism and Ecology,* ed. N.J. Girardot, James Miller and Liu Xiaogan, pp. 3–22. Cambridge, MA, Harvard University Center for the Study of World Religions/Harvard University Press

Penny, Benjamin. 2000. Immortality and Transcendence. In *Daoism Handbook,* ed. Livia Kohn, pp. 109–33. Leiden, E.J. Brill

Porkert, Manfred. 1979. *Biographie d'un Taoïste Légendaire: Tcheou Tseu-yang*. Mémoires de l'Institut des Hautes Études Chinoises, Vol. X. Paris, Collège de France

Porter, Bill. 1993. *The Road To Heaven: Encounters with Chinese Hermits*. San Francisco, Mercury House

Pregadio, Fabrizio. 2000. Elixirs and Alchemy. In *Daoism Handbook*, ed. Livia Kohn, pp. 165–95. Leiden, E.J. Brill

Raphals, Lisa. 2001. Metic Intelligence or Responsible Non-Action? Further Reflection on the *Zhuangzi, Daode jing* and *Neiye*. In *Daoism and Ecology*, ed. N.J. Girardot, James Miller and Liu Xiaogan, pp. 305–14. Cambridge, MA, Harvard University Center for the Study of World Religions/Harvard University Press

Robinet, Isabelle. 1993. *The Mao-shan Tradition of Great Purity*. Berkeley, University of California Press

—— 1995. *Introduction à l'alchimie intérieure taoïste: De l'unité et de la multiplicité*. Paris, Éditions Cerf

—— 1997. *Taoism: Growth of a Religion*, trans. Phyllis Brooks. Stanford, Stanford University Press

—— 1998. Later Commentaries: Textual and Syncretistic Interpretations. In *Lao-tzu and the Tao-te-ching*, ed. Livia Kohn and Michael LaFargue, pp. 119–42. Albany, NY, State University of New York Press

—— 2000. Shangqing–Highest Clarity. In *Daoism Handbook*, ed. Livia Kohn, pp. 196–224. Leiden, E.J. Brill

Robson, James. 1995. The polymorphous space of the southern march-mount. *Cahiers d'Extrême-Asie*, 8:221-64

Roth, Harold. 1999. *Original Tao*. New York, NY, Columbia University Press

Schafer, Edward. 1977. *Pacing the Void: Tang Approaches to the Stars*. Berkeley, University of California Press

Schipper, Kristofer Marinus. 1993. *The Taoist Body*. Berkeley, University of California Press

—— 2001. Daoist Ecology: The Inner Transformation. A Study of the Precepts of the Early Daoist Ecclesia. In *Daoism and Ecology*, ed. N.J. Girardot, James Miller and Liu Xiaogan, pp. 79–94. Cambridge, MA, Harvard University Center for the Study of World Religions/Harvard University Press

Schwartz, Benjamin. 1985. *The World of Thought in Ancient China*. Cambridge, Belknap Press

Seidel, Anna. 1969. *La divinisation du Lao-tseu dans le taoïsme des Han*. Paris, École Française d'Extrême-Orient

—— 1987. Post-Mortem Immortality, or: The Taoist Resurrection of the Body. In *Gilgul: Essays on Transformation, Revolution and Permanence in the History of Religions*, ed. S. Shaked, D. Shulman and G.G. Stroumsa, pp. 223–37. Leiden, E.J. Brill

Seigler, Elijah. 2003. The History and Practice of Daoism in North America. Ph.D. Dissertation. Santa Barbara, University of California, Santa Barbara

Selin, Helaine, ed. 2003. *Nature Across Cultures: Non-Western Views of Nature and Environment.* The Hague, Kluwer Academic Publishers

Shiga, Ichiko. 2002. Manifestations of Lüzu in Modern Guangdong and Hong Kong: The Rise and Growth of Spirit-Writing Cults. In *Daoist Identity: History, Lineage and Ritual,* ed. Livia Kohn and Harold D. Roth, pp. 185–209. Honolulu, University of Hawai'i Press

Sivin, Nathan. 1995. *Medicine, Philosophy and Religion in Ancient China.* Aldershot, Variorum

Skar, Lowell and Fabrizio Pregadio. 2000. Inner Alchemy (*Neidan*). In *Daoism Handbook,* ed. Livia Kohn, pp. 464–97. Leiden, E.J. Brill

Strickmann, Michel. 1979. On the Alchemy of T'ao Hung-ching. In *Facets of Taoism: Essays in Chinese Religion,* ed. Holmes Welch and Anna Seidel, pp. 123–92. New Haven, CT, Yale University Press

Surin, Kenneth. 1998. Liberation. In *Critical Terms for Religious Studies,* ed. Mark C. Taylor. Chicago, University of Chicago Press

Tsui, Bartholomew P. 1991. *Taoist Tradition and Change: The Story of the Complete Perfection Sect in Hong Kong.* Hong Kong, Christian Study Centre on Chinese Religion and Culture

Unschuld, Paul U. 1085. *Medicine in China: A History of Ideas.* Berkeley, University of California Press

Vervoorn, Aat. 1990. Cultural Strata of Hua Shan, the Holy Peak of the West. *Monumenta Serica,* 39:1–30

Waley, Arthur. 1931. *The Travels of an Alchemist.* London: George Routledge & Sons, Ltd.

—— 1955. *The Nine Songs: A Study of Shamanism in China.* London, Allen & Unwin

Ware, James R. 1966. *Alchemy, Medicine and Religion in the China of A.D. 320: The Nei p'ien of Ko Hung (Pao-p'u tzu).* Cambridge, MA, MIT Press

Wile, Douglas. 1992. *Art of the Bedchamber: The Chinese Sexology Classics Including Women's Solo Meditation Texts.* Albany State University of New York Press

Wong, Eva. 1992. *Cultivating Stillness: A Taoist Manual for Transforming Body and Mind.* Boston, Shambhala

Yamada, Toshiaki. 2000. The Lingbao School. In *Daoism Handbook,* ed. Livia Kohn, pp. 225–55. Leiden, E.J. Brill

Yao, Ted. Quanzhen – Complete Perfection. In *Daoism Handbook,* ed. Livia Kohn, pp. 567–93. Leiden, E.J. Brill

Yu, David C., trans. 2000. *History of Chinese Daoism,* vol. 1, ed. Qing Xitai. Lanham, MD, University Press of America, Inc.

Zhang Jiyu. 2001. A Declaration of the Chinese Daoist Association on Global Ecology. In *Daoism and Ecology,* ed. N.J. Girardot, James Miller and Liu Xiaogan, pp. 261–72. Cambridge, MA, Harvard University Center for the Study of World Religions/Harvard University Press

Index

Abrahamic religions, temporal framework
    of 107–108
Addiss, Stephen 55
alchemy
    immortality
        elixir of, first record of ingestion of
            xvi, 108
        fascination with 108
        time, cyclical and linear aspects of
            108–109
    internal (neidan)
        'cinnabar fields' in body 113
        gods, visualization of 112
        jing energy, and creation of immortal
            embryo 113–114
        lead and mercury (yang-yin),
            allegorical understanding of 113
        linear cosmogeny (yin-yang), reversal
            of 113
    outer (waidan) 'laboratory'
        elixir, concoction of as religious
            endeavour 110–111
        Ge Hong, exponent of 111
        linear cosmogony, (yin-yang), reversal
            of 109–110
        mercury, ingestion of as fatal
            111–112
    tradition, independent development of
        108–109
    see also Complete Perfection, Way of;
        transformation
Allan, Sarah 76, 140–141
Ames, Roger 38
Analects (Confucius) 39–40
analogical thinking see correlative thinking

animals, as bearers of transcendence 148
art, and nature
    spontaneity, Daoist aesthetic of
        calligraphy 150
        landscape painting 150
        wilderness and domestic space,
            complementarity of 150–151
Aslaksen, Helmer 23
astral journeys see under light practices
Austin, J.L. 39
Axial Age 36, 37, 90

Benn, Charles 128, 129, 131, 149
Big Dipper (constellation) 9, 50, 98–101,
    104–106
bigu (fasting) 97–98
Biographies of Divine Transcendents
    (Shenxian zhuan) (Ge Hong) 81,
    111
Bo He 149
body
    body gods, visualization of 65, 101–104
    food for ('five grains') 97
    human physiology, as central theme of
        spirituality 53–54
    see also correlative thinking, and the
        body; longevity practices; qi
Bokenkamp, Stephen 70, 78, 136
Book of Burial (Zangshu) 146
Book of Changes (Yijing or Zhouyi)
    109–110
Buddhism
    brought to China 2
    and Falun dafa 68
    and religious syncretism 3, 11, 116

and ritual of purification 51–52
texts and talismans, application for
    salvation of all beings 10
see also Lingbao movement
Buddhist-Daoist rivalry
    Daoist theocracy movement 85–87
    'earlier as better' attitude, and cosmic
        history 119–120
    first formal debates xvii
    monasteries 10, 117–118
    and myth of Laozi's journey west 85–86,
        117–118
    supremacy, Daoist during Tang dynasty
        2
Bumbacher, Stephan P. 72

calendar, Chinese
    apocalypse, expectation of 78
    lunar and solar elements, festivals based
        on 23
    sixty-year cycle 22–23
Campany, Robert F. 146, 148
Cao Cao xvii
Capra, Fritjof 64
caves (dong)
    and communication with Heaven 47
    physical aspects 47–48
    revelation of texts in 48, 148–150
    subterranean networks, symbolism of
        149–150
Celestial Masters, Way of
    bureaucratic religion 94
    classical Daoism 2, 8–9
    ending of xvi
    expiation of sins 51
    founding of xvi, 2, 8, 83
    Laozi
        solidification of central role of 81–82
        Zhang Daoling's 'awesome covenant'
            with 8–9, 26
    lineage of supplanted 95
    and messianic interventions 82, 83–84
    ordination of Highest Clarity priests,
        authority over xvii, xviii, 95
    organization of 8
    precepts of, and concerned for natural
        environment 49, 141–142
    registers of spirits, for petitions 9, 25,
        26–27, 127–128
    sexual initiation rite of 68, 69–70, 84
    Xiang'er commentary, origination of
        135–136
Central Scripture of the Nine Perfected 102
Chan, Alan, K.L. 133
*Chart of Being in Accord with Good
    Fortune (Ruiying tu)* 148

Chenivesse, Sandrine 130, 149
Chia, Mantak 33
Chiang Kai-Shek 13
Chinese characters
    pronunciation of xii–xiii
    and spirit-communication 122–123
    systems for representing xiii
Chinese Communist Party, as atheist 87
Chinese script, use of for Daoist texts 21
Ching, Julia 89
Chinggis Khan, meeting with Qiu
    Changchun (Chuji) xviii, 3, 12,
    115–116
Chu ci (Songs of Chu) (Qu Yuan) xvi, 50,
    97
cinnabar, refining of 110
classical Daoism 1–2, 7–11, 41–42
Cohn, Norman 78–79
communication
    caves, symbolism of 47–48
    Dao, as pathway between humans, earth
        and Heaven 42, 46–47
    humans, role in promotion of
        harmonious communication 48–49
    mediumship 50
    public rituals 50–52
    shamanism 49–50
Complete Perfection, Way of
    civil life, incorporation of Daoism into
        12–13
    Dragon Gate branch, establishment of
        xviii, 13, 115–116
    flourishing of, under Qiu Chuji 12
    founding of xvii, 2–3, 11–12, 114–115
    internal alchemy, and energy practices
        12, 28, 29, 68, 91–92
    lay movements, flourishing of 13
    Lüzu cults 126–127
    main form of Daoism in mainland China
        today 118
    mind-body, cultivation of 116–117
    monasticism, establishment of 28–29,
        115–117
    three teachings, harmonization of 3, 11,
        116
    see also alchemy
*Complete Writings of Patriarch Lü (Lüzu
    quanshu)* 127
*Comprehensive Treatise on the Regulation
    of the Spirit in Accord with the Four
    Seasons (Siji tiaoshen dalun)* 59
Confucianism
    Analects, and shared pleasures of
        teaching and learning 39–40
    cultural markers, reestablishment of 38
    de, as moral virtue 76

as foundation of social, economic, and
    political life 40
harmony, and hierarchy 39
inherent conservatism of 40
morality, understanding by analogy with
    nature 141
normalization of five cardinal
    relationships 38
ritual and aesthetic, recovery of 38–39
Confucius
    dates of xvi
    instructed by Laozi 4
    morality, understanding by analogy with
        nature 141
contemporary Daoism 1, 3, 13–15
correlative thinking, and the body
    body/state/cosmos, analogous
        functioning of 60–61
    deities, therapeutic function of 64–65
    dimensions of reality, resonances
        between 63–64
    five phases (elements)
        cycle of control 62
        cycle of generation 62
        phases of cycles, and process of
            extension (tui) 62–63
    goodness, medical definition of 61
    versus logical thinking 60
    see also light practices, astral journeys
cosmography, transformation as purpose
    of 107–108
creativity, as Dao ix
Crouching Tiger, Hidden Dragon (film)
    (Ang Lee) 66
Cultural Revolution, impact of 3, 87
culture, understanding Chinese x–xii

Dao see Way
Daode jing (Scripture of the Way and its
    Power)
    bamboo-strip version xvi, 4, 30, 133
    as canonical scripture 48–52
    and Dao as (transcendent) cosmic
        principle 41
    'earlier as better' attitude, and cosmic
        history 120
    earliest versions, dates of ix
    and environmentalism 139
    form of 133
    hymn to Dao as mother of the universe
        41–44
    intellectual values of, and Way as
        manifested in person of Laozi 44–45
    interpretations of
        'Collected Interpretations' (Dong
            Sijing) 132–133

Heshang Gong commentary
    134–135
influential western 137
and language 132–133
Wang Bi commentary xvii, 4,
    133–134
Xiang'er commentary xvii, 82,
    135–136
jing energy, conservation of 112
Laozi, composer of 5–6
non-assertive action (wuwei) 41
proto-Daoism period 1–2
qi, as key to maintaining life 55
recitation of 81
silk cloth version xvi, 4, 30, 133
as standing for whole of Daoism in
    Western imagination 30–31
transmission of, and myth of Laozi's
    journey west 85–86, 117–118
two-part structure of (Daojing and
    Dejing) 4–5
Way (Dao), and its Power (De) xvi, 4–5
Daoism and Chinese Culture (Kohn) x
Daoism Handbook (Kohn) xiv
Daoist Canon (Daozang) 128–129
Daoist Cultivation (Komjathy) xiv
Daoist theocracy movement xvii
    Buddhist rivalry 85–87
    Daoist precepts and practices, integration
        of 84–85
daojia, school of the Way (Philosophical
    Daoism) 17
daojiao, traditions of the Way (Religious
    Daoism) 17
daoshu, arts of the Way (Daoist practices)
    17
Daoyin tu (gymnastics chart) 71
'Dark Learning' (Xuanxue) school of
    intellectuals 133
Darwin, Charles 19
Davis, Edward L. 11, 25, 50, 95, 126
de see power
De Bruyn, Pierre-Henry 87
De Groot, J.J.M. 20
De Woskin, Kenneth J. 108, 130
Dean, Kenneth 52, 130
Declaration of the Chinese Daoist
    Association 142
Declarations of the Perfected (Zhen'gao)
    95
Deleuze, Gilles 120
Deng Xiaoping xviii, 14
Despeux, Catherine 125, 130, 148
destiny (ming), negotiating with 6
    cultivation of body, and reciprocal nature
        of cosmos 91

and cultivation of one's nature 90–91
and longevity, cultivation of 91
and revolutionary social movement of Way of Great Peace 91
dong *see* caves
Dong Sijing 132–133
Dragon Gate (Longmen), establishment of xviii, 13, 115–116
Dunhuang caves excavation 82, 148

Early Chinese Mysticism (Kohn) 56
Eckhart, Meister 56
'Eight Immortals' 72–73
elements *see* five phases
embodiment, emphasis on as challenge to Western academic intellectualism 34–35
Englehardt, Ute 147, 148
Eskildsen, Stephen 97, 145
Esposito, Monica 127
exorcism 126
expansion and contraction principle (yin-yang) 59

Falun dafa organization 67–68
Fengdu (underworld) 98–99, 131, 149
fengshui 145–146
festivals, and Chinese calendar 23
Field, Stephen L. 146, 147
Fifteen Discourses (Wang Zhe) 116, 117
five phases (elements)
    and authority to rule 76–78
    cycle of control 62
    cycle of generation 62
    extension (tui), process of 62–63
    five organs, and five spirits 64, 102–104, 135
    five talismans 130
    formalization of system of xvi
Foucault, Michel 53
founder, none of Daoism ix
fugang (absorption of light) 97
Fung Loy Kok 67, 122
funghi, numinous 147

Ge Chaofu xvii, 10
Ge Hong xvii, 26, 49, 81, 146, 148
Geil, William E. 143
geomancy *see* fengshui
Al-Ghazzali 56
Girardot, Miller and Liu xiii
Girardot, N.J. 147
gourds 147–148
Graham, Angus Charles 72, 148
Granet, Marcel 20
Great Bear *see* Big Dipper

Great Clarity (Taiqing) movement xvii, 110–111
Great Peace, Way of
    classical Daoism 8
    cyclical cosmology, rejection of 80
    expiation of sins 51
    heaven/earth/human, harmony between, and human prosperity 79, 142–143
    inherited guilt (cheng-fu), and need for revolutionary new order 79–80
    Taiping jing (Scripture of Great Peace) 79
    Yellow Turbans 8, 78, 80, 84
Great Proletarian Cultural Revolution xviii
grottos *see* caves
Guanzi texts 7
Gui Xi 150
Guo Xiang 6
Guodian excavations xvi, 4, 30, 133

Haedong chōndo rok (Han Muwae) 2
Hahn, Thomas 48, 144–145, 149, 151
Hall, David 38
Han dynasty
    fall of 76–78, 80–82
    Former xvi
    Later xvi–xvii, 108
Hanyu pinyin (Pinyin) system xiii
Harper, Donald 68
Hawkes, David 50
Healing Tao organization (Mantak Chia) 104–105
Hendrischke, Barbara 82
herbalism, Chinese 147–148
Heshang Gong commentary *(Daode jing)* 134–135
Highest Clarity, Way of
    interiorization process 94, 104
    Maoshan Daoism 95
    personal self-cultivation, emphasis on 9
    texts, revelation of 9, 50, 94–95, 124, 125
    see also light practices; Shangqing Daoism
historical approach, to Daoism x
Hong Kong xviii
Huang-Lao naturalistic philosophy 76
Huang Ziyang 72
Huangdi neijing suwen (Simple Questons on the Yellow Emperor's Internal Classic) 61
Huxley, Aldous 32
Huxley, Thomas 19

I-Ching *see* Book of Changes

identity, Daoist
    and Chinese identity, assertion of unity of
        disunity, and Warring States period 18
        nationalism, rise of 18–19
        Qin state, and unification of central
            China 18
    Chinese script, use of for Daoist texts 21
    construction of definitions of 16
    daojia, school of the Way ('Philosophical
        Daoism') 17
    daojiao, traditions of the Way ('Religious
        Daoism) 17
    daoshu, arts of the Way (Daoist
        practices) 17
    embodiment, emphasis on as challenge to
        Western academic intellectualism
        34–35
    non-Chinese religion, Daoism as 21
    reasons for asserting 34
    understanding of 16
    see also lineages of transmission; religion;
        universal path, Daoism as
immortals see perfected persons
inward training see Neiye
Ishimpo (Japanese medical compendium)
    69
Ivanhoe, Philip J. 119

James, William 56
Jaspers, Karl 36
Jin dynasty xviii, 115
Jindan qiuzheng pian (Seeking Instruction
    on the Golden Elixir) 70
jing energy
    conservation of 112
    and creation of immortal embryo
        113–114
    internal alchemy, and cultivation of jing
        68–69
    vital energy (qi), training to produce 7,
        55
    see also qi
Jiudan shanghua taijing zhong jijing 99
Jiuzhen zhongjing 102, 103
Jung, Jae-Seo 1, 97

Kirkland, Russell 57, 95
Kjellberg, Paul 119
Kleeman, Terry 27–28
Kobayashi, Masayoshi 82
Kohn, Livia x, xiv, 42, 56, 69, 77, 78, 80,
    83, 86, 95, 97, 116, 147
Komjathy, Louis xiv
Korea, Daoism in 1, 2, 97
Kou Qianzhi xvii, 84–85
Kruykov, Vassili 75

Kublai xviii, 12, 115, 118
Kunlun 147

Lady Wei, and revelation of Highest Clarity
    texts 9, 50, 94–95, 124, 125
LaFargue, Michael 132, 140
Lai Chi-tim 49, 80
Landt, Frank A. 143
Laozi
    and Buddha, relative status of 86
    cult of 81–82
    Daode jing, composer of 4–6
    identified as archivist 81, 82
    and myth of journey west 85–86,
        117–118
    Way, as manifested in person of 44–45
    Way of Celestial Masters, central role in
        81–82
    Zhang Daoling, 'awesome covenant'
        with 8–9, 26
Laozi (the Old Master) 4
Lee, Ang 66
Li Er (Laozi) 82
Li Hongzhi 68
light practices
    astral journeys
        Big Dipper, adept's journey to
            98–101, 104–106
        dead ancestors, liberation of 99, 101
        death as possibility for
            transformation 99–100
        embryonic knots concept 99
        stars, as symbolism of 98–99
    body gods, visualization of
        bodies, as residence for gods 101–102
        five bodily organs, correspondences of
            102
        journeying (to stars), as internal
            (meditative) process 101–102
        Method of the Nine Perfected
            technique 102–104
        visualization text, example of 102–104
    cosmic light, absorption as food 97–98
    hagiographies, encouragement from
        96–97
    salutation to the sun 96
    transfiguration into celestial body of pure
        light , goal as 96–97
lineages of transmission
    'awesome covenant', Zhan Daoling's
        with Laozi 8–9, 26
    content of 29
    Daoist priests, important function of
        128–129
    ethnic-based definitions, avoidance of
        27–28

monasticism 28–29
  priestly ordinations, system of 26–27
  registers for spiritual petitions, and
    Daoists as functionaries 27–28
Lingbao movement (Numinous Treasure)
  Buddhism and Daoism, encounter
    between 9–10, 93
  classical Daoism 2, 9–10
  rituals, standardization of 10, 14,
    51–52, 129
  scriptures xvii, 48, 123–125
  talismanic objects and texts 9–10
Little, Stephen 150
Liu Dabin xviii, 95
Liu Feng 108
Liu Xiaogan 118, 140
Liu Xin 77–78
Lizong, Emperor of Southern Song dynasty
  95
*Lofty Message of Streams and Mountains
  (Linquan gaozhi ji)* 150
Lombardo, Stephen and Stanley 55
longevity practices
  and animals 148
  Daoism and sex
    jing, conservation of 68–69
    reproduction, cosmic significance of
      70–71
    sexual initiation rite (of Celestial
      Masters), and 'sexual vampirism'
      69–70
  longevity and transcendence, relationship
    between 71–72, 73
  Qigong, circulation and stimulation of qi,
    as aim of 67–68
  religion and health, connection between
    65–66
  Taiji quan (Tai-Chi) 66–67
Lord Lao (*Taishan Laojun;* the deified
  Laozi) 84
Lü Dongbin 11–12, 73, 114
Lu Xiujing xvii, 10, 52, 94–95, 142
Lüzu cults 126–127

Ma Yu 115
Macao xviii
MacInnis, Donald E. 87
Mair, Victor 119
Mandarin Chinese xii, xiii
Mao Zedong 13
Maoshan Daoism 95
Map of the True form of the Five Peaks
  131
martial arts *see* Qigong; Taiji quan
Master who Embraces Spirituality, The (Ge
  Hong) 111

Master Zhuang (Zhuangi) 6
Mawangdui excavations xvi, 4, 30, 68, 71,
  133
medicine, Chinese
  correlative thinking, and diagnosis of
    diseases 62–63
  microcosm, body as 59
  pathology, and blockages in circulation
    of qi 58
  vital energy, continuous exchange of (yin-
    yang) 58–59
mediumism
  and spirit-possession 50
  and spirit-writing cults 125–127
  texts, revelation of 9, 50, 94, 124, 125
mercury, refining of 110
messianism
  messiah, meaning of 82–83
  religious and political elements, fusion
    of 83–84
  religious authority of ruler, ideological
    tool for 82
  'seed people', cosmic redemption of
    83–84
  textual evidence for 83
  see also Daoist theocracy movement
Meyer, Jeffrey F. 144
millenarianism
  Chinese imperial power and Daoist
    movements, relationship between
    78
  Laozi, cult of 81–82
  linear *versus* cyclical time 78–79
  modern academic meaning of 78
  Way of Orthodox Unity 80–81
  see also Great Peace, Way of
Ming dynasty xviii, 79
  civil life, incorporation of Daoism into
    12–13
  flourishing of Daoism during 3, 86–87
modern Daoism 1, 2–3, 11–13
monasticism
  Complete Perfection, Way of xviii,
    28–29, 115–117
  influence of Buddhism 85
morality
  goodness, medical definition of 61
  popular 127
  understanding by analogy with nature
    141
Mount Fengdu 131, 149
Mount Mao, and establishment of
  Maoshan Daoism 95
Mount Qingcheng (Grotto of the Celestial
  Master) 47, 144
Mount Tai 108

Mount Wudang (Wudang shan), promotion of as Daoist centre 12–13, 66, 144

mountains
  and eremitical tradition 145
  five sacred 143–144
  nature and religion, shifting relationship between 144–145
  religious symbolism, levels of 145
  temples, construction of 144

Moy Lin-Shin 66

Mr. Lü's Springs and Autumns (Lüshi chunqiu) 60

Munakata Kiyohiko 144

mysticism, and Daoism 56– 57

Mysticism and Kingship in China: The Heart of Chinese Wisdom (Ching) 89

nationalism, rise of Chinese
  People's Republic of China, as nation state 21
  Qing dynasty, overthrow of and upsurge of Han nationalism 19–20
  single Chinese people, impression of 20–21
  Yellow Empire, myth of 19–20
  'yellow race', and cultural superiority 19

Nature Across Cultures: Non-Western Views of Nature and Environment (Selin) xiv

nature (ziran)
  and alchemy 146
  and dwellings of the immortals
    animals, as bearers of transcendence 148
    vegetation, interest in and Chinese herbalism 147–148
  environmental protection, and human conduct 141–143
  as model for the Dao 139
  and wuwei as 'action as non-action' 140
  see also art, and nature; caves; sacred space

Needham, Joseph 62, 77, 137

Neiye (inward training)
  longevity practices, forerunner of 7
  vital energy (qi), cultivation of 7, 55
  see also alchemy, internal

Nickerson, Peter 25, 27, 83, 84

Northern Bushel *see* Big Dipper

Northern Celestial Masters *see* Daoist theocracy movement

Northern Wei dynasty xvii

Numinous Treasure, Way of *see* Lingbao movement

One Hundred and Eighty Precepts (Yibaibashi jie) 141–142

oracle bones 75

Oral Instructions Declared by the Celestial Master of Orthodox Unity to Zhao Sheng (Zhengyi tianshi gao Zhao Sheng koujue) 83

organs, deities corresponding to 64, 102–104, 107–108, 135

Orthodox Unity, Way of *see* Celestial Masters, Way of

Paper, Jordan 139

peaches 147

Penglai islands, dwelling of the immortals 147

Penny, Benjamin 72, 108–109, 147

People's Daily 87

People's Republic of China xviii

Perennial Philosophy 32–33, 56–57

Perfect Text of Numinous Treasure in Five Tablets 130

perfected persons (zhenren) 5, 24–25, 71–73, 96–97, 147–148

Perfected Purple Yang (Zhou Yishan), hagiography of 96, 149–150

performative utterances, theory of (Austin) 39

phases, five *see* five phases

pine trees 147

Pinyin (Hanyu pinyin) system xiii

pole star, and importance of Big Dipper 98

Porkert, Manfred 96

Porter, Bill 145

power (*de*)
  Five Virtues, and authority to rule 76–78
  as manifestation of the Way (Dao) 45–46, 75
  and metaphor of cultivation 45–46
  and non-action (wuwei) 45
  self-transformative of universe 46
  as virtue, and mandate of heaven (tianming) 75–76, 89–90

Pregadio, Fabrizio 108, 110, 113

priests
  in Daoist theocracy 85
  and expiation of sins 51
  jiao rituals (offerings) 10
  lineage of ordination 2
  and registers of spirits, for petitions 9, 25, 26–27, 127–129
  and spirit-possession 50
  and spirit-writing cults 126

projection and reception (yin-yang principle) 59

proto-Daoism 1–2, 4–7, 56, 57, 118–119

qi (breath of life)
  biospiritual practices 57
  blockages, and pathology 57–58, 59
  cultivation of 55
  expansion-contraction principle 54–55
  internal alchemy, and energy practices 12, 28, 29, 68, 91–92
  and light, as subtlest form of food 97–98
  One, and essential energy (jingqi) of all life 134–135
  pre- and post-natal 57–58
  yin and yang, cosmic and human significance of 58–59
  see also jing energy; longevity practices; Qigong; Taiji Quan
Qigong 3, 67–68
Qin dynasty 108
Qin shi huangdi (First Qin Emperor), date of xvi
Qing dynasty
  Buddhism, favouring of 86
  and flourishing of lay movements 13
  morality books 127
  overthrow of, and upsurge of Han nationalism 19–20
  popular texts, publication of 3
  and spirit-writing cults 126
  taiji quan (Tai Chi) and Qigong (Ch'i-kung), practice of 3, 66
Qingyang temple 88
Qiui Changchun xviii, 3, 12, 115–116
quantum physics, and correlative thinking 64
Quanzhen Daoism see Complete Perfection, Way of
Que Yuan 50, 97

ranks and titles, preoccupation with 96, 100–101
Raphals, Lisa 55
religion
  Daoism as organized indigenous religion of China 17–18
  as faith and belief 53
  and health, connection between 65–66
  and political authority
    cosmos, state, and body, relationship between 89
    destiny, negotiating with 90–91
    Mandate of Heaven, as applicable to all 89–90
    sage-king paradigm, analogy of 89–90
  popular Chinese 21–22
    ambiguity in 25
    deceased ancestors, treatment of 24–25

timekeeping (calendar) 22–23
true (versus popular superstition), toleration of 87–88
Religion of the Chinese, The (De Groot) 20
Religion of the Chinese People, The (Granet) 20
Republic of China xviii, 13
Ritual of Salvation of the Yellow Book of Highest Clarity 70
rituals
  and humans/earth/heaven communication 50–52
  interiorization process 104
  loss of understanding of 14
  of purification (zhai) 51–52
  standardization of 10, 14
Road to Heaven, The (Porter) 145
Robinet, Isabelle xii, 94, 99, 110, 119, 124, 130
Robson, James 144
Roots of Sins, The (Zuigen pin) 124–125
Roth, Harold 7, 55

Sacred Land, Sacred Sex – Rapture of the Deep (LaChapelle) 139
sacred space
  cultural metaphors, from images of nature 141
  fengshui (geomancy) 145–146
  natural environment as 142
  versus profane space 143
  see also mountains
Sandon zhu'nang 98
Sankara 56
scapulimancy 75
Schafer, Edward 98
Schall, Adam 23
Schipper, Kristofer 25, 49, 70, 141–142
Scripture of Great Peace 142
Scripture of Purity and Tranquillity (Qingjing jing) 116
Scripture of the Opening of Heaven (Kaitian jing) 86
Scripture of the Salvation of Humankind (Duren jing) 124
Scripture of the Transformations of Laozi (Laozi bianhua jing) 82
Scripture of the Yellow Court (Huangting jing) 64–65
Scriptures of the Cavern-Divine 149
sects (popular contemporary), persecution of 88
Seidel, Anna 24, 80, 82
Seigler, Elijah 67
Selin, Helaine xiv

sexual yoga, Chinese 68, 70
 see also jing energy
shamanism 49–50, 93, 97
Shang Dynasty 75
Shangqing Daoism
 development of 93–95
 influence of *Zhuangzi* on 6
 lineage, ending of power of 95
 versus Maoshan Daoism 95
 revelations of xvii, 123–124, 130
 shamanism, incorporation of 93
 transcendence, personal quest for 94
 see also Highest Clarity, Way of
*Shennong's Materia Medica (Shennong
 bencao jing)* (Tao Hongjing) 147
Shenxian Zhuan (Biographies of Divine
 Immortals) 26
Shiga, Ichiko 126
Shiji (Records of the Historian) 4
Sima Chengzhen xvii, 95
Sima Qian 4, 6, 62, 81
Sivin, Nathan 61
Skar, Lowell 113
Song dynasty xvii–xviii, 2, 11, 25, 50, 115,
 150
spatial concepts, importance of 107–108
spirit-writing cults
 Lüzu cults 126–127
 morality books 127
 spirit-mediums, phenomenon of
  125–126
stars see light practices, astral journeys
Strickman, Michel 27, 28, 95
Sui dynasty xvii, 82, 93
Sun Bu'er xviii, 12
Sun Youyue 95
Supreme Purity see Highest Clarity, Way of
Surin, Kenneth 120
syncretism, religious 2, 3, 11, 116

Taiji Quan (Tai Chi) 3, 33
 invention of 66
 name, meaning of 66
 as qi cultivation 66
 religion/health duality 67
 Tai-Chi Society, Toronto 66–67
 yin-yang principle, embodiment of 66
taiji (Supreme Ultimate), astrological
 significance of 98
Taiqing (Great Clarity) alchemical
 movement xvii, 110–111
Taishang Laojun jiejin (Scripture of
 Precepts of the Highest Lord) 77
talismans (fu)
 as instrumental in founding of Numinous
  Treasure tradition 130

 and 'magico-technicians' of Han period
  130
 and ordination rituals 130–131
 and texts 129–130
Tang dynasty 86, 93
 break-up of 2–3
 high point of Shangqing Daoism under
  95
 integration of Daoism with imperial
  court system 2, 10–11
 Xuanzong Emperor ordained xvii
Tao Hongjing xvii, 94, 147
Tao of Pooh (Hoff) 137
Tao-te-ching see Daode jing
Taoism or Daoism? xii–xiii, 17
terracotta warriors mausoleum 108
texts
 chanting of 122
 charts/diagrams, use of 131–132
 and contexts 122
 as cosmic revelation
 Daoist Canon, publication of 128–129
 Lingbao tradition, (Buddhist influence)
  124–125
 Shanqing revelations 123–124, 130
 spirit-writing cults 122–123
 talismanic function of 122, 129–131
 transmission rituals 127–128
 Western *versus* traditional somatic
  interpretations 138
 see also caves; *Daode jing*,
  interpretations of; spirit-writing
  cults
*Three Ways to Cross the Heavenly Pass
 (Tianguan santu)* 100–101
time, cyclical and linear aspects of 108–109
 see also calendar, Chinese
transcendent bodies see perfected persons
transformation
 of aging process 120
 of deities 119
 'earlier as better' attitude, and cosmic
  history 119–120
 modern technologies, development of
  120–121
 natural/unnatural and supernatural,
  boundaries between 120
 within universe 118–119
Travels of an Alchemist (Li Zhichang) 115
trigrams, eight 109–110, 118–119
Tsui, Bartholemew P. 126

Uniting Yin and Yang (He yinyang) 68
universal path, Daoism as
 Chinese culture, influence on 30–31
 colonial attitudes 30–31

Perennial Philosophy, interest in 32–33
    Western markets, for Daoism 33–34
Unschuld, Paul U. 58
Upper Purity see Highest Clarity, Way of
Ursa Major see Big Dipper

Varieties of Mystical Experience, The
    (James) 56
vegetarianism 51
vegetation, and Chinese herbalism
    147–148
Vervoorn, Aat 145
visualization practices see light practices

Wade-Giles system xiii
Waley, Arthur 50, 115
Wang Bi commentary (Daode jing) xvii, 4,
    133–134
Wang Zhe xvii, 2, 3, 11–12, 114–115
    see also Complete Perfection, Way of
Warring States period
    de, and mandate of Heaven 76
    and question of the Way 37–38
    ruler, powers and virtues of 45
Way (Dao)
    as harmony with natural order 40–41
    hymn to, as mother of the universe
        (Daode jing) 41–42
    communication between forms of life,
        principle of 42
    harmony, as balance of opposites 44
    matrix of life 42–43
    progress and return, theme of 43
    self-transformation, constant of all
        things 44
    spontaneity, Dao as modelled on own
        43
    yin and yang, foundational pattern
        43–44
    as (transcendent) cosmic principle 41
    and Western categories of thought
        37–38
    see also communication; power
Way of Celestial Masters see Celestial
    Masters, Way of
Way of Complete Perfection see Complete
    Perfection, Way of
Way of Great Peace see Great Peace, Way of
Way of Highest Clarity see Highest Clarity,
    Way of
Way of Numinous Treasure see Lingbao
    movement
Way of Orthodox Unity see Celestial
    Masters, Way of
Wei dynasty 84
Wen Xuan 76

Wen Yiduo 19–20
Wendi emperor of Han dynasty 134
West
    colonial power, influence of and rise of
        nationalism 3, 18–19
    and contemporary Daoism 13, 14–15
    and Daoism as 'spiritual technology'
        106
    practice of Daoism in 3, 14, 33–34
Wile, Douglas 68, 69, 70
Women
    and alchemy 113
    immortals, see Sun Bu'er
Wong, Eva 116
wuwei
    as 'action as non-action' 140
    as personal life philosophy 137

Xiang'er commentary (Daode jing) xvii, 82,
    135–136
Xu family 94, 96
Xuanwu (or Zhenwu) deity 13

yang see yin and yang
Yang Xi xvii, 9, 50, 94–95, 124, 125
Yao, Ted 115, 116
Yao minority 28
Yellow Emperor 80
Yellow Emperor's Simple Questions
    (medical compendium) 58
Yellow Turbans see Great Peace, Way of
Yijing see Book of Changes
yin and yang
    alchemy and reversal of 109–110, 113
    and Big Dipper correspondences 98–99
    and 'Dark Room Enlightenment'
        practice 104–105
    as dynamic cosmic principle 58–59
    foundational pattern 43–44
    Taiji quan as physical embodiment of
        interplay of 66
Yin Tong 85
Yin Xi 85
Yongjo, King 97
Yuan dynasty xviii, 3, 115
Yufang bijue 69, 70

Zhang, Jiyu 142
Zhang Daoling (Ling)
    and 'awesome covenant' with Laozi 8–9,
        26
    and emergence of Daoism in alchemical
        tradition 111
    first Celestial Master, and founding
        patriarch of Daoist religion 8, 47,
        49, 81, 83, 91

Xiang'er commentary, attributed to 135–136
Zhang Jue 78, 80
Zhang Lu xvii, 81
Zhang Sanfeng 66
Zhengyi (Orthodox Daoism), absorption of Shangqing Daoism into 95
Zhongli Quan 11–12, 114
Zhou dynasty xvi, 18
Zhu Xi xviii, 40
Zhuangzi
    animals, and longevity practices 148
    authors of 6
    dates of ix
and environmentalism 139
Master Zhuang's reaction to wife's death, story of 73
philosophical aspects ix
and proto-Daoism 5–7
Shangqing movement, influence on 6
as standing for whole of Daoism in Western imagination 30–31
and view of wandering sage 5–6
ziran see nature
zodiac, Chinese 22–23
Zoroaster 78
Zou Yan xvi, 62
Zuangzi's dream 119